Enduring Issues in Philosophy

Other books in the Enduring Issues series:

Criminology
Psychology
Religion
Sociology

Enduring Issues in Philosophy

Gerald W. Eichhoefer

David L. Bender, *Publisher*
Bruno Leone, *Executive Editor*

Bonnie Szumski, *Series Editor*

Gerald W. Eichhoefer, Professor of Philosophy, William Jewell College, *Book Editor*

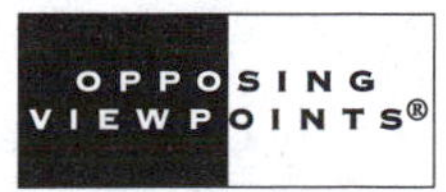

Greenhaven Press, Inc., San Diego, CA 92198-9009

This book is dedicated to my mother, Lucille Herman, and to Lorena, Mara, and Alethea, who have been long-suffering.

Library of Congress Cataloging-in-Publication Data

Enduring issues in philosophy : opposing viewpoints / Gerald W. Eichhoefer, book editor.
p. cm. — (Enduring issues series)
Includes bibliographical references and index.
ISBN 1-56510-252-5 (lib. bdg. : alk. paper)
ISBN 1-56510-251-7 (pbk. : alk. paper)
1. Philosophy. I. Eichhoefer, Gerald W., 1946- . II. Series.
B72.E53 1995
100—dc20 94-41045
CIP

P.O. Box 289009, San Diego, CA 92198-9009
Printed in the U.S.A.

Contents

FOREWORD

"When a thing ceases to be a subject of controversy, it ceases to be a subject of interest."

William Hazlitt

The Enduring Issues series is based on the concept that certain fundamental disciplines remain interesting and vibrant because they remain controversial, debatable, and mutable. Indeed, it is through controversy that these disciplines were forged, and through debate that they continue to be defined.

Each book in the Enduring Issues series aims to present the most seminal and thought-provoking issues in the most accessible way—by pitting the founders of each discipline side by side in a pro/con format. This running debate style allows readers to compare and contrast major philosophical views, noting the major and minor areas of disagreement. In this way, the chronology of the formation of the discipline itself is traced. As American clergyman Lyman Beecher argued, "No great advance has ever been made in science, politics, or religion, without controversy."

In an effort to collect the most representative opinions of these disciplines, every editor of each book in the Enduring Issues series has been chosen for his or her expertise in presenting these issues in the classroom. Each editor has chosen the materials for his or her book with these goals in mind: 1) To offer, both to the uninitiated and to the well read, classic questions answered by the leading historical and contemporary proponents for each question. 2) To create and stimulate an interest and excitement in these academic disciplines by revealing that even in the most esoteric areas there are questions and views common to every person's search for life's meaning. 3) To reveal the development of ideas, and, in the process, plant the notion in the reader's mind that truth can only be unearthed in thoughtful examination and reexamination.

The editors of the Enduring Issues series hope that readers will find in it a launching point to do their own investigation and form their own opinions about the issues raised by these academic disciplines. Because it is in the continued contemplation of these questions that these issues will remain alive.

Introduction

You may be reading this book as a course requirement, because you are curious about philosophy, or both. In any case, a few preliminary observations will help you along the way. First, do not assume that philosophy is something completely foreign to you. Whether you know it or not, you have already done some serious philosophical thinking. If you have ever wondered whether God exists or whether you did the right thing you have engaged in philosophical inquiry. Most philosophical thinkers are ordinary people who are not aware that they are engaging in philosophy. Other people are more systematic. They carefully explore philosophical ideas and discuss them with others. Sometimes they write down and even publish them. These people may be professional philosophers, who make their living "doing philosophy," or they may be people who have mastered other disciplines, like physics or religion or literature. A biologist, for example, may wonder about evolution and its implications for the existence of God, or a physicist may wonder how far the "scientific method" can be pushed to yield truth. The things these people have to say are interesting to ordinary people as well. Reading their reflections may help us answer or at least understand our own questions.

Second, do not make the mistake of thinking that philosophy is a waste of time. The study of philosophy helps develop clear and careful thought. It teaches people to make important distinctions and question assumptions. This book, which contains opposing points of view, makes it possible to develop these skills by comparing what different careful thinkers have to say about the same topics. The critical thinking that philosophy fosters can help a person be more successful in other areas of life, whether as a manager in a corporation or a parent dealing with children. It has been said that the unexamined life is not worth living. Philosophy is a systematic way of examining life and is a valuable tool for this purpose.

Third, do not think that philosophy is abstract and will not affect your personal values and beliefs. Examination of life as well as other topics will reveal both strengths and weaknesses in your own ideas. It is probably impossible for a person to critically examine his or her beliefs without finding ideas that are weak. This, obviously, is threatening. One way of dealing with this is to read several points of view, as you can with this text. You may find that although one philosopher may challenge an important belief another may find weaknesses in the challenger's point of view. Still another philosopher may agree with you and support your position with stronger and more valid reasons than yours. You may finally decide after reading more deeply about your position that you have to change your mind or suspend your judgment in some areas. Remember to remain unintimidated by philosophers or authors. Read and think some more. Consider what other, equally qualified, people have to say. Practice some philosophical detachment yourself.

Fourth, be prepared to spend some time and effort in your study of philosophy. Philosophical understanding, like most valuable things, comes at a price. You cannot speed-read philosophical material. You will probably have to read the material several times. First read the entire article to get some impression of the what and how of the argument. Use the glossary at the back of the book or a good dictionary to look up terms that are not obvious to you from the context. Next, read the text in an attempt to answer the study questions provided with each reading. Some of these are obvious after reading the material, while some require a good deal of thought and may have more than one very good answer. The purpose is not just to read someone's opinions but to bring your own ideas and knowledge to bear upon the reading and to interact with the author, your professor, and fellow students. Do not expect to completely understand everything the authors have to say. That is a lifelong journey, not a bridge to cross.

Finally, I would like to call your attention to the way this book is organized. Philosophers, like everybody else, classify things. One major area of philosophy is introduced in each chapter of this collection. The first chapter begins by asking what it is possible to know. There is little point to inquiry if we have no idea how or where to look. This question cannot be entirely separated from the question of what reality is ultimately like, the topic of the second chapter. After all, we want to know what is real, do we not? Some questions about reality have wider implications than others. The big reality question, in the minds of most people, concerns whether God exists, which the third chapter considers. Examining the purpose of human existence in a universe created by an all-powerful being is quite different than in one where creation was accidental or random. Chapter 4, as is much of human life, is centered around moral questions. Pursuing moral questions may tell us something about the ultimate nature of things and about the significance of the God question.

In some sense, the study of philosophy is the study of ourselves—we want to know about the universe because we want to know who and what we are. The fifth chapter discusses what role government should play in our lives given our concern for morality and justice and our value as conscious beings.

I hope that this book will be only a launching point for a lifelong exploration of self-knowledge and self-reflection. Humans are unique, at least in this small part of the cosmos, in their ability to communicate in detail with others their ideas, thoughts, and deepest self-doubts. By exploring these topics, you explore what it means to be human. Take on the journey.

To the Instructor

Suggestions for the Use of This Book

This collection is suitable for use with a one-semester introduction to philosophy course either as a stand-alone text, a book of readings to support a systematic or historical introductory text, or for independent study. If it is used as a text, the instructor will need to provide fairly extensive supporting lectures. For the most part, the selections are organized according to topic and an attempt is made to present them in an intuitive order that represents an ongoing discussion or set of discussions within each chapter. The discussions are generally in historical order, but clarity was a more important organizational consideration than sequence. For this reason Aristotle, for example, shows up near the middle rather than the beginning of Chapter 4, "What Is Morality?" A broad selection of classical and contemporary writers is included, so it is possible to choose selections in historical order rather than on the basis of chapter titles. Many of the selections could have been included under more than one topic.

Study questions specific to each reading are included and more general questions, suitable for extended class discussions and papers, are included at the end of the book. The questions are carefully thought out and are not designed simply to verify that chapters have been read. The reading-specific questions require a careful and thoughtful reading of the texts. In keeping with the philosophy of the *Opposing Viewpoints* series, a wide variety of viewpoints are included. Some philosophers are mentioned but viewpoints by them are not included because of space limitations. Viewpoints that are often neglected in general introductory collections, like process metaphysics, are included here.

What Can We Know?

Chapter Preface

It is common prudence to verify sources of information when that information is extremely important. When people claim to know the answers to significant questions like what is ultimately real or whether there is a God or a real right and wrong, it is philosophically prudent to ask them how they know. Philosophers are not merely interested in how someone obtained a particular set of facts, but whether it is even possible to obtain those facts. For example, when someone claims that there really are such things as souls or electrons, philosophers want to know how anyone could know such things.

This type of questioning stems from Renaissance thinkers, who developed a powerful skeptical tradition that questioned all major religious and philosophical beliefs. René Descartes, who had skeptical teachers, realized that many of his beliefs could not stand up to skeptical attack. He responded by using skepticism as a method for discovering truth. He did this by using his reason to doubt everything he could possibly doubt. He claimed that anything that could not possibly be doubted must be true. Modern philosophy, with its emphasis in epistemology, or the theory of truth, was born. Descartes' use of his reason to obtain certain knowledge was the beginning of what is called the rationalist school of philosophy.

This rationalist approach was opposed by a group of philosophers, known as the empiricists, who argued that all knowledge comes through the senses rather than through reason. John Locke and other members of this group believe that all of our ideas originate in experience. Despite the carefully reasoned arguments of both the rationalists and the empiricists, neither side succeeded in completely discrediting the other. Immanuel Kant, the great German philosopher, argued that neither side had the whole truth and that knowledge is the result of both the use of the mind and the senses. Kant argued that the mind contributed the basic structures, which he called categories or ideas, that made all human experience possible. He believed that the senses provided the content of these experiences. Early in the twentieth century Henri Bergson criticized this approach because he believed that reality is dynamic and flowing and that sharp rigid categories like those Kant proposed did more to distort reality than to reveal it. Bergson replaced reason and sensory experience with intuition. In contrast with reason and experience, which are external to reality, he argued that intuition placed the knower empathetically within the flow of reality.

With the considerable success of the physical and biological sciences in the twentieth century many philosophers were convinced that science held the only key to truth. These philosophers, who include Quine and Ullian, elevated the hypothetical-deductive method of science to the very highest status. They believe, in essence, that whatever humans can know will be discovered by using this method. Not all philosophers and scientists, however, share this opinion. The famous mathematical physicist James Jeans argued that the hypothetical-deductive method cannot lead to truth because the hypotheses of modern physics do not allow any way of looking at the world that makes sense to human beings. The difficulty in conceptualizing quantum mechanics especially has convinced many thinkers that the world simply cannot be understood by humans. Consciousness has proved to be equally conceptually difficult. Thomas Nagel, a brilliant philosopher and cognitive scientist, has reflected deeply on the problems of consciousness, much like Jeans and others have done with physics. Nagel argues that there are facts which humans must acknowledge as true but which we can never understand or even express. Thus the issue of human knowledge remains as hotly contested today as it ever was.

All Knowledge Is Gained Through Reason

René Descartes

René Descartes (1596-1650) made major contributions to mathematics and is regarded as the founder of modern philosophy because of his contributions to epistemology, the theory of knowledge and truth. The oft quoted "I think, therefore I am" first appeared in Descartes' best-known work, *Meditations on First Philosophy*. The following viewpoint contains the first and second meditations. Descartes begins by discussing many of his beliefs and deciding to examine his fundamental beliefs in order to eliminate error and lay secure foundations for truth. He does this by systematically doubting his beliefs until he finds something which he cannot doubt, which turns out to be the existence of his own mind or self. In the course of his doubting he finds that his belief in the physical world and even the truths of his beloved mathematics are uncertain. Descartes' quest for certain foundations for knowledge and truth set the agenda for modern philosophy, which insists upon asking how and what we can know before it attempts to answer questions about what is real.

QUESTIONS

1. How does Descartes justify the method of doubt?
2. Why does Descartes believe it is possible to doubt the senses?
3. What makes it possible, according to the author, to doubt even mathematics?
4. What, according to Descartes, must be true, even if we are dreaming? Do you agree with him?
5. What capacity does Descartes conclude is more reliable than the senses?
6. What kind of thing is the self, according to Descartes?

■ ■ ■

Some years ago I was struck by the large number of falsehoods that I had accepted as true in my childhood, and by the highly doubtful nature of the whole edifice that I had subsequently based on them. I realized that it was necessary, once in the course of my life, to demolish everything completely and start again right from the foundations if I wanted to establish anything at all in the sciences that was stable and likely to last. But the task looked an enormous one, and I began to wait until I should reach a mature enough age to ensure that no subsequent time of life would be more suitable for tackling such inquiries. This led me to put the project off for so long that I would now be to blame if by pondering over it any further I wasted the time still left for carrying it out. So today I have expressly rid my mind of all worries and arranged for myself a clear stretch of free time. I am here quite alone, and at last I will devote myself sincerely and without reservation to the general demolition of my opinions.

But to accomplish this, it will not be necessary for me to show that all my opinions are false, which is something I could perhaps never manage. Reason now leads me to think that I should hold back my assent from opinions which are not completely certain and indubitable just as carefully as I do from those which are patently false. So, for the purpose of rejecting all my opinions, it will be enough if I find in each of them at least some reason for doubt. And to do this I will not need to run through them all individually, which would be an endless task. Once the foundations of a building are undermined, anything built on them collapses of its own accord; so I will go straight for the basic principles on which all my former beliefs rested.

Whatever I have up till now accepted as most true I have acquired either from the senses or through the senses. But from time to time I have found that the senses deceive, and it is prudent never to trust completely those who have deceived us even once.

Yet although the senses occasionally deceive us with respect to objects which are very small or in the distance, there are many other beliefs about which doubt is quite impossible, even though they are derived from the senses—for example, that I am here, sitting by the fire, wearing a winter dressing-gown, holding this piece of paper in my hands, and so on. Again, how could it be denied that these hands or this whole body are mine? Unless perhaps I were to liken myself to madmen, whose brains are so damaged by the persistent vapours of melancholia that they firmly maintain they are kings when they are paupers, or say they are dressed in purple when they are naked, or that their heads are made of earthenware, or that they are pumpkins, or made of glass. But such people are insane, and I would be thought equally mad if I took anything from them as a model for myself.

A brilliant piece of reasoning! As if I were not a man who sleeps at night, and regularly has all the same experiences[1] while asleep as madmen do when awake—indeed sometimes even more improbable ones. How often, asleep at night, am I convinced of just such familiar events—that I am here in my dressing-gown, sitting by the fire—when in fact I am lying undressed in bed! Yet at the moment my eyes are certainly wide awake when I look at this piece of paper; I shake my head and

[1] '. . . and in my dreams regularly represent to myself the same things' (French version).

it is not asleep; as I stretch out and feel my hand I do so deliberately, and I know what I am doing. All this would not happen with such distinctness to someone asleep. Indeed! As if I did not remember other occasions when I have been tricked by exactly similar thoughts while asleep! As I think about this more carefully, I see plainly that there are never any sure signs by means of which being awake can be distinguished from being asleep. The result is that I begin to feel dazed, and this very feeling only reinforces the notion that I may be asleep.

Suppose then that I am dreaming, and that these particulars—that my eyes are open, that I am moving my head and stretching out my hands—are not true. Perhaps, indeed, I do not even have such hands or such a body at all. Nonetheless, it must surely be admitted that the visions which come in sleep are like paintings, which must have been fashioned in the likeness of things that are real, and hence that at least these general kinds of things—eyes, head, hands and the body as a whole—are things which are not imaginary but are real and exist. For even when painters try to create sirens and satyrs with the most extraordinary bodies, they cannot give them natures which are new in all respects; they simply jumble up the limbs of different animals. Or if perhaps they manage to think up something so new that nothing remotely similar has ever been seen before—something which is therefore completely fictitious and unreal—at least the colours used in the composition must be real. By similar reasoning, although these general kinds of things—eyes, head, hands and so on—could be imaginary, it must at least be admitted that certain other even simpler and more universal things are real. These are as it were the real colours from which we form all the images of things, whether true or false, that occur in our thought.

This class appears to include corporeal nature in general, and its extension; the shape of extended things; the quantity, or size and number of these things; the place in which they may exist, the time through which they may endure[1] and so on.

So a reasonable conclusion from this might be that physics, astronomy, medicine, and all other disciplines which depend

[1] '. . . the place where they are, the time which measures their duration' (French version).

on the study of composite things, are doubtful; while arithmetic, geometry and other subjects of this kind, which deal only with the simplest and most general things, regardless of whether they really exist in nature or not, contain something certain and indubitable. For whether I am awake or asleep, two and three added together are five, and a square has no more than four sides. It seems impossible that such transparent truths should incur any suspicion of being false.

And yet firmly rooted in my mind is the long-standing belief that there is an omnipotent God who made me the kind of creature that I am. How do I know that he has not brought it about that there is no earth, no sky, no extended thing, no shape, no size, no place, while at the same time ensuring that all these things appear to me to exist just as they do now? Moreover, since I sometimes consider that others go astray in cases where they think they have the most perfect knowledge, may I not similarly go wrong every time I add two and three or count the sides of a square, or in some even simpler matter, if that is imaginable? But perhaps God would not have wished me to be deceived in this way, since he is said to be supremely good. But if it were inconsistent with his goodness to have created me such that I am deceived all the time, it would seem equally foreign to his goodness to allow me to be deceived even occasionally; yet this last assertion cannot be made.[1]

Perhaps there may be some who would prefer to deny the existence of so powerful a God rather than believe that everything else is uncertain. Let us not argue with them, but grant them that everything said about God is a fiction. According to their supposition, then, I have arrived at my present state by fate or chance or a continuous chain of events, or by some other means; yet since deception and error seem to be imperfections, the less powerful they make my original cause, the more likely it is that I am so imperfect as to be deceived all the time. I have no answer to these arguments, but am finally compelled to admit that there is not one of my former beliefs about which a doubt may not properly be raised; and this is not a flippant or ill-considered conclusion, but is based on powerful and well thought-out reasons. So in future I must

[1] '. . . yet I cannot doubt that he does allow this' (French version).

withhold my assent from these former beliefs just as carefully as I would from obvious falsehoods, if I want to discover any certainty.[1]

But it is not enough merely to have noticed this; I must make an effort to remember it. My habitual opinions keep coming back, and, despite my wishes, they capture my belief, which is as it were bound over to them as a result of long occupation and the law of custom. I shall never get out of the habit of confidently assenting to these opinions, so long as I suppose them to be what in fact they are, namely highly probable opinions—opinions which, despite the fact that they are in a sense doubtful, as has just been shown, it is still much more reasonable to believe than to deny. In view of this, I think it will be a good plan to turn my will in completely the opposite direction and deceive myself, by pretending for a time that these former opinions are utterly false and imaginary. I shall do this until the weight of preconceived opinion is counter-balanced and the distorting influence of habit no longer prevents my judgement from perceiving things correctly. In the meantime I know that no danger or error will result from my plan, and that I cannot possibly go too far in my distrustful attitude. This is because the task now in hand does not involve action but merely the acquisition of knowledge.

I will suppose therefore that not God, who is supremely good and the source of truth, but rather some malicious demon of the utmost power and cunning has employed all his energies in order to deceive me. I shall think that the sky, the air, the earth, colours, shapes, sounds and all external things are merely the delusions of dreams which he has devised to ensnare my judgement. I shall consider myself as not having hands or eyes, or flesh, or blood or senses, but as falsely believing that I have all these things. I shall stubbornly and firmly persist in this meditation; and, even if it is not in my power to know any truth, I shall at least do what is in my power,[2] that is, resolutely guard against assenting to any falsehoods, so that the deceiver, however powerful and cunning he may be, will be unable to impose on me in the slightest degree.

---

[1] '. . . in the sciences' (French version). [2] '. . . nevertheless it is in my power to suspend my judgement' (French version).

But this is an arduous undertaking, and a kind of laziness brings me back to normal life. I am like a prisoner who is enjoying an imaginary freedom while asleep; as he begins to suspect that he is asleep, he dreads being woken up, and goes along with the pleasant illusion as long as he can. In the same way, I happily slide back into my old opinions and dread being shaken out of them, for fear that my peaceful sleep may be followed by hard labour when I wake, and that I shall have to toil not in the light, but amid the inextricable darkness of the problems I have now raised.

So serious are the doubts into which I have been thrown as a result of yesterday's meditation that I can neither put them out of my mind nor see any way of resolving them. It feels as if I have fallen unexpectedly into a deep whirlpool which tumbles me around so that I can neither stand on the bottom nor swim up to the top. Nevertheless I will make an effort and once more attempt the same path which I started on yesterday. Anything which admits of the slightest doubt I will set aside just as if I had found it to be wholly false; and I will proceed in this way until I recognize something certain, or, if nothing else, until I at least recognize for certain that there is no certainty. Archimedes used to demand just one firm and immovable point in order to shift the entire earth; so I too can hope for great things if I manage to find just one thing, however slight, that is certain and unshakable.

I will suppose then, that everything I see is spurious. I will believe that my memory tells me lies, and that none of the things that it reports ever happened. I have no senses. Body, shape, extension, movement and place are chimeras. So what remains true? Perhaps just the one fact that nothing is certain.

Yet apart from everything I have just listed, how do I know that there is not something else which does not allow even the slightest occasion for doubt? Is there not a God, or whatever I may call him, who puts into me[1] the thoughts I am now having? But why do I think this, since I myself may perhaps be the author of these thoughts? In that case am not I, at least, something? But I have just said that I have no senses and no body. This is the sticking point: what follows from this? Am I not so

[1] '. . . puts into my mind' (French version).

bound up with a body and with senses that I cannot exist without them? But I have convinced myself that there is absolutely nothing in the world, no sky, no earth, no minds, no bodies. Does it now follow that I too do not exist? No: if I convinced myself of something[1] then I certainly existed. But there is a deceiver of supreme power and cunning who is deliberately and constantly deceiving me. In that case I too undoubtedly exist, if he is deceiving me; and let him deceive me as much as he can, he will never bring it about that I am nothing so long as I think that I am something. So after considering everything very thoroughly, I must finally conclude that this proposition, *I am, I exist*, is necessarily true whenever it is put forward by me or conceived in my mind.

But I do not yet have a sufficient understanding of what this 'I' is, that now necessarily exists. So I must be on my guard against carelessly taking something else to be this 'I', and so making a mistake in the very item of knowledge that I maintain is the most certain and evident of all. I will therefore go back and meditate on what I originally believed myself to be, before I embarked on this present train of thought. I will then subtract anything capable of being weakened, even minimally, by the arguments now introduced, so that what is left at the end may be exactly and only what is certain and unshakable.

What then did I formerly think I was? A man. But what is a man? Shall I say 'a rational animal'? No; for then I should have to inquire what an animal is, what rationality is, and in this way one question would lead me down the slope to other harder ones, and I do not now have the time to waste on subtleties of this kind. . . .

As to the body, however, I had no doubts about it, but thought I knew its nature distinctly. If I had tried to describe the mental conception I had of it, I would have expressed it as follows: by a body I understand whatever has a determinable shape and a definable location and can occupy a space in such a way as to exclude any other body; it can be perceived by touch, sight, hearing, taste or smell, and can be moved in various ways, not by itself but by whatever else comes into contact with it. For, according to my judgement, the power of self-

[1] '. . . or thought anything at all' (French version).

movement, like the power of sensation or of thought, was quite foreign to the nature of a body; indeed, it was a source of wonder to me that certain bodies were found to contain faculties of this kind.

But what shall I now say that I am, when I am supposing that there is some supremely powerful and, if it is permissible to say so, malicious deceiver, who is deliberately trying to trick me in every way he can? Can I now assert that I possess even the most insignificant of all the attributes which I have just said belong to the nature of a body? I scrutinize them, think about them, go over them again, but nothing suggests itself; it is tiresome and pointless to go through the list once more. But what about the attributes I assigned to the soul? Nutrition or movement? Since now I do not have a body, these are more fabrications. Sense-perception? This surely does not occur without a body, and besides, when asleep I have appeared to perceive through the senses many things which I afterwards realized I did not perceive through the senses at all. Thinking? At last I have discovered it—thought; this alone is inseparable from me. I am, I exist—that is certain. But for how long? For as long as I am thinking. For it could be that were I totally to cease from thinking, I should totally cease to exist. At present I am not admitting anything except what is necessarily true. I am, then, in the strict sense only a thing that thinks;[1] that is, I am a mind, or intelligence, or intellect, or reason—words whose meaning I have been ignorant of until now. But for all that I am a thing which is real and which truly exists. But what kind of a thing? As I have just said—a thinking thing.

What else am I? . . . It would indeed be a case of fictitious invention if I used my imagination to establish that I was something or other; for imagining is simply contemplating the shape or image of a corporeal thing. Yet now I know for certain both that I exist and at the same time that all such images and, in general, everything relating to the nature of body, could be mere dreams <and chimeras>. Once this point has been

[1] '. . . The word 'only' is most naturally taken as going with 'a thing that thinks', and this interpretation is followed in the French version. When discussing this passage with Gassendi, however, Descartes suggests that he meant the 'only' to govern 'in the strict sense'; cf. AT IXA 215; CSM II 276.

grasped, to say 'I will use my imagination to get to know more distinctly what I am' would seem to be as silly as saying 'I am now awake, and see some truth; but since my vision is not yet clear enough, I will deliberately fall asleep so that my dreams may provide a truer and clearer representation.' I thus realize that none of the things that the imagination enables me to grasp is at all relevant to this knowledge of myself which I possess, and that the mind must therefore be most carefully diverted from such things[1] if it is to perceive its own nature as distinctly as possible.

But what then am I? A thing that thinks. What is that? A thing that doubts, understands, affirms, denies, is willing, is unwilling, and also imagines and has sensory perceptions.

This is a considerable list, if everything on it belongs to me. But does it? Is it not one and the same 'I' who is now doubting almost everything, who nonetheless understands some things, who affirms that this one thing is true, denies everything else, desires to know more, is unwilling to be deceived, imagines many things even involuntarily, and is aware of many things which apparently come from the senses? Are not all these things just as true as the fact that I exist, even if I am asleep all the time, and even if he who created me is doing all he can to deceive me? Which of all these activities is distinct from my thinking? Which of them can be said to be separate from myself? The fact that it is I who am doubting and understanding and willing is so evident that I see no way of making it any clearer. But it is also the case that the 'I' who imagines is the same 'I'. For even if, as I have supposed, none of the objects of imagination are real, the power of imagination is something which really exists and is part of my thinking. Lastly, it is also the same 'I' who has sensory perceptions, or is aware of bodily things as it were through the senses. For example, I am now seeing light, hearing a noise, feeling heat. But I am asleep, so all this is false. Yet I certainly *seem* to see, to hear, and to be warmed. This cannot be false; what is called 'having a sensory perception' is strictly just this, and in this restricted sense of the term it is simply thinking. . . .

Let us consider the things which people commonly think

[1] '. . . from this manner of conceiving things' (French version).

they understand most distinctly of all; that is, the bodies which we touch and see. I do not mean bodies in general—for general perceptions are apt to be somewhat more confused—but one particular body. Let us take, for example, this piece of wax. It has just been taken from the honeycomb; it has not yet quite lost the taste of the honey; it retains some of the scent of the flowers from which it was gathered; its colour, shape and size are plain to see; it is hard, cold and can be handled without difficulty; if you rap it with your knuckle it makes a sound. In short, it has everything which appears necessary to enable a body to be known as distinctly as possible. But even as I speak, I put the wax by the fire, and look: the residual taste is eliminated, the smell goes away, the colour changes, the shape is lost, the size increases; it becomes liquid and hot; you can hardly touch it, and if you strike it, it no longer makes a sound. But does the same wax remain? It must be admitted that it does; no one denies it, no one thinks otherwise. So what was it in the wax that I understood with such distinctness? Evidently none of the features which I arrived at by means of the senses; for whatever came under taste, smell, sight, touch or hearing has now altered—yet the wax remains.

Perhaps the answer lies in the thought which now comes to my mind; namely, the wax was not after all the sweetness of the honey, or the fragrance of the flowers, or the whiteness, or the shape, or the sound, but rather a body which presented itself to me in these various forms a little while ago, but which now exhibits different ones. But what exactly is it that I am now imagining? Let us concentrate, take away everything which does not belong to the wax, and see what is left: merely something extended, flexible and changeable. But what is meant here by 'flexible' and 'changeable'? Is it what I picture in my imagination: that this piece of wax is capable of changing from a round shape to a square shape, or from a square shape to a triangular shape? Not at all; for I can grasp that the wax is capable of countless changes of this kind, yet I am unable to run through this immeasurable number of changes in my imagination, from which it follows that it is not the faculty of imagination that gives me my grasp of the wax as flexible and changeable. And what is meant by 'extended'? Is the extension of the wax also unknown? For it increases if the wax melts, increases again if it boils, and is greater still if the heat is increased. I would not be making a correct judgement about the nature of wax unless I believed it capable of being extended in many more different ways than I will ever encompass in my imagination. I must therefore admit that the nature of this piece of wax is in no way revealed by my imagination, but is perceived by the mind alone. (I am speaking of this particular piece of wax; the point is even clearer with regard to wax in general.) But what is this wax which is perceived by the mind alone?[1] It is of course the same wax which I see, which I touch, which I picture in my imagination, in short the same wax which I thought it to be from the start. And yet, and here is the point, the perception I have of it[2] is a case not of vision or touch or imagination—nor has it ever been, despite previous appearances—but of purely mental scrutiny; and this can be imperfect and confused, as it was before, or clear and distinct as it is now, depending on how carefully I concentrate on what the wax consists in. . . .

So let us proceed, and consider on which occasion my perception of the nature of the wax was more perfect and evident. Was it when I first looked at it, and believed I knew it by my external senses, or at least by what they call the 'common' sense—that is, the power of imagination? Or is my knowledge more perfect now, after a more careful investigation of the nature of the wax and of the means by which it is known? Any doubt on this issue would clearly be foolish; for what distinctness was there in my earlier perception? Was there anything in it which an animal could not possess? But when I distinguish the wax from its outward forms—take the clothes off, as it were, and consider it naked—then although my judgement may still contain errors, at least my perception now requires a human mind.

But what am I to say about this mind, or about myself? (So far, remember, I am not admitting that there is anything else in me except a mind.) What, I ask, is this 'I' which seems to perceive the wax so distinctly? Surely my awareness of my own self is not merely much truer and more certain than my awareness of the wax, but also much more distinct and evident. For

[1]'. . . which can be conceived only by the understanding or the mind' (French version). [2]'. . . or rather the act whereby it is perceived' (added in French version).

if I judge that the wax exists from the fact that I see it, clearly this same fact entails much more evidently that I myself also exist. It is possible that what I see is not really the wax; it is possible that I do not even have eyes with which to see anything. But when I see, or think I see (I am not here distinguishing the two), it is simply not possible that I who am now thinking am not something. By the same token, if I judge that the wax exists from the fact that I touch it, the same result follows, namely that I exist. If I judge that it exists from the fact that I imagine it, or for any other reason, exactly the same thing follows. And the result that I have grasped in the case of the wax may be applied to everything else located outside me. Moreover, if my perception of the wax seemed more distinct[1] after it was established not just by sight or touch but by many other considerations, it must be admitted that I now know myself even more distinctly. This is because every consideration whatsoever which contributes to my perception of the wax, or of any other body, cannot but establish even more effectively the nature of my own mind. But besides this, there is so much else in the mind itself which can serve to make my knowledge of it more distinct, that it scarcely seems worth going through the contributions made by considering bodily things.

I see that without any effort I have now finally got back to where I wanted. I now know that even bodies are not strictly perceived by the senses or the faculty of imagination but by the intellect alone, and that this perception derives not from their being touched or seen but from their being understood; and in view of this I know plainly that I can achieve an easier and more evident perception of my own mind than of anything else. But since the habit of holding on to old opinions cannot be set aside so quickly, I should like to stop here and meditate for some time on this new knowledge I have gained, so as to fix it more deeply in my memory.

---

[1] The French version has 'more clear and distinct' and, at the end of this sentence, 'more evidently, distinctly and clearly'.

All Knowledge Is Gained Through the Senses

JOHN LOCKE

John Locke (1632-1704) made major contributions to epistemology and political philosophy. In his classic *Essay Concerning Human Understanding* he argues for empiricism, the thesis that all of human knowledge is ultimately derived from the five senses. Locke explains that human ideas come either from sensation or from the process of reflection when the mind looks at itself and its own operations. Ideas are either simple, like the idea of a colored patch, or complex, like the idea of a tree. The mind forms complex ideas by putting together or compounding simple ideas. For Locke, this means that there is no need to assume that any ideas are innate or exist in the mind prior to experience. We can only know about the external world through sensations which are caused by external objects when they touch us or when we see or hear or smell or taste them. This means that we cannot

Excerpted from *An Essay Concerning Human Understanding* by John Locke. Oxford: Clarendon Press, 1924.

be certain that the external world exists since all we strictly experience are our sensations, not the objects which caused them. We only infer that these objects exist. There are, however, a number of good reasons to believe that our sensations really are the result of objects in a real external physical world. The lack of philosophical certainty we have about the external world is understandable since human knowledge seems designed for practical survival rather than for philosophical speculation.

QUESTIONS

1. What does Locke mean by "ideas"?
2. What does the author believe are the sources of our ideas?
3. How does the mind construct complex ideas, according to Locke?
4. Does Locke believe that we could imagine what senses other than our own would be like? Can you imagine senses other than our own?
5. Why doesn't it make any difference to Locke whether there are more than five senses?
6. Does Locke distinguish between his ideas of external things and the things themselves?
7. What reasons does Locke give for believing in the external world? Do you think these are good reasons?

■ ■ ■

Of Ideas in General and Their Original

1. *Idea is the object of thinking.* Every man being conscious to himself that he thinks, and that which his mind is applied about whilst thinking being the ideas that are there, it is past doubt that men have in their minds several ideas, such as are those expressed by words, 'whiteness, hardness, sweetness, thinking, motion, man, elephant, army, drunkenness', and others. It is in the first place then to be enquired, How he comes by them? I know it is a received doctrine, that men have native

ideas and original characters stamped upon their minds in their very first being. . . .

2. *All ideas come from sensation or reflection.* Let us then suppose the mind to be, as we say, white paper, void of all characters, without any ideas; how comes it to be furnished? Whence comes it by that vast store, which the busy and boundless fancy of man has painted on it with an almost endless variety? Whence has it all the materials of reason and knowledge? To this I answer, in one word, from EXPERIENCE; in that all our knowledge is founded, and from that it ultimately derives itself. Our observation, employed either about external sensible objects, or about the internal operations of our minds, perceived and reflected on by ourselves, is that which supplies our understandings with all the materials of thinking. These two are the fountains of knowledge, from whence all the ideas we have, or can naturally have, do spring.

3. *The objects of sensation one source of ideas.* First, our senses, conversant about particular sensible objects, do convey into the mind several distinct perceptions of things, according to those various ways wherein those objects do affect them; and thus we come by those *ideas* we have of yellow, white, heat, cold, soft, hard, bitter, sweet, and all those which we call sensible qualities; which when I say the senses convey into the mind, I mean, they from external objects convey into the mind what produces there those perceptions. This great source of most of the ideas we have, depending wholly upon our senses, and derived by them to the understanding, I call, SENSATION.

4. *The operations of our minds the other source of them.* Secondly, the other fountain, from which experience furnisheth the understanding with ideas, is the perception of the operations of our own minds within us, as it is employed about the ideas it has got; which operations, when the soul comes to reflect on and consider, do furnish the understanding with another set of ideas which could not be had from things without: and such are perception, thinking, doubting, believing, reasoning, knowing, willing, and all the different actings of our own minds; which we being conscious of, and observing in ourselves, do from these receive into our understanding as distinct ideas, as we do from bodies affecting our senses. This source of ideas every man has wholly in himself: and though it be not sense, as having nothing to do with external objects, yet it is very like it, and might properly enough be called internal sense. But as I call the other Sensation, so I call this REFLECTION, the ideas it affords being such only as the mind gets by reflecting on its own operations within itself. By Reflection, then, in the following part of this discourse, I would be understood to mean that notice which the mind takes of its own operations, and the manner of them, by reason whereof there comes to be ideas of these operations in the understanding. These two, I say, viz., external material things as the objects of Sensation, and the operations of our own minds within as the objects of Reflection, are, to me, the only originals from whence all our ideas take their beginnings. The term *operations* here, I use in a large sense, as comprehending not barely the actions of the mind about its ideas, but some sort of passions arising from any thought.

5. *All our ideas are of the one or the other of these.* The understanding seems to me not to have the least glimmering of any ideas which it doth not receive from one of these two. *External objects* furnish the mind with the ideas of sensible qualities, which are all those different perceptions they produce in us; and *the mind* furnishes the understanding with ideas of its own operations. These, when we have taken a full survey of them, and their several modes, combinations, and relations, we shall find to contain all our whole stock of ideas; and that we have nothing in our minds which did not come in one of these two ways. Let any one examine his own thoughts, and thoroughly search into his understanding, and then let him tell me, whether all the original ideas he has there, are any other than of the objects of his senses, or of the operations of his mind considered as objects of his reflection; and how great a mass of knowledge soever he imagines to be lodged there, he will, upon taking a strict view, see that he has not any idea in his mind but what one of these two have imprinted, though perhaps with infinite variety compounded and enlarged by the understanding. . . .

Of Simple Ideas

1. *Uncompounded appearances.* The better to understand the nature, manner, and extent of our knowledge, one thing is carefully to be observed concerning the ideas we have; and that is, that some of them are *simple*, and some *complex*.

Though the qualities that affect our senses are, in the things themselves, so united and blended that there is no separation, no distance between them; yet it is plain the ideas they produce in the mind enter by the senses simple and unmixed. For though the sight and touch often take in from the same object at the same time different ideas; as a man sees at once motion and colour, the hand feels softness and warmth in the same piece of wax; yet the simple ideas thus united in the same subject are as perfectly distinct as those that come in by different senses. The coldness and hardness which a man feels in a piece of ice being as distinct ideas in the mind as the smell and whiteness of a lily, or as the taste of sugar and smell of a rose: and there is nothing can be plainer to a man than the clear and distinct perception he has of those simple ideas; which, being each in itself uncompounded, contains in it nothing but one uniform appearance or conception in the mind, and is not distinguishable into different ideas.

2. *The mind can neither make nor destroy them.* These simple ideas, the materials of all our knowledge, are suggested and furnished to the mind only by those two ways above mentioned, viz., sensation and reflection. When the understanding is once stored with these simple ideas, it has the power to repeat, compare, and unite them, even to an almost infinite variety, and so can make at pleasure new complex ideas. But it is not in the power of the most exalted wit or enlarged understanding, by any quickness or variety of thought, to invent or frame one new simple idea in the mind, not taken in by the ways before mentioned; nor can any force of the understanding destroy those that are there. The dominion of man in this little world of his own understanding, being much-what the same as it is in the great world of visible things, wherein his power, however managed by art and skill, reaches no farther than to compound and divide the materials that are made to his hand, but can do nothing towards the making the least particle of new matter, or destroying one atom of what is already in being. The same inability will every one find in himself, who shall go about to fashion in his understanding any simple idea not received in by his senses from external objects, or by reflection from the operations of his own mind about them. I would have any one try to fancy any taste which had never affected his palate, or frame the idea of a scent he had never smelt; and when he can do this, I will also conclude, that a blind man hath ideas of colours, and a deaf man true distinct notions of sounds.

3. This is the reason why, though we cannot believe it impossible to God to make a creature with other organs, and more ways to convey into the understanding the notice of corporeal things than those five, as they are usually counted, which he has given to man: yet I think it is *not possible* for any one *to imagine* any other qualities in bodies, howsoever constituted, whereby they can be taken notice of, besides sounds, tastes, smells, visible and tangible qualities. And had mankind been made with but four senses, the qualities then which are the object of the fifth sense, had been as far from our notice, imagination, and conception, as now any belonging to a sixth, seventh, or eighth sense, can possibly be: which, whether yet some other creatures, in some other parts of this vast and stupendous universe, may not have, will be a great presumption to deny. He that will not set himself proudly at the top of all things, but will consider the immensity of this fabric, and the great variety that is to be found in this little and inconsiderable part of it which he has to do with, may be apt to think, that in other mansions of it there may be other and different intelligible beings, of whose faculties he has as little knowledge or apprehension, as a worm shut up in one drawer of a cabinet hath of the senses or understanding of a man; such variety and excellency being suitable to the wisdom and power of the Maker. I have here followed the common opinion of man's having but five senses, though perhaps there may be justly counted more; but either supposition serves equally to my present purpose. . . .

Of Our Knowledge of the Existence of Other Things

1. *It is to be had only by sensation.* The knowledge of our own being we have by intuition. The existence of a God reason clearly makes known to us, as has been shown.

The knowledge of the existence of any other thing we can have only by sensation: for there being no necessary connexion of real existence with any idea a man hath in his memory; nor of any other existence but that of God with the existence of any particular man: no particular man can know the existence of any other being, but only when, by actual operating upon him, it makes itself perceived by him. For the having the idea of anything in our mind no more proves the existence of that thing than the picture of a man evidences his being in the world, or the visions of a dream make thereby a true history.

2. It is therefore the actual receiving of ideas from without that gives us notice of the existence of other things, and makes us know that something doth exist at that time without us which causes that idea in us, though perhaps we neither know nor consider how it does it. For it takes not from the certainty of our senses, and the ideas we receive by them, that we know not the manner wherein they are produced: v.g., whilst I write this, I have, by the paper affecting my eyes, that idea produced in my mind, which whatever object causes, I call white; by which I know that that quality or accident (i.e., whose appearance before my eyes always causes that idea) doth really exist, and hath a being without me. And of this, the greatest assurance I can possibly have, and to which my faculties can attain, is the testimony of my eyes, which are the proper and sole judges of this thing; whose testimony I have reason to rely on as so certain, that I can no more doubt, whilst I write this, that I see white and black, and that something really exists that causes that sensation in me, than that I write or move my hand; which is a certainty as great as human nature is capable of, concerning the existence of anything but a man's self alone, and of God.

3. *This, though not so certain as demonstration, yet may be called knowledge, and proves the existence of things without us.* The notice we have by our senses of the existing of things without us, though it be not altogether so certain as our intuitive knowledge, or the deductions of our reason employed about the clear abstract ideas of our minds; yet it is an assurance that deserves the name of *knowledge*. If we persuade ourselves that our faculties act and inform us right concerning the existence of those objects that affect them, it cannot pass for an ill-grounded confidence: for I think nobody can, in earnest, be so sceptical as to be uncertain of the existence of those things which he sees and feels. At least, he that can doubt so far (whatever he may have with his own thoughts) will never have any controversy with me; since he can never be sure I say anything contrary to his opinion. As to myself, I think God has given me assurance enough of the existence of things without me; since by their different application I can produce in myself both pleasure and pain, which is one great concernment of my present state. This is certain, the confidence that our faculties do not herein deceive us is the greatest assurance we are capable of concerning the existence of material beings. For we cannot act anything but by our faculties, nor talk of knowledge itself, but by the help of those faculties which are fitted to apprehend even what knowledge is. But besides the assurance we have from our senses themselves, that they do not err in the information they give us of the existence of things without us, when they are affected by them, we are farther confirmed in this assurance by other concurrent reasons.

4. *Because we cannot have them but by the inlet of the senses.* First, It is plain those perceptions are produced in us by exterior causes affecting our senses, because those that want the organs of any sense never can have the ideas belonging to that sense produced in their minds. The organs themselves, it is plain, do not produce them; for then the eyes of a man in the dark would produce colours, and his nose smell roses in the winter: but we see nobody gets the relish of a pine-apple till he goes to the Indies where it is, and tastes it.

5. *Because an idea from actual sensation and another from memory are very distinct perceptions*. Secondly, Because sometimes I find that I cannot avoid the having those ideas produced in my mind. For though when my eyes are shut, or windows fast, I can at pleasure recall to my mind the ideas of light or the sun, which former sensations had lodged in my memory; so I can at pleasure lay by that idea, and take into my view that of the smell of a rose, or taste of sugar. But if I turn my eyes at noon towards the sun, I cannot avoid the ideas which the light or sun then produces in me. So that there is a manifest difference between the ideas laid up in my memory, and those which force themselves upon me, and I cannot avoid having. And therefore it must needs be some exterior cause, and the brisk acting of some objects without me, whose efficacy I cannot resist, that produces those ideas in my mind, whether I will or no. . . .

6. *Pleasure or pain, which accompanies actual sensation, accompanies not the returning of those ideas without the external objects.* Thirdly, Add to this, that many of those ideas are produced in us with pain, which afterwards we remember without the least offence. . . . Thus the pain of heat or cold, when the idea of it is revived in our minds, gives us no disturbance; which, when felt, was very troublesome, and is again, when actually repeated: which is occasioned by the disorder the external object causes in our bodies when applied to it. And we remember the pain of hunger, thirst, or the headache, without any pain at all; which would either never disturb us, or else constantly do it as often as we thought of it, were there nothing more but ideas floating in our minds, and appearances entertaining our fancies, without the real existence of things affecting us from abroad. . . .

7. *Our senses assist one another's testimony of the existence of outward things.* Fourthly, Our senses, in many cases, bear witness to the truth of each other's report concerning the existence of sensible things without us. He that sees a fire may, if he doubt whether it be anything more than a bare fancy, feel it too, and be convinced by putting his hand in it; which certainly could never be put into such exquisite pain by a bare idea or phantom, unless that the pain be a fancy too; which yet he cannot, when the burn is well, by raising the idea of it, bring upon himself again. . . .

8. *This certainty is as great as our condition needs.* But yet, if after all this any one will be so sceptical as to distrust his senses, and to affirm that all we see and hear, feel and taste, think and do, during our whole being, is but the series and deluding appearances of a long dream whereof there is no reality; and therefore will question the existence of all things or our knowledge of anything: I must desire him to consider, that if all be a dream, then he doth but dream that he makes the question; and so it is not much matter that a waking man should answer him. But yet, if he pleases, he may dream that I make him this answer, that the certainty of things existing *in rerum natura*, when we have the testimony of our senses for it, is not only as great as our frame can attain to, but as our condition needs. For our faculties being suited not to the full extent of being, nor to a perfect, clear, comprehensive knowledge of things free from all doubt and scruple; but to the preservation of us, in whom they are; and accommodated to the use of life: they serve to our purpose well enough, if they will but give us certain notice of those things which are convenient or inconvenient to us.

Intuition Gives Us Knowledge

Henri Bergson

Henri Bergson (1859-1941) was a distinguished French intellectual and a leading twentieth-century philosopher. He held one of the leading academic positions in France, the chair of modern philosophy at the Collège de France. His main works include *Creative Evolution* and *An Introduction to Metaphysics*, the source of this viewpoint. Bergson asserts that we can either know a thing from an outside perspective, by analysis, or from the inside, by intuition. Knowledge from the outside is merely relative and fails to capture the inner dynamic and unity of the real. Once analysis breaks things up it cannot put the pieces together again. What is left is a distorted set of static perspectives, not a real dynamic thing. Intuitive knowledge, like the kind we have of our own consciousness, grasps all of the complex and changing parts of a thing from the inside and as a unified whole. This intuitive knowledge is true

From Henri Bergson, *An Introduction to Metaphysics*, trans. by T.E. Hulme. New York: G.P. Putnam's Sons, 1912.

metaphysical knowledge, which cannot even be comprehended or communicated using the concepts of analysis, which are too rigid to capture the dynamic flow of things.

QUESTIONS

1. Bergson uses the example of absolute and relative motion to illustrate the difference between absolute and relative knowledge. Describe this difference in your own words.
2. According to the author, what is mere representation and why is it inadequate?
3. How does Bergson distinguish between representation and analysis?
4. Bergson believes that we can know our personalities by intuition. What kind of metaphors does he use to describe this process?
5. According to the author, exactly how incomprehensible are humanly inaccessible facts? Can we eventually achieve an understanding of such facts?
6. What does Bergson mean when he says that concepts become "too large" to fit a particular object?

■ ■ ■

A comparison of the definitions of metaphysics and the various concepts of the absolute leads to the discovery that philosophers, in spite of their apparent divergencies, agree in distinguishing two profoundly different ways of knowing a thing. The first implies that we move round the object; the second, that we enter into it. The first depends on the point of view at which we are placed and on the symbols by which we express ourselves. The second neither depends on a point of view nor relies on any symbol. The first kind of knowledge may be said to stop at the *relative*; the second, in those cases where it is possible, to attain the *absolute*.

Consider, for example, the movement of an object in space. My perception of the motion will vary with the point of view, moving or stationary, from which I observe it. My expression of it will vary with the systems of axes, or the points of reference, to which I relate it; that is, with the symbols by which I translate it. For this double reason I call such motion *relative*: in the one case, as in the other, I am placed outside the object itself. But when I speak of an *absolute* movement, I am attributing to the moving object an interior and, so to speak, states of mind; I also imply that I am in sympathy with those states, and that I insert myself in them by an effort of imagination. Then, according as the object is moving or stationary, according as it adopts one movement or another, what I experience will vary. And what I experience will depend neither on the point of view I may take up in regard to the object, since I am inside the object itself, nor on the symbols by which I may translate the motion, since I have rejected all translations in order to possess the original. In short, I shall no longer grasp the movement from without, remaining where I am, but from where it is, from within, as it is in itself. I shall possess an absolute.

Consider, again, a character whose adventures are related to me in a novel. The author may multiply the traits of his hero's character, may make him speak and act as much as he pleases, but all this can never be equivalent to the simple and indivisible feeling which I should experience if I were able for an instant to identify myself with the person of the hero himself. Out of that indivisible feeling, as from a spring, all the words, gestures, and actions of the man would appear to me to flow naturally. They would no longer be accidents which, added to the idea I had already formed of the character, continually enriched that idea, without ever completing it. The character would be given to me all at once, in its entirety, and the thousand incidents which manifest it, instead of adding themselves to the idea and so enriching it, would seem to me, on the contrary, to detach themselves from it, without, however, exhausting it or impoverishing its essence. All the things I am told about the man provide me with so many points of view from which I can observe him. All the traits which describe him, and which can make him known to me only by so many comparisons with persons or things I know already, are signs by which he is expressed more or less symbolically. Symbols and points of view, therefore, place me outside him; they give me only what he has in common with others, and not what belongs to him and to him alone. But that which is properly himself, that which constitutes his essence, cannot be perceived from without, being internal by definition, nor be expressed by symbols, being incommensurable with everything else. Description, history, and analysis leave me here in the relative. Coincidence with the person himself would alone give me the absolute.

It is in this sense, and in this sense only, that *absolute* is synonymous with *perfection*. Were all the photographs of a town, taken from all possible points of view, to go on indefinitely completing one another, they would never be equivalent to the solid town in which we walk about. Were all the translations of a poem into all possible languages to add together their various shades of meaning and, correcting each other by a kind of mutual retouching, to give a more and more faithful image of the poem they translate, they would yet never succeed in rendering the inner meaning of the original. A representation taken from a certain point of view, a translation made with certain symbols, will always remain imperfect in comparison with the object of which a view has been taken, or which the symbols seek to express. But the absolute, which is the object and not its representation, the original and not its translation, is perfect, by being perfectly what it is.

It is doubtless for this reason that the *absolute* has often been identified with the *infinite.* Suppose that I wished to communicate to someone who did not know Greek the extraordinarily simple impression that a passage in Homer makes upon me; I should first give a translation of the lines, I should then comment on my translation, and then develop the commentary; in this way, by piling up explanation on explanation, I might approach nearer and nearer to what I wanted to express; but I should never quite reach it. When you raise your arm, you accomplish a movement of which you have, from within, a simple perception; but for me, watching it from the outside, your arm passes through one point, then through another, and between these two there will be still other points; so that, if I began to count, the operation would go on forever. Viewed from the inside, then, an absolute is a simple thing; but looked at from the outside, that is to say, relatively to other things; it becomes, in relation to these signs which express it, the gold coin for which we never seem able to finish giving small change. Now, that which lends itself at the same time both to an indivisible apprehension and to an inexhaustible enumeration is, by the very definition of the word, an infinite.

It follows from this that an absolute could only be given in an *intuition*, whilst everything else falls within the province of *analysis*. By intuition is meant the kind of *intellectual sympathy* by which one places oneself within an object in order to coincide with what is unique in it and consequently inexpressible. Analysis, on the contrary, is the operation which reduces the object to elements already known, that is, to elements common both to it and other objects. To analyze, therefore, is to express a thing as a function of something other than itself. All analysis is thus a translation, a development into symbols, a representation taken from successive points of view from which we note as many resemblances as possible between the new object which we are studying and others which we believe we know already. In its eternally unsatisfied desire to embrace the object around which it is compelled to turn, analysis multiplies without end the number of its points of view in order to complete its always incomplete representation, and ceaselessly varies its symbols that it may perfect the always imperfect translation. It goes on, therefore, to infinity. But intuition, if intuition is possible, is a simple act.

Now it is easy to see that the ordinary function of positive science is analysis. Positive science works, then, above all, with symbols. Even the most concrete of the natural sciences, those concerned with life, confine themselves to the visible form of living beings, their organs and anatomical elements. They make comparisons between these forms, they reduce the more complex to the more simple; in short, they study the workings of life in what is, so to speak, only its visual symbol. If there exists any means of possessing a reality absolutely instead of knowing it relatively, of placing oneself within it instead of looking at it from outside points of view, of having the intuition instead of making the analysis: in short, of seizing it without any expression, translation, or symbolic representation—metaphysics is that means. *Metaphysics, then, is the science which claims to dispense with symbols.*

There is one reality, at least, which we all seize from within, by intuition and not by simple analysis. It is our own personality in its flowing through time—our self which endures. We may sympathize intellectually with nothing else, but we certainly sympathize with our own selves.

When I direct my attention inward to contemplate my own

self (supposed for the moment to be inactive), I perceive at first, as a crust solidified on the surface, all the perceptions which come to it from the material world. These perceptions are clear, distinct, juxtaposed or juxtaposable one with another; they tend to group themselves into objects. Next, I notice the memories which more or less adhere to these perceptions and which serve to interpret them. These memories have been detached, as it were, from the depth of my personality, drawn to the surface by the perceptions which resemble them; they rest on the surface of my mind without being absolutely myself. Lastly, I feel the stir of tendencies and motor habits—a crowd of virtual actions, more or less firmly bound to these perceptions and memories. All these clearly defined elements appear more distinct from me, the more distinct they are from each other. Radiating, as they do, from within outwards, they form, collectively, the surface of a sphere which tends to grow larger and lose itself in the exterior world. But if I draw myself in from the periphery towards the center, if I search in the depth of my being that which is most uniformly, most constantly, and most enduringly myself, I find an altogether different thing.

There is, beneath these sharply cut crystals and this frozen surface, a continuous flux which is not comparable to any flux I have ever seen. There is a succession of states, each of which announces that which follows and contains that which precedes it. They can, properly speaking, only be said to form multiple states when I have already passed them and turn back to observe their track. Whilst I was experiencing them they were so solidly organized, so profoundly animated with a common life, that I could not have said where any one of them finished or where another commenced. In reality no one of them begins or ends, but all extend into each other.

This inner life may be compared to the unrolling of a coil, for there is no living being who does not feel himself coming gradually to the end of his role; and to live is to grow old. But it may just as well be compared to a continual rolling up, like that of a thread on a ball, for our past follows us, it swells incessantly with the present that it picks up on its way; and consciousness means memory. . . .

Let us, then, rather, imagine an infinitely small elastic body, contracted, if it were possible, to a mathematical point. Let this be drawn out gradually in such a manner that from the point comes a constantly lengthening line. Let us fix our attention not on the line as a line, but on the action by which it is traced. Let us bear in mind that this action, in spite of its duration, is indivisible if accomplished without stopping, that if a stopping-point is inserted, we have two actions instead of one, that each of these separate actions is then the indivisible operation of which we speak, and that it is not the moving action itself which is divisible, but, rather, the stationary line it leaves behind it as its track in space. Finally, let us free ourselves from the space which underlies the movement in order to consider only the movement itself, the act of tension or extension; in short, pure mobility. We shall have this time a more faithful image of the development of our self in duration.

However, even this image is incomplete, and, indeed, every comparison will be insufficient, because the unrolling of our duration resembles in some of its aspects the unity of an advancing movement and in others the multiplicity of expanding states; and, clearly, no metaphor can express one of these two aspects without sacrificing the other. If I use the comparison of the spectrum with its thousand shades, I have before me a thing already made, whilst duration is continually in the making. If I think of an elastic which is being stretched, or of a spring which is extended or relaxed, I forget the richness of color, characteristic of duration that is lived, to see only the simple movement by which consciousness passes from one shade to another. The inner life is all this at once: variety of qualities, continuity of progress, and unity of direction. It cannot be represented by images.

But it is even less possible to represent it by *concepts*, that is by abstract, general, or simple ideas. It is true that no image can reproduce exactly the original feeling I have of the flow of my own conscious life. . . .

For, on the one hand, these concepts, laid side by side, never actually give us more than an artificial reconstruction of the object, of which they can only symbolize certain general and, in a way, impersonal aspects; it is therefore useless to believe that with them we can seize a reality of which they present to us the shadow alone. And, on the other hand, besides the illusion there is also a very serious danger. For the concept generalizes at the same time as it abstracts. The concept can only symbolize a particular property by making it common to an infinity of things. It therefore always more or less deforms the property by the extension it gives to it. Replaced in the metaphysical object to which it belongs, a property coincides with the object, or at least molds itself on it, and adopts the same outline. Extracted from the metaphysical object, and presented in a concept, it grows indefinitely larger, and goes beyond the object itself, since henceforth it has to contain it, along with a number of other objects. Thus the different concepts that we form of the properties of a thing inscribe round it so many circles, each much too large and none of them fitting it exactly. And yet, in the thing itself the properties coincided with the thing, and coincided consequently with one another. So that if we are bent on reconstructing the object with concepts, some artifice must be sought whereby this coincidence of the object and its properties can be brought about. For example, we may choose one of the concepts and try, starting from it, to get round to the others. But we shall then soon discover that according as we start from one concept or another, the meeting and combination of the concepts will take place in an altogether different way. According as we start, for example, from unity or from multiplicity, we shall have to conceive differently the multiple unity of duration. Everything will depend on the weight we attribute to this or that concept, and this weight will always be arbitrary, since the concept extracted from the object has no weight, being only the shadow of a body. In this way, as many different *systems* will spring up as there are external points of view from which the reality can be examined, or larger circles in which it can be enclosed. Simple concepts have, then, not only the inconvenience of dividing the concrete unity of the object into so many symbolical expressions; they also divide philosophy into distinct schools, each of which takes its seat, chooses its counters, and carries on with the others a game that will never end. Either metaphysics is only this play of ideas, or else, if it is a serious occupation of the mind, if it is a science and not simply an exercise, it must transcend concepts in order to reach intuition. Certainly, concepts are necessary to it, for all the other sciences work as a rule with concepts, and metaphysics cannot dispense with the other sciences. But it is only truly itself when it goes beyond the concept, or at least when it frees itself from rigid and ready-made concepts in order to create a kind very different from those which we habitually use; I mean supple, mobile, and almost fluid representations, always ready to mold themselves on the fleeting forms of intuition. . . . Let it suffice us for the moment to have shown that our duration can be presented to us directly in an intuition, that it can be suggested to us indirectly by images, but that it can never—if we confine the word concept to its proper meaning—be enclosed in a conceptual representation.

The Scientific Method Gives Us Knowledge

W.V. Quine and J.S. Ullian

W.V. Quine (1908-   ) rates as one of the leading philosophers of the twentieth century by virtue of his contributions to logic and the philosophy of language. He is famous, for, among other things, the way he relates ontology (the study of what is real) with logic and for his theory of the meaning of language. J.S. Ullian (1930-   ) is an influential philosopher at Washington University in St. Louis. He specializes in logic, mathematics, and computer science. In this selection, Quine and Ullian assert that self-evident truths and observations must be supplemented by hypotheses in order to yield the general truths of nature. They argue that good hypotheses possess five virtues (conservatism, modesty, simplicity, generality, refutability) which allow them to guide science in a credible and practical manner. These virtues have to be balanced against one another to develop good hypotheses.

From *The Web of Belief*, 2nd ed., by W.V. Quine and J.S. Ullian. New York: Random House, 1978. Reprinted by permission.

Even scientific revolutions can be described, according to the authors, in terms of a balance of these virtues. They are optimistic that the hypothetical/deductive method will continue to produce more and more general hypotheses which predict the future and explain the past.

QUESTIONS

1. According to the authors, what two things will a successful hypothesis do? Do you think a successful hypothesis is the same as a true one?
2. How do Quine and Ullian use the "leap in the dark" analogy? Do you think it is a good analogy?
3. Do the authors think the more modest alternative among competing conservative alternatives is the best one?
4. Which do the authors value more, the simplicity of a hypothesis or the simplicity of some entire part of science?
5. What reasons do Quine and Ullian give for preferring simplicity over complexity whenever possible?
6. According to the authors, what factors contribute to the plausibility of a hypothesis?
7. What do the authors see as the tradeoffs that lead to a scientific revolution?
8. Why, according to Quine and Ullian, are *ad hoc* hypotheses bad?
9. What do the authors believe is the only good likely to follow from a hypothesis that is not falsifiable?

■ ■ ■

Some philosophers once held that whatever was true could in principle be proved from self-evident beginnings by self-evident steps. The trait of absolute demonstrability, which we attributed to the truths of logic in a narrow sense and to relatively little else, was believed by those philosophers to pervade all truth. They thought that but for our intellectual limitations we could find proofs for any truths, and so, in particular, predict the future to any desired extent. These philosophers were the *rationalists*. Other philosophers, a little less sanguine, had it that whatever was true could be proved by self-evident steps from two-fold beginnings: self-evident truths and observations. . . .

What then of the truths of nature? Might these be derivable still by self-evident steps from self-evident truths together with observations? Surely not. Take the humblest generalization from observation: that giraffes are mute, that sea water tastes of salt. We infer these from our observations of giraffes and sea water because we expect instinctively that what is true of all observed samples is true of the rest. The principle involved here, far from being self-evident, does not always lead to true generalizations. It worked for the giraffes and the sea water, but it would have let us down if we had inferred from a hundred observations of swans that all swans are white.

Such generalizations already exceed what can be proved from observations and self-evident truths by self-evident steps. Yet such generalizations are still only a small part of natural science. Theories of molecules and atoms are not related to any observations in the direct way in which the generalizations about giraffes and sea water are related to observations of mute giraffes and salty sea water.

It is now recognized that deduction from self-evident truths and observation is not the sole avenue to truth nor even to reasonable belief. A dominant further factor, in solid science as in daily life, is *hypothesis*. In a word, hypothesis is guesswork; but it can be enlightened guesswork.

It is the part of scientific rigor to recognize hypothesis as hypothesis and then to make the most of it. Having accepted the fact that our observations and our self-evident truths do not together suffice to predict the future, we frame hypotheses to make up the shortage.

Calling a belief a hypothesis says nothing as to what the belief is about, how firmly it is held, or how well founded it is. Calling it a hypothesis suggests rather what sort of reason we have for adopting or entertaining it. People adopt or entertain a hypothesis because it would explain, if it were true, some things that they already believe. Its evidence is seen in its consequences. . . .

Hypothesis, where successful, is a two-way street, extending back to explain the past and forward to predict the future. What we try to do in framing hypotheses is to explain some otherwise unexplained happenings by inventing a plausible story, a plausible description or history of relevant portions of the world. What counts in favor of a hypothesis is a question not to be lightly answered. We may note five virtues that a hypothesis may enjoy in varying degrees.

Virtue I is *conservatism*. In order to explain the happenings that we are inventing it to explain, the hypothesis may have to conflict with some of our previous beliefs; but the fewer the better. Acceptance of a hypothesis is of course like acceptance of any belief in that it demands rejection of whatever conflicts with it. The less rejection of prior beliefs required, the more plausible the hypothesis—other things being equal.

Often some hypothesis is available that conflicts with no prior beliefs. Thus we may attribute a click at the door to arrival of mail through the slot. Conservatism usually prevails in such a case; one is not apt to be tempted by a hypothesis that upsets prior beliefs when there is no need to resort to one. When the virtue of conservatism deserves notice, rather, is when something happens that cannot evidently be reconciled with our prior beliefs.

There could be such a case when our friend the amateur magician tells us what card we have drawn. How did he do it? Perhaps by luck, one chance in fifty-two; but this conflicts with our reasonable belief, if all unstated, that he would not have volunteered a performance that depended on that kind of luck. Perhaps the cards were marked; but this conflicts with our belief that he had had no access to them, they being ours. Perhaps he peeked or pushed, with help of a sleight-of-hand; but this conflicts with our belief in our perceptiveness. Perhaps he resorted to telepathy or clairvoyance; but this would wreak havoc with our whole web of belief. The counsel of conservatism is the sleight-of-hand.

Conservatism is rather effortless on the whole, having inertia in its favor. But it is sound strategy too, since at each step it sacrifices as little as possible of the evidential support, whatever that may have been, that our overall system of beliefs has hitherto been enjoying. The truth may indeed be radically remote from our present system of beliefs, so that we may need a long series of conservative steps to attain what might have been attained in one rash leap. The longer the leap, however, the more serious an angular error in the direction. For a leap in the dark the likelihood of a happy landing is severely limited. Conservatism holds out the advantages of limited liability and a maximum of live options for each next move.

Virtue II, closely akin to conservatism, is *modesty*. One hypothesis is more modest than another if it is weaker in a logical sense: if it is implied by the other, without implying it. A hypothesis *A* is more modest than *A* and *B* as a joint hypothesis. Also, one hypothesis is more modest than another if it is more humdrum: that is, if the events that it assumes to have happened are of a more usual and familiar sort, hence more to be expected.

Thus suppose a man rings our telephone and ends by apologizing for dialing the wrong number. We will guess that he slipped, rather than that he was a burglar checking to see if anyone was home. It is the more modest of the two hypotheses, butterfingers being rife. We could be wrong, for crime is rife too. But still the butterfingers hypothesis scores better on modesty than the burglar hypothesis, butterfingers being rifer.

We habitually practice modesty, all unawares, when we identify recurrent objects. Unhesitatingly we recognize our car off there where we parked it, though it may have been towed away and another car of the same model may have happened to pull in at that spot. Ours is the more modest hypothesis, because staying put is a more usual and familiar phenomenon than the alternative combination.

It tends to be the counsel of modesty that the lazy world is the likely world. We are to assume as little activity as will suffice to account for appearances. This is not all there is to modesty. It does not apply to the preferred hypothesis in the telephone example, since Mr. Butterfingers is not assumed to be a less active man than one who might have plotted burglary. Modesty figured there merely in keeping the assumptions down, rather than in actually assuming inactivity. In the example of the parked car, however, the modest hypothesis does expressly assume there to be less activity than otherwise. This is a policy that guides science as well as common sense. It is even erected into an explicit principle of mechanics under the name of the law of least action.

Between modesty and conservatism there is no call to draw a sharp line. But by Virtue I we meant conservatism only in a literal sense—conservation of past beliefs. Thus there remain grades of modesty still to choose among even when Virtue I—compatibility with previous beliefs—is achieved to perfection; for both a slight hypothesis and an extravagant one might be compatible with all previous beliefs.

Modesty grades off in turn into Virtue III, *simplicity*. Where simplicity considerations become especially vivid is in drawing curves through plotted points on a graph. Consider the familiar practice of plotting measurements. Distance up the page represents altitude above sea level, for instance, and distance across represents the temperature of boiling water. We plot our measurements on the graph, one dot for each pair. However many points we plot, there remain infinitely many curves that may be drawn through them. Whatever curve we draw represents our generalization from the data, our prediction of what boiling temperatures would be found at altitudes as yet untested. And the curve we will choose to draw is the simplest curve that passes through or reasonably close to all the plotted points.

There is a premium on simplicity in any hypothesis, but the highest premium is on simplicity in the giant joint hypothesis that is science, or the particular science, as a whole. We cheerfully sacrifice simplicity of a part for greater simplicity of the whole when we see a way of doing so. Thus consider gravity. Heavy objects tend downward: here is an exceedingly simple hypothesis, or even a mere definition. However, we complicate matters by accepting rather the hypothesis that the heavy objects around us are slightly attracted also by one another, and by the neighboring mountains, and by the moon, and that all these competing forces detract slightly from the downward one. Newton propounded this more complicated hypothesis even though, aside from tidal effects of the moon, he had no means of detecting the competing forces; for it meant a great gain in the simplicity of physics as a whole. His hypothesis of universal gravitation, which has each body attracting each in proportion to mass and inversely as the square of the distance, was what enabled him to make a single neat system of celestial and terrestrial mechanics. . . .

What is simplicity? For curves we can make good sense of it in geometrical terms. A simple curve is continuous, and among continuous curves the simplest are perhaps those whose curvature changes most gradually from point to point. . . .

Simplicity is harder to define when we turn away from curves and equations. Sometimes in such cases it is not to be distinguished from modesty. Commonly a hypothesis *A* will count as simpler than *A* and *B* together; thus far simplicity and modesty coincide. On the other hand the simplicity gained by Newton's hypothesis of universal gravitation was not modesty, in the sense that we have assigned to that term; for the hypothesis was not logically implied by its predecessors, nor was it more humdrum in respect of the events that it assumed. Newton's hypothesis was simpler than its predecessors in that it covered in a brief unified story what had previously been covered only by two unrelated accounts. Similar remarks apply to the kinetic theory of gases.

In the notion of simplicity there is a nagging subjectivity. What makes for a brief unified story depends on the structure of our language, after all, and on our available vocabulary, which need not reflect the structure of nature. This subjectivity of simplicity is puzzling, if simplicity in hypotheses is to make for plausibility. Why should the subjectively simpler of two hypotheses stand a better chance of predicting objective events? Why should we expect nature to submit to our subjective standards of simplicity?

That would be too much to expect. Physicists and others are continually finding that they have to complicate their theories to accommodate new data. At each stage, however, when choosing a hypothesis subject to subsequent correction, it is still best to choose the simplest that is not yet excluded. This strategy recommends itself on much the same grounds as the strategies of conservatism and modesty. The longer the leap, we reflected, the more and wilder ways of going wrong. But likewise, the more complex the hypothesis, the more and wilder ways of going wrong; for how can we tell which complexities to adopt? Simplicity, like conservatism and modesty, limits liability. Conservatism can be good strategy even though one's present theory be ever so far from the truth, and simplicity can be good strategy even though the world be ever so complicated. Our steps toward the complicated truth can usually be laid out most dependably if the simplest hypothesis that is still tenable is chosen at each step. It has even been argued that this policy will lead us at least asymptotically toward a theory that is true. . . .

Virtue IV is *generality*. The wider the range of application of a hypothesis, the more general it is. When we find electricity conducted by a piece of copper wire, we leap to the hypothesis that all copper, not just long thin copper, conducts electricity.

The plausibility of a hypothesis depends largely on how compatible the hypothesis is with our being observers placed at random in the world. Funny coincidences often occur, but they are not the stuff that plausible hypotheses are made of. The more general the hypothesis is by which we account for our present observation, the less of a coincidence it is that our present observation should fall under it. Hence, in part, the power of Virtue IV to confer plausibility.

The possibility of testing a hypothesis by repeatable experiment presupposes that the hypothesis has at least some share of Virtue IV. For in a repetition of an experiment the test situation can never be exactly what it was for the earlier run of the experiment; and so, if both runs are to be relevant to the hypothesis, the hypothesis must be at least general enough to apply to both test situations.[1] One would of course like to have it much more general still.

Virtues I, II, and III made for plausibility. So does Virtue IV to some degree, we see, but that is not its main claim; indeed generality conflicts with modesty. But generality is desirable in that it makes a hypothesis interesting and important if true. . . .

When a way is seen of gaining great generality with little loss of simplicity, or great simplicity with no loss of generality, then conservatism and modesty give way to scientific revolution.

The aftermath of the famous Michelson-Morley experiment of 1887 is a case in point. The purpose of this delicate and ingenious experiment was to measure the speed with which the earth travels through the ether. For two centuries, from Newton onward, it had been a well-entrenched tenet that something called the ether pervaded all of what we think of as empty space. The great physicist Lorentz (1853-1928) had hypothesized that the ether itself was stationary. What the experiment revealed was that the method that was expected to enable measurement of the earth's speed through the ether was totally inadequate to that task. Supplementary hypotheses

---

[1]We are indebted to Nell E. Scroggins for suggesting this point.

multiplied in an attempt to explain the failure without seriously disrupting the accepted physics. Lorentz, in an effort to save the hypothesis of stationary ether, shifted to a new and more complicated set of formulas in his mathematical physics. Einstein soon cut through all this, propounding what is called the special theory of relativity.

This was a simplification of physical theory. Not that Einstein's theory is as simple as Newton's had been; but Newton's physics had been shown untenable by the Michelson-Morley experiment. The point is that Einstein's theory is simpler than Newton's as corrected and supplemented and complicated by Lorentz and others. It was a glorious case of gaining simplicity at the sacrifice of conservatism; for the time-honored ether went by the board, and far older and more fundamental tenets went by the board too. Drastic changes were made in our conception of the very structure of space and time. . . .

Yet let the glory not blind us to Virtue I. When our estrangement from the past is excessive, the imagination boggles; genius is needed to devise the new theory, and high talent is needed to find one's way about in it. Even Einstein's revolution, moreover, had its conservative strain; Virtue I was not wholly sacrificed. The old physics of Newton's classical mechanics is, in a way, preserved after all. For the situations in which the old and the new theories would predict contrary observations are situations that we are not apt to encounter without sophisticated experiment—because of their dependence on exorbitant velocities or exorbitant distances. This is why classical mechanics held the field so long. Whenever, even having switched to Einstein's relativity theory, we dismiss those exorbitant velocities and distances for the purpose of some practical problem, promptly the discrepancy between Einstein's theory and Newton's becomes too small to matter. Looked at from this angle, Einstein's theory takes on the aspect not of a simplification but a generalization. We might say that the sphere of applicability of Newtonian mechanics in its original simplicity was shown, by the Michelson-Morley experiment and related results, to be less than universal; and then Einstein's theory comes as a generalization, presumed to hold universally. Within its newly limited sphere, Newtonian mechanics retains its old utility. What is more, the evidence of past centuries for Newtonian mechanics even carries over, within these limits, as evidence for Einstein's physics; for, as far as it goes, it fits both.

What is thus illustrated by Einstein's relativity is more modestly exemplified elsewhere, and generally aspired to: the retention, in some sense, of old theories in new ones. If the new theory can be so fashioned as to diverge from the old only in ways that are undetectable in most ordinary circumstances, then it inherits the evidence of the old theory rather than having to overcome it. Such is the force of conservatism even in the context of revolution.

Virtues I through IV may be further illustrated by considering Neptune. That Neptune is among the planets is readily checked by anyone with reference material; indeed it passes as common knowledge, and there is for most of us no need to check it. But only through extensive application of optics and geometry was it possible to determine, in the first instance, that the body we call Neptune exists, and that it revolves around the sun. This required not only much accumulated science and mathematics, but also powerful telescopes and cooperation among scientists .

In fact it happens that Neptune's existence and planethood were strongly suspected even before that planet was observed. Physical theory made possible the calculation of what the orbit of the planet Uranus should be, but Uranus' path differed measurably from its calculated course. Now the theory on which the calculations were based was, like all theories, open to revision or refutation. But here conservatism operates: one is loath to revise extensively a well-established set of beliefs, especially a set so deeply entrenched as a basic portion of physics. And one is even more loath to abandon as spurious immense numbers of observation reports made by serious scientists. Given that Uranus had been observed to be as much as two minutes of arc from its calculated position, what was sought was a discovery that would render this deviation explicable within the framework of accepted theory. Then the theory and its generality would be unimpaired, and the new complexity would be minimal.

It would have been possible in principle to speculate that some special characteristic of Uranus exempted that planet from the physical laws that are followed by other planets. If such a hypothesis had been resorted to, Neptune would not have been discovered; not then, at any rate. There was a reason, however, for not resorting to such a hypothesis. It would have been what is called an *ad hoc hypothesis*, and ad hoc hypotheses are bad air; for they are wanting in Virtues III and IV. Ad hoc hypotheses are hypotheses that purport to account for some particular observations by supposing some very special forces to be at work in the particular cases at hand, and not generalizing sufficiently beyond those cases. The vice of an ad hoc hypothesis admits of degrees. The extreme case is where the hypothesis covers only the observations it was invented to account for, so that it is totally useless in prediction. Then also it is insusceptible of confirmation, which would come of our verifying its predictions. . . .

These reflections bring a fifth virtue to the fore: *refutability*, Virtue V. It seems faint praise of a hypothesis to call it refutable. But the point, we have now seen, is approximately this: some imaginable event, recognizable if it occurs, must suffice to refute the hypothesis. Otherwise the hypothesis predicts nothing, is confirmed by nothing, and confers upon us no earthly good beyond perhaps a mistaken peace of mind.

This is too simple a statement of the matter. Just about any hypothesis, after all, can be held unrefuted no matter what, by making enough adjustments in other beliefs—though sometimes doing so requires madness. We think loosely of a hypothesis as implying predictions when, strictly speaking, the implying is done by the hypothesis together with a supporting chorus of ill-distinguished background beliefs. It is done by the whole relevant theory taken together.

Properly viewed, therefore, Virtue V is a matter of degree, as are its four predecessors. The degree to which a hypothesis partakes of Virtue V is measured by the cost of retaining the hypothesis in the face of imaginable events. The degree is measured by how dearly we cherish the previous beliefs that would have to be sacrificed to save the hypothesis. The greater the sacrifice, the more refutable the hypothesis.

A prime example of deficiency in respect of Virtue V is astrology. Astrologers can so hedge their predictions that they are devoid of genuine content. We may be told that a person will "tend to be creative" or "tend to be outgoing," where the evasiveness of a verb and the fuzziness of adjectives serve to insulate the claim from repudiation. But even if a prediction should be regarded as a failure, astrological devotees can go on believing that the stars rule our destinies; for there is always some item of information, perhaps as to a planet's location at a long gone time, that may be alleged to have been overlooked. Conflict with other beliefs thus need not arise.

All our contemplating of special virtues of hypotheses will not, we trust, becloud the fact that the heart of the matter is observation. Virtues I through V are guides to the framing of hypotheses that, besides conforming to past observations, may plausibly be expected to conform to future ones. When they fail on the latter score, questions are reopened. Thus it was that the Michelson-Morley experiment led to modifications, however inelegant, of Newton's physics at the hands of Lorentz. When Einstein came out with a simpler way of accommodating past observations, moreover, his theory was no mere reformulation of the Newton-Lorentz system; it was yet a third theory, different in some of its predicted observations and answerable to them. Its superior simplicity brought plausibility to its distinctive consequences.

Hypotheses were to serve two purposes: to explain the past and predict the future. Roughly and elliptically speaking, the hypothesis serves these purposes by implying the past events that it was supposed to explain, and by implying future ones. More accurately speaking, as we saw, what does the implying is the whole relevant theory taken together, as newly revised by adoption of the hypothesis in question. Moreover, the predictions that are implied are mostly not just simple predictions of future observations or other events; more often they are conditional predictions. The hypothesis will imply that we will make these further observations if we look in such and such a place, or take other feasible steps. If the predictions come out right, we can win bets or gain other practical advantages. Also, when they come out right, we gain confirmatory evidence for our hypotheses. When they come out wrong, we go back and tinker with our hypotheses and try to make them better. . . .

We talk of framing hypotheses. Actually we inherit the main ones, growing up as we do in a going culture. The continuity of belief is due to the retention, at each particular time, of most beliefs. In this retentiveness science even at its most progressive is notably conservative. Virtue I looms large. A reasonable person will look upon some of his or her retained beliefs as self-evident, on others as common knowledge though not self-evident, on others as vouched for by authority in varying degree, and on others as hypotheses that have worked all right so far.

But the going culture goes on, and each of us participates in adding and dropping hypotheses. Continuity makes the changes manageable. Disruptions that are at all sizable are the work of scientists, but we all modify the fabric in our small way, as when we conclude on indirect evidence that the schools will be closed and the planes grounded or that an umbrella thought to have been forgotten by one person was really forgotten by another.

There Is Knowledge That Humans Cannot Know

THOMAS NAGEL

Thomas Nagel (1937-) has written significant works in ethics and the philosophy of the mind. He is a professor of philosophy and law at New York University and has been a visiting professor at Oxford University. He is known for asking important questions that elude other philosophers. His writings include *Mortal Questions* and *The View from Nowhere*. In this excerpt, he argues that conscious experience has an irreducibly subjective character—there are facts such as "what it is like to be a human being" or "what it is like to be a bat." He claims that these facts cannot be completely explained or even conceived of using conceptual resources derived from and limited by human experience. Since he does not think that denying the existence of such facts is an option, we are left with the existence of facts which are in principle inaccessible to humans.

From Thomas Nagel, "What Is It Like to Be a Bat?" *Philosophical Review*, 84 (1974).

QUESTIONS

1. How does Nagel define the "subjective character of experience"?
2. What attempts to explain the subjective character of experience have failed, according to the author?
3. Why, according to Nagel, can't we imagine what it is like for a bat to be a bat as opposed to merely imagining what it would be like for a human to behave like a bat?
4. What argument does the author make using the analogy of intelligent Martians?
5. According to the author, exactly how incomprehensible are humanly inaccessible facts? Can we eventually achieve an understanding of such facts?
6. Does Nagel believe that we can at least state these inaccessible facts?

■ ■ ■

Conscious experience is a widespread phenomenon. It occurs at many levels of animal life, though we cannot be sure of its presence in the simpler organisms, and it is very difficult to say in general what provides evidence of it. (Some extremists have been prepared to deny it even of mammals other than man.) No doubt it occurs in countless forms totally unimaginable to us, on other planets in other solar systems throughout the universe. But no matter how the form may vary, the fact that an organism has conscious experience *at all* means, basically, that there is something it is like to *be* that organism. There may be further implications about the form of the experience; there may even (though I doubt it) be implications about the behavior of the organism. But fundamentally an organism has conscious mental states if and only if there is something that it is like to *be* that organism—something it is like *for* the organism.

We may call this the subjective character of experience. It is not captured by any of the familiar, recently devised reductive analyses of the mental, for all of them are logically compatible with its absence. It is not analyzable in terms of any explanatory system of functional states, or intentional states, since these could be ascribed to robots or automata that behaved like people though they experienced nothing.* It is not analyzable in terms of the causal role of experiences in relation to typical human behavior—for similar reasons.† I do not deny that conscious mental states and events cause behavior, nor that they may be given functional characterizations. I deny only that this kind of thing exhausts their analysis. . . .

Let me first try to state the issue somewhat more fully than by referring to the relation between the subjective and the objective, or between the *pour soi* and the *en soi*. This is far from easy. Facts about what it is like to be an X are very peculiar, so peculiar that some may be inclined to doubt their reality, or the significance of claims about them. To illustrate the connection between subjectivity and a point of view, and to make evident the importance of subjective features, it will help to explore the matter in relation to an example that brings out clearly the divergence between the two types of conception, subjective and objective.

I assume we all believe that bats have experience. After all, they are mammals, and there is no more doubt that they have experience than that mice or pigeons or whales have experience. I have chosen bats instead of wasps or flounders because if one travels too far down the phylogenetic tree, people gradually shed their faith that there is experience there at all. Bats, although more closely related to us than those other species, nevertheless present a range of activity and a sensory apparatus so different from ours that the problem I want to pose is exceptionally vivid (though it certainly could be raised with other species). Even without the benefit of philosophical reflection, anyone who has spent some time in an enclosed space with an excited bat knows what it is to encounter a fundamentally *alien* form of life.

I have said that the essence of the belief that bats have ex-

---

*Perhaps there could not actually be such robots. Perhaps anything complex enough to behave like a person would have experiences. But that, if true, is a fact which cannot be discovered merely by analyzing the concept of experience.

†It is not equivalent to that about which we are incorrigible, both because we are not incorrigible about experience and because experience is present in animals lacking language and thought, who have no beliefs at all about their experiences.

perience is that there is something that it is like to be a bat. Now we know that most bats (microchiroptera, to be precise) perceive the external world primarily by sonar, or echolocation, detecting the reflections, from objects within range, of their own rapid, subtly modulated, high-frequency shrieks. Their brains are designed to correlate the outgoing impulses with the subsequent echoes, and the information thus acquired enables bats to make precise discriminations of distance, size, shape, motion, and texture comparable to those we make by vision. But bat sonar, though clearly a form of perception, is not similar in its operation to any sense that we possess, and there is no reason to suppose that it is subjectively like anything we can experience or imagine. This appears to create difficulties for the notion of what it is like to be a bat. We must consider whether any method will permit us to extrapolate to the inner life of the bat from our own case, and if not, what alternative methods there may be for understanding the notion.

Our own experience provides the basic material for our imagination, whose range is therefore limited. It will not help to try to imagine that one has webbing on one's arms, which enables one to fly around at dusk and dawn catching insects in one's mouth; that one has very poor vision, and perceives the surrounding world by a system of reflected high-frequency sound signals; and that one spends the day hanging upside down by one's feet in an attic. Insofar as I can imagine this (which is not very far), it tells me only what it would be like for *me* to behave as a bat behaves. But that is not the question. I want to know what it is like for *a bat* to be a bat. Yet if I try to imagine this, I am restricted to the resources of my own mind, and those resources are inadequate to the task. I cannot perform it either by imagining additions to my present experience, or by imagining segments gradually subtracted from it, or by imagining some combination of additions, subtractions, and modifications.

To the extent that I could look and behave like a wasp or a bat without changing my fundamental structure, my experiences would not be anything like the experiences of those animals. On the other hand, it is doubtful that any meaning can be attached to the supposition that I should possess the internal neurophysiological constitution of a bat. Even if I could by gradual degrees be transformed into a bat, nothing in my present constitution enables me to imagine what the experiences of such a future stage of myself thus metamorphosed would be like. The best evidence would come from the experiences of bats, if we only knew what they were like.

So if extrapolation from our own case is involved in the idea of what it is like to be a bat, the extrapolation must be incompletable. We cannot form more than a schematic conception of what it *is* like. For example, we may ascribe general *types* of experience on the basis of the animal's structure and behavior. Thus we describe bat sonar as a form of three-dimensional forward perception; we believe that bats feel some versions of pain, fear, hunger, and lust, and that they have other, more familiar types of perception besides sonar. But we believe that these experiences also have in each case a specific subjective character, which it is beyond our ability to conceive. And if there is conscious life elsewhere in the universe, it is likely that some of it will not be describable even in the most general experiential terms available to us. (The problem is not confined to exotic cases, however, for it exists between one person and another. The subjective character of the experience of a person deaf and blind from birth is not accessible to me, for example, nor presumably is mine to him. This does not prevent us each from believing that the other's experience has such a subjective character.)

If anyone is inclined to deny that we can believe in the existence of facts like this whose exact nature we cannot possibly conceive, he should reflect that in contemplating the bats we are in much the same position that intelligent bats or Martians* would occupy if they tried to form a conception of what it was like to be us. The structure of their own minds might make it impossible for them to succeed, but we know they would be wrong to conclude that there is not anything precise that it is like to be us: that only certain general types of mental state could be ascribed to us (perhaps perception and appetite would be concepts common to us both; perhaps not). We know they would be wrong to draw such a skeptical conclusion because we know what it is like to be us. And we know that while it includes an enormous amount of variation and complexity, and while we do

---

*Any intelligent extraterrestrial beings totally different from us.

not possess the vocabulary to describe it adequately, its subjective character is highly specific, and in some respects describable in terms that can be understood only by creatures like us. The fact that we cannot expect ever to accommodate in our language a detailed description of Martian or bat phenomenology should not lead us to dismiss as meaningless the claim that bats and Martians have experiences fully comparable in richness of detail to our own. It would be fine if someone were to develop concepts and a theory that enabled us to think about those things; but such an understanding may be permanently denied to us by the limits of our nature. And to deny the reality or logical significance of what we can never describe or understand is the crudest form of cognitive dissonance.

This brings us to the edge of a topic that requires much more discussion than I can give it here: namely, the relation between facts on the one hand and conceptual schemes or systems of representation on the other. My realism about the subjective domain in all its forms implies a belief in the existence of facts beyond the reach of human concepts. Certainly it is possible for a human being to believe that there are facts which humans never *will* possess the requisite concepts to represent or comprehend. Indeed, it would be foolish to doubt this, given the finiteness of humanity's expectations. After all, there would have been transfinite numbers even if everyone had been wiped out by the Black Death before Cantor discovered them. But one might also believe that there are facts which *could* not ever be represented or comprehended by human beings, even if the species lasted forever—simply because our structure does not permit us to operate with concepts of the requisite type. This impossibility might even be observed by other beings, but it is not clear that the existence of such beings, or the possibility of their existence, is a precondition of the significance of the hypothesis that there are humanly inaccessible facts. (After all, the nature of beings with access to humanly inaccessible facts is presumably itself a humanly inaccessible fact.) Reflection on what it is like to be a bat seems to lead us, therefore, to the conclusion that there are facts that do not consist in the truth of propositions expressible in a human language. We can be compelled to recognize the existence of such facts without being able to state or comprehend them.

What Is Ultimately Real?

Chapter Preface

Most of us do not have trouble accepting the reality of the ordinary objects of our experience. We believe that there are cars and dogs and stars and people. Many of us, however, are less sure about souls or justice or numbers. When we begin to ask questions like "What are things like cars ultimately made of?" or "Is everything material?" or "What kind of reality does justice have?" we are asking metaphysical questions. Metaphysics is the branch of philosophy which asks questions about what is really real. Maybe the car we see is ultimately just an idea or maybe it is actually mostly empty space. Western philosophy itself started with metaphysics when ancient Greek wise men attempted to explain the properties of the world by claiming that everything consists of water or fire or mind. Today metaphysical questions are argued against the backdrop of modern physics and biology, which have provided us with powerful descriptions of the world. An equally powerful contribution to metaphysics has come from the study of language and attempts to understand how language works.

There are a variety of respected philosophical perspectives that attempt to explain what is ultimately real. When philosophers like John Locke attempted to explain our knowledge of the physical world in terms of sensory impressions, Bishop Berkeley asked an obvious question: If all we have are our impressions and the ideas they cause, how can we know that there is any physical world at all? Maybe all we really know are our ideas themselves. Maybe those ideas are all there is and anything else is unjustified inference. People who argue this way are called idealists. The relationship between our ideas and the things, if any, that they are ideas *of* remains an important philosophical question.

David Hume was most impressed by the particular things that he believed caused our ideas. He believed that our ideas themselves were particular things in the same sense that physical objects are particular things. Other philosophers, including Plato, have long argued that there must be a special kind of reality made up of universals or general things which are much different from particular things like physical objects. Such people are called realists. They argue that these universals correspond to general ideas like *dog* and *triangle* which make it possible for us to use the words "dog" and "triangle" to refer to many different individual dogs and triangles. Since Hume believed that there were only individual things part of his philosophical responsibility was to explain how general terms like *triangle* can refer to groups of individual things. People, like Hume, who do not believe that there are universals are called nominalists. Hume makes a powerful argument based upon the similarity between various individual triangles. They can be grouped together and carry a common name because they are similar to each other, not because there is a universal *triangle* somewhere. This sort of argument does not satisfy every philosopher. Bertrand Russell took a hard look at language and concluded that similarity itself was a universal.

Materialism, the view that everything is made of matter, has a long and distinguished philosophical history beginning with the early Greek philosophers and continuing to the present. Newtonian physics and Darwinian evolution are generally used to argue in favor of materialistic explanations of even life and consciousness. Modern materialists like James Feibleman continue to make powerful arguments for materialism that reflect deeper insights into matter than were available to early materialists. Other philosophers, like Alfred North Whitehead and Charles Hartshorne, believe that some principle of consciousness or creativity is more fundamental than matter. They argue that the universe is not made up of static material things or substances, but of dynamic processes which are ultimately more like conscious experiences than stones or marbles. They are called process philosophers and are very influential in theological circles.

What is real and what only appears to be real? What is appearance itself? The viewpoints in this chapter attempt to answer these metaphysical questions.

Ideas Are Ultimately Real

GEORGE BERKELEY

George Berkeley (1685-1753) was a bishop in the Church of England who wrote important philosophical works as a young man. His writings include *A Treatise Concerning the Principles of Human Understanding*, from which this viewpoint is taken, and *Dialogues Between Hylas and Philonous*. Berkeley was impressed by John Locke, but he was convinced that many unnecessary philosophical problems stemmed from Locke's unwarranted idea of matter or material substance which in some unknowable way supports our experiences through the senses. Berkeley argued that all we actually know are our own ideas whose very existence consists in our knowing them. For these ideas "to be is to be perceived." Locke and others argued that qualities like taste and color were subjective and existed only in the mind while qualities like figure and extension exist objectively in matter. Berkeley argued that so-called objective qualities like extension cannot exist without so-called subjective qualities like color. We cer-

From *A Treatise Concerning the Principles of Human Knowledge* by George Berkeley. New York: Doubleday, Doran and Co., 1935.

tainly do not experience colorless extensions. Berkeley concludes that extension is as much an idea in the mind as color. This eliminates the need for matter and the world we experience consists entirely of ideas. Our ideas appear to be passive insofar as we can control them by using our minds as when we imagine or remember things. Berkeley accounts for the vivid and orderly ideas we have of the physical world in terms of the Author of nature, God. God is the powerful spirit whose will controls the ideas which make up the world. The being of the material world, like our ideas, is "to be perceived," but God perceives the world even when we do not.

QUESTIONS

1. According to Berkeley, what are the objects of human knowledge?
2. What does Berkeley mean by "a distinct thing signified by a name"?
3. Does Berkeley think the soul is an idea like a color or odor?
4. What kind of existence do objects in the world have, according to the author?
5. What does Berkeley assert is impossible to conceive in thought?
6. Why does Berkeley deny that qualities can exist in an unthinking substance?
7. According to Berkeley, what sorts of things do some philosophers think exist outside the mind even if colors and sounds and tastes do not?
8. How does Berkeley use the example of sweet and bitter tastes to argue his point?
9. What does the author mean by "material substance" and why does he deny that it exists?
10. What kinds of substances does Berkeley believe actually exist?
11. What does Berkeley think God explains?

■ ■ ■

It is evident to anyone who takes a survey of the objects of human knowledge, that they are either ideas (1) actually imprinted on the senses, or else such as are (2) perceived by attending to the passions and operations of the mind, or lastly (3) ideas formed by help of memory and imagination, either compounding, dividing, or barely representing those originally perceived in the aforesaid ways. By sight I have the ideas of lights and colors, with their several degrees and variations. By touch I perceive hard and soft, heat and cold, motion and resistance, and of all these more and less either as to quantity or degree. Smelling furnishes me with odors, the palate with tastes, and hearing conveys sounds to the mind in all their variety of tone and composition. And as several of these are observed to accompany each other, they come to be marked by one name, and so to be reputed as one thing. Thus, for example, a certain color, taste, smell, figure, and consistence, having been observed to go together, are accounted one distinct thing, signified by the name 'apple.' Other collections of ideas constitute a stone, a tree, a book, and the like sensible things; which, as they are pleasing or disagreeable, excite the passions of love, hatred, joy, grief, and so forth.

2. But besides all that endless variety of ideas or objects of knowledge, there is likewise something which knows or perceives them, and exercises divers operations, as willing, imagining, remembering, about them. This perceiving, active being is what I call *mind, spirit, soul*, or *myself*. By which words I do not denote any one of my ideas, but a thing entirely distinct from them wherein they exist, or, which is the same thing, whereby they are perceived; for the existence of an idea consists in being perceived.

3. That neither our thoughts, nor passions, nor ideas formed by the imagination, exist without the mind, is what everybody will allow. And it seems no less evident that the various sensations or ideas imprinted on the sense, however blended or combined together (that is, whatever objects they compose), cannot exist otherwise than in a mind perceiving them. I think an intuitive knowledge may be obtained of this by anyone that shall attend to what is meant by the term 'exist' when applied to sensible things. The table I write on I say exists—that is, I see and feel it; and if I were out of my study I should say it existed—meaning thereby that if I was in my study I might perceive it, or that some other spirit actually does perceive it. There was an odor, that is, it was smelt; there was a sound, that is, it was heard; a color or figure, and it was

perceived by sight or touch. This is all that I can understand by these and the like expressions. For as to what is said of the absolute existence of unthinking things without any relation to their being perceived, that seems perfectly unintelligible. Their *esse* is *percipi,* nor is it possible they should have any existence out of the minds or thinking things which perceive them.

4. It is indeed an opinion strangely prevailing amongst men, that houses, mountains, rivers, and in a word all sensible objects, have an existence, natural or real, distinct from their being perceived by the understanding. But with how great an assurance and acquiescence soever this principle may be entertained in the world, yet whoever shall find in his heart to call it in question may, if I mistake not, perceive it to involve a manifest contradiction. For what are the forementioned objects but the things we perceive by sense? and what do we perceive *besides our own ideas or sensations?* and is it not plainly repugnant that any one of these, or any combination of them, should exist unperceived?

5. If we thoroughly examine this tenet it will perhaps be found at bottom to depend on the doctrine of *abstract ideas.* For can there be a nicer strain of abstraction than to distinguish the existence of sensible objects from their being perceived, so as to conceive them existing unperceived? Light and colors, heat and cold, extension and figures—in a word the things we see and feel—what are they but so many sensations, notions, ideas, or impressions on the sense? And is it possible to separate, even in thought, any of these from perception? For my part, I might as easily divide a thing from itself. I may, indeed, divide in my thoughts, or conceive apart from each other, those things which perhaps I never perceived by sense so divided. Thus I imagine the trunk of a human body without the limbs, or conceive the smell of a rose without thinking on the rose itself. So far, I will not deny, I can abstract, if that may properly be called abstraction which extends only to the conceiving separately such objects as it is possible may really exist or be actually perceived asunder. But my conceiving or imagining power does not extend beyond the possibility of real existence or perception. Hence, as it is impossible for me to see or feel anything without an actual sensation of that thing, so it is impossible for me to conceive in my thoughts any sensible thing or object distinct from the sensation or perception of it.

6. Some truths there are so near and obvious to the mind

that a man need only open his eyes to see them. Such I take this important one to be, to wit, that all the choir of heaven and furniture of the earth, in a word all those bodies which compose the mighty frame of the world, have not any subsistence without a mind, that their *being* is to be perceived or known; that consequently so long as they are not actually perceived by me, or do not exist in my mind or that of any other created spirit, they must either have no existence at all, or else subsist in the mind of some Eternal Spirit; it being perfectly unintelligible, and involving all the absurdity of abstraction, to attribute to any single part of them an existence independent of a spirit. To be convinced of which, the reader need only reflect and try to separate in his own thoughts the *being* of a sensible thing from its *being perceived*.

7. From what has been said it follows there is not any other substance than *spirit*, or that which perceives. But for the fuller proof of this point, let it be considered the sensible qualities are color, figure, motion, smell, taste, etc.—that is, the ideas perceived by sense. Now, for an idea to exist in an unperceiving thing is a manifest contradiction, for to have an idea is all one as to perceive; that therefore wherein color, figure, and the like qualities exist must perceive them; hence it is clear there can be no unthinking substance or *substratum* of those ideas.

8. But, say you, though the ideas themselves do not exist without the mind, yet there may be things *like* them, whereof they are copies or resemblances, which things exist without the mind in an unthinking substance. I answer, an idea can be like nothing but an idea; a color or figure can be like nothing but another color or figure. If we look but never so little into our thoughts, we shall find it impossible for us to conceive a likeness except only between our ideas. Again, I ask whether those supposed originals or external things, of which our ideas are the pictures or representations, be themselves perceivable or no? If they are, then they are ideas and we have gained our point; but if you say they are not, I appeal to any one whether it be sense to assert a color is like something which is invisible; hard or soft, like something which is intangible; and so of the rest.

9. Some there are who make a distinction betwixt *primary* and *secondary* qualities. By the former they mean extension, figure, motion, rest, solidity or impenetrability, and number; by the latter they denote all other sensible qualities, as colors,

sounds, tastes, and so forth. The ideas we have of these they acknowledge not to be the resemblances of anything existing without the mind, or unperceived, but they will have our ideas of the primary qualities to be patterns or images of things which exist without the mind, in an unthinking substance which they call *matter*. By *matter*, therefore, we are to understand an inert, senseless substance, in which extension, figure, and motion do actually subsist. But it is evident from what we have already shown, that extension, figure, and motion are only ideas existing in the mind, and that an idea can be like nothing but another idea, and that consequently neither they nor their archetypes can exist in an unperceiving substance. Hence, it is plain that the very notion of what is called *matter*, or *corporeal substance*, involves a contradiction in it.

10. They who assert that figure, motion, and the rest of the primary or original qualities do exist without the mind in unthinking substances, do at the same time acknowledge that color, sounds, heat, cold, and suchlike secondary qualities, do not; which they tell us are sensations existing in the mind alone, that depend on and are occasioned by the different size, texture, and motion of the minute particles of matter. This they take for an undoubted truth, which they can demonstrate beyond all exception. Now, if it be certain that those original qualities are inseparably united with the other sensible qualities, and not, even in thought, capable of being abstracted from them, it plainly follows that they exist only in the mind. But I desire any one to reflect and try whether he can, by any abstraction of thought, conceive the extension and motion of a body without all other sensible qualities. For my own part, I see evidently that it is not in my power to frame an idea of a body extended and moving, but I must withal give it some color or other sensible quality which is acknowledged to exist only in the mind. In short, extension, figure, and motion, abstracted from all other qualities, are inconceivable. Where therefore the other sensible qualities are, there must these be also, to wit, in the mind and nowhere else. . . .

14. I shall further add that, after the same manner as modern philosophers prove certain sensible qualities to have no existence in matter, or without the mind, the same thing may be likewise proved of all other sensible qualities whatsoever. Thus, for instance, it is said that heat and cold are affections only of the

mind, and not at all patterns of real beings, existing in the corporeal substances which excite them, for that the same body which appears cold to one hand seems warm to another. Now, why may we not as well argue that figure and extension are not patterns or resemblances of qualities existing in matter, because to the same eye at different stations, or eyes of a different texture at the same station, they appear various, and cannot therefore be the images of anything settled and determinate without the mind? Again, it is proved that sweetness is not really in the sapid thing, because the thing remaining unaltered the sweetness is changed into bitter, as in case of a fever or otherwise vitiated palate. Is it not as reasonable to say that motion is not without the mind, since if the succession of ideas in the mind become swifter, the motion, it is acknowledged, shall appear slower without any alteration in any external object?

15. In short, let any one consider those arguments which are thought manifestly to prove that colors and tastes exist only in the mind, and he shall find they may with equal force be brought to prove the same thing of extension, figure, and motion—though it must be confessed this method of arguing does not so much prove that there is no extension or color in an outward object, as that we do not know by sense which is the true extension or color of the object. But the arguments foregoing plainly show it to be impossible that any color or extension at all, or other sensible quality whatsoever, should exist in an unthinking subject without the mind, or in truth, that there should be any such thing as an outward object.

16. But let us examine a little the received opinion. It is said extension is a mode or accident of matter, and that matter is the *substratum* that supports it. Now I desire that you would explain to me what is meant by matter's *supporting* extension. Say you, I have no idea of matter and therefore cannot explain it. I answer, though you have no positive, yet, if you have any meaning at all, you must at least have a relative idea of matter; though you know not what it is, yet you must be supposed to know what relation it bears to accidents, and what is meant by its supporting them. It is evident 'support' cannot here be taken in its usual or literal sense—as when we say that pillars support a building; in what sense therefore must it be taken?

17. If we inquire into what the most accurate philosophers declare themselves to mean by *material substance*, we shall find

them acknowledge they have no other meaning annexed to those sounds but the idea of *Being in general*, together with the relative notion of its supporting accidents. The general idea of Being appeareth to me the most abstract and incomprehensible of all other; and as for its supporting accidents, this, as we have just now observed, cannot be understood in the common sense of those words; it must therefore be taken in some other sense, but what that is they do not explain. So that when I consider the two parts or branches which make the signification of the words *material substance*, I am convinced there is no distinct meaning annexed to them. But why should we trouble ourselves any farther, in discussing this material *substratum* or support of figure and motion, and other sensible qualities? Does it not suppose they have an existence without the mind? And is not this a direct repugnancy, and altogether inconceivable?

18. But though it were possible that solid, figured, movable substances may exist without the mind, corresponding to the ideas we have of bodies, yet how is it possible for us to know this? Either we must know it by sense or by reason. As for our senses, by them we have the knowledge only of our sensations, ideas, or those things that are immediately perceived by sense, call them what you will; but they do not inform us that things exist without the mind, or unperceived, like to those which are perceived. This the materialists themselves acknowledge. It remains therefore that if we have any knowledge at all of external things, it must be by reason, inferring their existence from what is immediately perceived by sense. But what reason can induce us to believe the existence of bodies without the mind, from what we perceive, since the very patrons of matter themselves do not pretend there is any necessary connection betwixt them and our ideas? I say it is granted on all hands (and what happens in dreams, frenzies, and the like, puts it beyond dispute) that *it is possible we might be affected with all the ideas we have now, though there were no bodies existing without, resembling them.* Hence, it is evident the supposition of external bodies is not necessary for the producing our ideas; since it is granted they are produced sometimes, and might possibly be produced always in the same order we see them in at present, without their concurrence. . . .

25. All our ideas, sensations, notions, or the things which we perceive, by whatsoever names they may be distinguished, are visibly inactive: there is nothing of power or agency included in

them. So that one idea or object of thought cannot produce or make any alteration in another. To be satisfied of the truth of this, there is nothing else requisite but a bare observation of our ideas. For, since they and every part of them exist only in the mind, it follows that there is nothing in them but what is perceived: but whoever shall attend to his ideas, whether of sense or reflection, will not perceive in them any power or activity; there is, therefore, no such thing contained in them. A little attention will discover to us that the very being of an idea implies passiveness and inertness in it, insomuch that it is impossible for an idea to do anything, or, strictly speaking, to be the cause of anything: neither can it be the resemblance or pattern of any active being. Whence it plainly follows that extension, figure, and motion cannot be the cause of our sensations. To say, therefore, that these are the effects of powers resulting from the configuration, number, motion, and size of corpuscles, must certainly be false.

26. We perceive a continual succession of ideas, some are anew excited, others are changed or totally disappear. There is therefore some cause of these ideas, whereon they depend, and which produces and changes them. That this cause cannot be any quality or idea or combination of ideas, is clear from the preceding section. It must therefore be a substance; but it has been shewn that there is no corporeal or material substance: it remains therefore that the cause of ideas is an incorporeal active substance or Spirit.

27. A spirit is one simple, undivided, active being: as it perceives ideas it is called the *understanding*, and as it produces or otherwise operates about them it is called the *will*. Hence there can be no *idea* formed of a soul or spirit; for all ideas whatever, being passive and inert, they cannot represent unto us, by way of image or likeness, that which acts. A little attention will make it plain to any one, that to have an idea which shall be like that active principle of motion and change of ideas is absolutely impossible. Such is the nature of *spirit*, or that which acts, that it cannot be of itself perceived, but only by the effects which it produceth. If any man shall doubt of the truth of what is here delivered, let him but reflect and try if he can frame the idea of any power or active being, and whether he hath ideas of two principal powers, marked by the names *will* and *understanding*, distinct from each other as well as from a third idea of

substance or being in general, with a relative notion of its supporting or being the subject of the aforesaid powers—which is signified by the name *soul* or *spirit*. This is what some hold; but, so far as I can see, the words *will, soul, spirit*, do not stand for different ideas, or, in truth, for any idea at all, but for something which is very different from ideas, and which, being an agent, cannot be like unto, or represented by, any idea whatsoever. Though it must be owned at the same time that we have some *notion* of soul, spirit, and the operations of the mind such as willing, loving, hating; inasmuch as we know or understand the meaning of these words.

28. I find I can excite ideas in my mind at pleasure, and vary and shift the scene as oft as I think fit. It is no more than willing, and straightway this or that idea arises in my fancy; and by the same power it is obliterated and makes way for another. This making and unmaking of ideas doth very properly denominate the mind active. Thus much is certain and grounded on experience; but when we think of unthinking agents or of exciting ideas exclusive of volition, we only amuse ourselves with words.

29. But, whatever power I may have over my own thoughts, I find the ideas actually perceived by sense have not a like dependence on my will. When in broad daylight I open my eyes, it is not in my power to choose whether I shall see or no, or to determine what particular objects shall present themselves to my view; and so likewise as to the hearing and other senses, the ideas imprinted on them are not creatures of my will. There is therefore some other will or spirit that produces them.

30. The ideas of sense are more strong, lively, and distinct than those of the imagination; they have likewise a steadiness, order, and coherence, and are not excited at random, as those which are the effects of human wills often are, but in a regular train or series, the admirable connection whereof sufficiently testifies the wisdom and benevolence of its Author. Now the set rules or established methods wherein the mind we depend on excites in us the ideas of sense, are called the *laws of nature*; and these we learn by experience, which teaches us that such and such ideas are attended with such and such other ideas, in the ordinary course of things.

31. This gives us a sort of foresight which enables us to regulate our actions for the benefit of life. And without this we

should be eternally at a loss: we could not know how to act anything that might procure us the least pleasure, or remove the least pain of sense. That food nourishes, sleep refreshes, and fire warms us; that to sow in the seed-time is the way to reap in the harvest; and, in general, that to obtain such or such ends, such or such means are conducive—all this we know, not by discovering any necessary connection between our ideas, but only by the observation of the settled laws of nature, without which we should be all in uncertainty and confusion, and a grown man no more know how to manage himself in the affairs of life than an infant just born.

32. And yet this consistent uniform working, which so evidently displays the goodness and wisdom of that governing Spirit whose will constitutes the laws of nature, in so far from leading our thoughts to Him, that it rather sends them wandering after second causes. For, when we perceive certain ideas of sense constantly followed by other ideas and we know this is not of our own doing, we forthwith attribute power and agency to the ideas themselves, and make one the cause of another, than which nothing can be more absurd and unintelligible. Thus, for example, having observed that when we perceive by sight a certain round luminous figure we at the same time perceive by touch the idea or sensation called heat, we do from thence conclude the sun to be the cause of heat. And in like manner perceiving the motion and collision of bodies to be attended with sound, we are inclined to think the latter the effect of the former.

33. The ideas imprinted on the senses by the Author of nature are called *real things*; and those excited in the imagination, being less regular, vivid, and constant, are more properly termed *ideas*, or *images of things*, which they copy and represent. But then our sensations, be they never so vivid and distinct, are nevertheless ideas, that is, they exist in the mind, or are perceived by it, as truly as the ideas of its own framing. The ideas of sense are allowed to have more reality in them, that is, to be more strong, orderly, and coherent than the creatures of the mind; but this is no argument that they exist without the mind. They are also less dependent on the spirit, or thinking substance which perceives them, in that they are excited by the will of another and more powerful spirit; yet still they are *ideas*, and certainly no idea, whether faint or strong, can exist otherwise than in a mind perceiving it.

Matter, Including the Mind, Is Ultimately Real

JAMES FEIBLEMAN

James Feibleman (1904-) is a prolific writer who has made significant contributions to diverse philosophical fields including philosophy of science, epistemology, social philosophy, metaphysics, and moral philosophy. His writings include *Foundations of Empiricism*, a book of poetry, and *The New Materialism*, from which this reading is taken. Feibleman argues that materialism—the idea that reality is composed of matter—is an implicit part of the actual practice of science today, just as it has always been. He believes the earlier conceptions of matter were not refined enough to explain all reliable knowledge about the universe, but that current conceptions of matter are adequate. This makes him a materialist, i.e., someone who believes that all reality is ultimately material. Feibleman includes energy as a form of matter and claims that scientists have discovered no things in the universe that are not composed of some form of matter. Even consciousness and so-called spiritual things, Feibleman believes, can be explained in materialist terms when they are properly understood.

From pp. 39-51 of *The New Materialism* by James Feibleman. The Hague, Netherlands: Martinus Nijhoff, 1970. Reprinted by permission of Kluwer Academic Publishers.

QUESTIONS

1. According to the author, what kinds of philosophical interpretations immediately followed the revolution in physics?
2. What does Feibleman mean when he says that all scientists are formal materialists?
3. According to Feibleman, how has the scientific understanding of matter changed over the last quarter-century?
4. What five characteristics of matter does the author claim we have learned from the physical sciences?
5. Does Feibleman think the five properties of matter are displayed on all levels of complexity?
6. According to Feibleman, are there any parts of reality that cannot be explained by materialism?

■ ■ ■

The history of science is an account not of steady development but rather of progress in bursts. One such burst occurred in the seventeenth century, sparked by Galileo. Another, in the eighteenth century, was led by Newton, and a third in the nineteenth century owed much to Darwin. The latest, in the twentieth century, is due chiefly to Planck and Einstein.

Each such advance is followed by a period of consolidation. Scientists busy themselves working out the consequences of great discoveries which they interpret as breakthroughs to more widespread research. Philosophers undertake the task of interpretation which has been posed for them afresh.

The revolution in physics has had an effect upon philosophy from which it has not yet recovered. By the end of the first quarter of the twentieth century, the first phase of the revolution was substantially completed. It cried aloud for interpretation. The first volunteers for the task were the physicists themselves. Planck and Einstein, as it happened, were realists; but their contentions were drowned out by the cries of the idealists, Eddington and Jeans, whose subjective interpretation became the fashionable one. The special theory of relativity, it was claimed, required that everything physical be relative to an observer, which is to say a knowing subject, who constituted the frame of reference. Planck's quantum constant was accepted as evidence that matter evaporates when examined closely, so that nothing remains of the physical world but the mathematical thoughts about it. Heisenberg's principle of indeterminacy, as defended and interpreted by Bohr and the Copenhagen school generally, meant that there is nothing objective to know; whether a material object is a wave or a particle depends upon how the observer takes his readings—relies, in short, upon the observer himself. The positivists, who seemed to disagree with this extreme subjectivism, nevertheless wished to confine scientific interpretation to a description of the physical world and ultimately to the performance of the physicists themselves, as for instance in the crude physicalism of Carnap and the operationalism of Bridgman.

The early epistemologists who followed in the wake of these interpretations made by the scientists were quick to seek support for Kantian subjectivism. Some, like Russell with his sense-datum theory, tried to find an intermediate position, but in general the surrender to the subject of knowledge was complete. That such a reading of the conclusions of a given period in physics did not check with the assumptions of a philosophical nature underlying the procedures called for and followed by the experimental method, was not particularly noticed. The problem of interpretation was assumed to have been settled and there was a pause.

A quarter of a century has now elapsed, and it is time to take another reading. The consolidation of the scientific revolution lies more clearly in one direction than in others. Moreover, there had already taken place developments in philosophy which were overlooked at the time. Formal materialism, at least as practiced if not as preached, had been around for some centuries, and had already influenced the development of "experimental philosophy."

All scientists are formal materialists in so far as their philosophies can be deduced from their behavior. They differ in their avowed beliefs about the philosophical foundations of their sciences but not about their methods, and it is the methods that they practice, not the beliefs. For they investigate matter in order to determine its formal properties. The theory of materialism has always existed as a thing apart from the study of matter as conducted for instance by such sciences as physics and chemistry.

The historical evidence indicates that science in fact arose as a product of materialism. There was Xenophanes, there was the tradition of mechanical materialism in Aristippus and Democritus, and there was the more dynamic materialism of Aristotle. Aristotle defined matter as potentiality to the actuality of the forms, the indeterminate underlying the determinate. From Aristotle's day to our own matter has meant a gross stuff perceptible to the senses and resistant to change, and lending to things such reality as they have. It is possible to see in this common sense version of formal materialism something of the influence of Aristotle, although perhaps lacking in the element of dynamism. The early scientists certainly behaved professionally like materialists, for they sought knowledge through an examination of matter. Despite the reaffirmation of the materialism of Democritus by Epicurus, there was no addition to the assertion of the truth of materialism between the death of Aristotle and the careers of the early scientists but they behaved professionally like materialists, for they sought reliable knowledge through an examination of matter. From Grosseteste to Newton, that is to say, from the twelfth century to the seventeenth, whatever the professed philosophy may have been, the behavior disclosed an adherence to materialism. For the scientific method relied primarily upon experiments by means of which sense experience was asked to discover evidence of natural regularities which could be formulated mathematically as laws. The nineteenth century development of dialectical materialism came out of science as much as it did out of Feuerbach, as the writings of both Marx and Engels—especially the latter—testify. But an exclusively materialist interpretation of the new physics was rejected on the grounds that any complete understanding of the physical world must include mind, and the mental is the opposite pole of the material.

It would be logical, then, to suppose that the variety of materialism which had given rise to science would be adequate for its interpretation. But this is not the case. Science, with respect both to its techniques and its interpretation, has changed and developed. It has become far more complex. The "matter" of traditional materialism, from the conception of the Greek atomists to the later version which was responsible for the philosophy of dialectical materialism, enjoyed a certain measure of continuity. Matter consisted in hard, round, impenetrable bits of stuff which were ultimately simple and solid. All were falling, the heavier falling faster. The kinds of motion and of interaction it was called on to carry were also simple. The heavier collided with the lighter, and when not directly in the line of centers produced a sideways motion. But there were limitations to the explanatory value of this conception. Other values, the so-called spiritual values, had to find another vehicle.

It is important to remember that to defend a coherent position or to follow a consistent procedure means to assume a philosophy. With the advent of the scientific method and the consequent development of science has come an increased knowledge of matter. We know more about it now than we did when materialism first became prominent. Matter is no longer considered a simple, inert stuff which resists analysis and has to be reckoned with only in the round, but has been acknowledged to be a highly dynamic agent capable of sustaining the most complex activities. It is no more composed of atoms, that is to say, uncuttable and irreducible bits of stuff. The new atom is complex, and its indefinitely analyzable levels and properties make it possible to sustain not only the physical properties, such as mass, density and dimension, but also all of the qualities that were once carried only by the spiritual values, or according to idealism by the consciousness of human subjects.

In order to understand what the term "matter" will be taken to mean in the following pages, a definition is necessary; but since matter is a kind of substance, a definition of substance is first required.

Substance is the irrational ground of individual reaction. It has two subdivisions, matter and energy. Matter is static substance; energy, dynamic. Matter and energy are demonstrably interconvertible in accordance with the Einstein formula.

In what it may be possible to call the new materialism matter can now support all of the properties of which we have knowledge, whether these be substantial or logical. The richness of matter renders it capable of containing everything which has been attributed to it by the philosophers, from the Greeks to the moderns. Matter is no longer a term confined to familiar objects. It applies equally to objects accessible only through instruments and mathematical calculations: microscopic objects, such as atoms and cells, and macroscopic objects, such as star clusters and eclipsing binaries. It is clear that throughout the lower integrative levels of the physical and the chemical the same basic though complex and tenuous "stuff" is under consideration. As science progresses, more and more is learned about it, but there always is still more to be learned.

It is perhaps the insight of Heraclitus and Bergson that what exists objectively exceeds what can be comprehended subjectively in our limited schemes. However, the consideration of time as the past and future in relation to the present, was needed to make their conceptions convincing. Much more is involved in the time categories than the mere succession of the things and events they order. There are certain properties of matter which have existed in the past and will exist again in the future (or at least may exist) but which are not to be found now in the material world. How for instance is matter to support the properties which are not present? For these we need another type of explanation. The acceptance of naive materialism would be a simple affair were it not for the matter and energy which existed in the past and will exist in the future. Logical place-holders are needed to represent absent objects. Thus the minimun philosophy is some logical version of materialism consisting in a conception of movement from past to future in a manner which allows present material objects to be exchanged for others. The single category of matter must be supplemented by one more category designed to account for absent material objects.

It is not possible to prove the truth of any philosophy. All that a philosophy can offer is an explanation. The argument in favor of formal materialism, therefore, is not whether it can explain everything but whether it can provide explanations which are a little more adequate than those of other philosophies. Simplicity as well as thoroughness must be taken into consideration in such a judgment, with consistency furnishing the criterion for simplicity, and completeness the one for thoroughness.

The major contention already stated, namely, that matter as currently understood is quite capable of supporting as properties all of reliable knowledge, will require some evidence. Such evidence will be furnished in the next two parts. In the first of these, the evidence of the experimental sciences will be adduced. From each of their broad divisions, something of the structure of matter will be learned. In the second part, given an understanding of the structure of matter, it will be shown how some of the properties previously thought to be excluded from matter, such as the so-called spiritual values, can now be shown to be included.

The justification for the definitions of substance, matter and energy, as stated above, comes from the findings of the experimental sciences. The chief source for the contemporary knowledge of matter, and hence for the formulation of a new version of materialism, comes of course from the physical sciences. We have learned from the physics of the last few decades that matter is (a) complex, (b) indefinitely divisible, (c) averagely distributed, (d) rare, and (e) uniform.

(a) Something of the complexity of matter is shown by the enormously wide variety of subatomic constituents. A recent count discloses forty or more different particles. Atoms are composed not only of protons and electrons but also of positrons, neutrons, pi mesons, muons, photons and many others. More are still being discovered. If it is legitimate to speak of the basic structure of matter, perhaps this refers to the hydrogen atom consisting of one proton with an electron in the ground state. In the heavier atoms additional entities and processes are involved. The best description of matter probably requires the addition of de Broglie's "standing waves," electrons in vibratory motion. The model of the atom itself offers considerable evidence for the contention that matter is exceedingly complex. The orbital model has been exchanged recently for the powder model, according to which the electron within the shell is understood to be a sort of averagely distributed affair.

Further evidence for the complexity of matter comes from the discovery of an additional state. Matter hitherto has been supposed to consist in three states: the solid, the liquid and the gaseous. Now an additional state has been discovered, the plasma state. This is the ionic, or excited, state of matter.

(b) Claims for the indefinite divisibility of matter have been supported by the failure to exhaust the list of atomic constituents. New ones are in fact frequently announced. Then, too, there is the problematic question of energy levels. There is the atom itself, to say nothing of the molecules it composes. Then there is the nucleus, with its particles and short-range forces. And below that the hypothesis of a sub-quantum-mechanical causal level. The wave-particle duality, like the matter-energy transformation, is additional evidence for complexity and divisibility.

(c) Knowledge of the character of the distribution of matter comes from the science of astronomy. Every successive estimation of the size of the universe revises the figure upward. Some half million galaxies catalogued, another half million observed, and no limit to the outer edges of the observed field, that is the story to date. Matter, then, is extremely prevalent; yet it is also scarce. The scattering gives a very low average density for the matter in metagalactic space. There is roughly as much matter between the stars as there is within the stars. Matter is bunched, but the bunches are separated by great expanses. The distribution of matter in space is uniform, with an overwhelming preponderance of volumes of empty space over volumes of matter.

(d) Matter is a rare enough phenomenon, but since we know nothing that can be done without at least a material base, it is highly valuable. Bearing in mind the material range, from that of gross objects in the solid state to that of extremely weak forms of energy such as gravitation, matter is an essential component of all activity. Nothing can be accomplished with matter alone—or without it. Matter as something rare and valuable may be a new conception; it is a demonstrable one.

(e) The chemical analysis of the stars has been a much more limited affair, since it relies chiefly on spectrometer studies. But the familiar elements, those ordinarily present on the surface of the earth, are the only ones detected thus far, and they are very common. This evidence lends some support to the contention that the matter of the stars although in different chemical compounds and in varying states, is very much the same as the matter of the earth. But although earthlike planets are probably common enough in many of the galaxies, planets and stars are no longer the chief features of the cosmos. There are, first of all, a number of different types of galaxies, such as star clusters and occulting binaries, and there are also vast hydrogen clouds, and fields of ionic radiation.

Another piece of evidence from astronomy concerning distribution comes from studies of the decay and death of the stars. Everywhere we look in the material universe we find the same entities and the same processes at work. No single configuration of matter persists indefinitely but all is change and recombination. Due to the interconvertibility of matter and energy, what recurs is the structures while the underlying substance remains capable of sustaining the structures.

Chemistry is the study of the molecular level of matter. The chemical elements with their isotopes, together with the organic compounds of biochemistry, yield an almost inexhaustible set of combinations of a basic group of elements. What chemistry shows is the prevalence of a material foundation capable of supporting a number of fixed forms. Stones, planets, interstellar gases, all of the gross material objects perceptible by the unaided senses, consist in huge repetitions of simple chemical structures.

We have been examining the nature of matter from the evidence furnished by the physical sciences: physics, astronomy and chemistry. As we continue our examination upward in the empirical sciences, moving from chemistry to the biological sciences, we find additional evidence of the same kind of matter but now supporting more elaborate forms. We shall find that the matter of which the biological organisms are composed discloses the same five properties.

An intricate but continuous series of steps leads from the molecule to the cell. Cells are enormously complex structures of giant molecules, and there are actually borderline cases, such as the tobacco mosaic virus, studied by W. M. Stanley and others, which is both a crystal and a virus by turns. Protein molecules have been synthesized from less organized materials and their patterns discovered.

From biochemistry and biology it has been possible to learn of the deep affinity to matter of living organisms. It would seem that organisms are enormously complex chemical compounds still more complexly organized and integrated. They are not generically different even though they may be structurally higher. Animals, including the human, evolved from lower forms, and some of them are still evolving. Animals, historically speaking, ride to their adventures: death for the dinosaur and the dodo, four million years of life unchanged for the horseshoe crab, and evolution for the ancestors of man.

There is considerable evidence that life was produced spontaneously from inorganic materials. Protons and electrons combine into atoms, atoms combine into molecules, molecules combine into cells, cells combine into organisms, organisms combine into societies. The series is continuous and the dividing line between the inorganic and the organic a thin and perhaps non-existent one. Amino-acids have been produced in the laboratory by subjecting a mixture of gases such as might have been present in the atmosphere of the early earth to repeated spark discharges. It is known that proteins consist of long chains of amino-acid residues. Also, it is meaningful that the tobacco mosaic virus can be crystallized. Although cells behave in the body quite differently from what they do in vitro, and although there are no doubt autonomous organic structures, so are there chemical structures and even physical structures more complex than, and qualitatively different from, the basic atoms of hydrogen. But this does not detract from the fact that all of the higher structures are the result of the complications of matter.

Additional evidence of the nature of matter is furnished by the combination of scientific findings. Such evidence occurs in many ways. We shall here consider one.

The universe is large, and the conditions here on earth must occur many times. If life has been produced spontaneously from inorganic materials, then it could exist wherever there is the same set of conditions. Estimates of the number of planets capable of sustaining life give 100,000 as the figure for our galaxy alone. If Darwinian evolution holds, then there is no reason to suppose that the evolutionary processes which produced man necessarily stop there. Other planets might be the scene for the development of species higher than man, provided only that life on them has gone on somewhat longer.

We are now in a position to say little more about matter. The properties of matter were once held to be few and known, now they are understood to be many and largely unknown. This weakens the assumptions and widens the implications. We have learned that matter can be analyzed into atomic and nuclear constituents, and that it can be integrated into higher structures. There are limits in both directions, but science has not yet arrived at them. Even the smallest physical entities possess structures which are fabulously intricate, and the extent of the universe remains for all of astronomy's efforts largely unknown. There has not yet been a successful penetration inside the electron or outside the metagalaxy. The lower structures remain intact in the higher. Thus chemical compounds and living organisms are equally material objects. The decomposition of any higher structure if carried sufficiently far will result in a material object with a lower structure. But at whatever analytical or integrative level we are dealing, it is still the same matter, a static substance having as its property a potentiality of reaction. The unity of the universe is a material unity.

The thesis of this study is that matter as presently understood is capable of supporting as properties all of reliable knowledge. We have noted some of these properties as disclosed by the experimental sciences. It is now our task to show how certain other properties which had been previously thought to be excluded from matter can now be considered as included.

What are these other properties? They could best be characterized perhaps as the spiritual qualities. A conventional set may be noted here. "Mind," "consciousness," "spirit," "purpose," "goodness," and "beauty" will serve as typical items. It will be well to discuss them one at a time.

Let us begin with "mind." From the general use of such terms as "mind," it is difficult to know what is meant. Descartes, for instance, divided the universe into thinking things and extended things. It is clear that by the last term he meant material things—matter. By the former, therefore, everything was included that was excluded from matter: thoughts, certainly, since the term for mental things was *res cogitans*. But also probably consciousness, and an unnamed and undefined spiritual property.

Certainly, the term "mind" is used to include memory and thought: the retention and manipulation of logical entities and their combination. That mind as so conceived can be shown to be connected with the brain is not difficult to demonstrate. In the traditional materialism, there was no explanation for mental events. They were not supposed to be material and so were assigned to a separate though often parallel series without interaction, as for instance by Malebranche. In the newer materialism, mental events take place in the brain, and consist in signals and signalling systems both of which are at the very least material. Experiments with the electroencephalogram, with drugs, and with ablation procedures have indicated that an intimate relation exists between mind and brain.

"Consciousness" would seem to depend upon a particular area of the brain, namely, upon the midbrain section of the upper brain stem reticular formation.

"Spirit" is a more difficult concept to pin down. Its use has been varied. Among the meanings which may be distinguished are: the animating or vital principle of man, the soul, immaterial being, the unknown.

The first two can be quickly disposed of, for if there is a vital principle or a soul, of what could the evidence consist? Not in anything material; not, that is to say, in any data the sciences of biology or psychology could bring forward. In what, then? In the religious experience, presumably, or in some sort of introspection. But this is a domain into which the modern empiricist may not enter; so far as he is concerned, it is inadmissible evidence. Oddly enough, in other matters, the defender of spirit will accept the findings of the materialist. The spiritualist believes in matter, he simply thinks that there is something more.

Much the same argument applies to the concept of immaterial being. If being is defined as matter and energy, and logic is to mean the representation of absent material things and forces, then immaterial being becomes a contradiction in terms. Presumably the meaning is the same as the former one we were just discussing, that there is matter in the world—and something more. And so the conclusion, given the premises of materialism and its rules of admissible evidence, will be the same.

Spirit as the unknown is easy to understand but difficult to dismiss. There is always an unknown area. Nature in any one of its many subdivisions seems always to be indefinitely larger than our limited formulations. There are more galaxies than our telescopes can reach, there is more depth to the atom than our methods of investigation can sound. Thus the area of the unknown may move away a little, but it is never altogether dissipated. It is always there.

But there is a marked difference in the attitudes toward the unknown of the materialist and the spiritualist. The materialist finds an inexplicable mystery in the known, the spiritualist finds it only in the unknown. Moreover, the materialist wishes to penetrate farther into the unknown. Through his investigations he wishes to reduce the unknown to the known, for it is knowledge that he seeks. The spiritualist, on the other hand, would leave the unknown alone, and only wishes to stand in awe before it, for it is wonder that he seeks, and mystification. At the same time he wishes to regard such responses as a kind of superior knowledge which he is justified in using.

The difference between the character and extent of the

knowledge of primitive man and that of civilized man is remarkable. The former is lost in superstitions unsubstantiated, the latter finds himself with scientific principles partially verified. But the comparison veers sharply when we compare the religions of primitive man and civilized man, for both so to speak are full of wonder. Each claims avenues of knowledge of a supernatural and trans-sensory variety which authorizes actions on matter however violent they may be. The consistency of the materialist is that he would use his knowledge of matter to influence the actions on matter. The inconsistency of the spiritualist is that he would use his knowledge of spirit to influence the actions on matter.

Next we have to examine the property of "purpose." For individual man it means quite simply that which the individual is for, his reason for existence. Purpose lies in the present, and consciousness of purpose belongs to sentient organisms. Ends lie in the future: for instance at such and such a time it is hoped that such and such configurations of matter will be present. In material terms, this could be the service of society, with the *terminus ad quem* unknown. For society itself it is necessary to appeal to the principle of biological evolution. *Homo sapiens* is working itself out to an end which lies invisible in the greater expanses of the material universe. But we do know this much. A state of maximum entropy would seem to be the *terminus ad quem* of the universe, with a state of maximum evolution falling somewhat short but consisting in the perfection of the human successor animal.

The last properties we shall have to consider are those of "goodness" and "beauty."

That "goodness" could be considered a property of matter is not a currently conventional proposition, yet it is one which could conceivably be entertained. Let us define the good as the quality which emerges from the attraction between material objects. It would not be too difficult to show that all material objects are so related. The qualities change in accordance with the complexity of structure of the objects. Thus the quality of goodness at the level of the physical is the pull of gravitation. At the psychological level, it is friendship or love. The good, in the conventional ethical sense, would be the latter, an attraction between human individuals. In the domain of logic the good is represented by completeness.

"Beauty" as a property of matter is perhaps more unfamiliar. Artists have been proclaiming the beauties of nature for millennia. We can define beauty as the quality which emerges from the relation of perfection between the parts of a material object. Beauty is thus an internal property. Art in the conventional aesthetic sense is the quality of beauty produced in a material object through human agency. In the domain of logic beauty is represented by consistency. It does not belong in the eye of the beholder which would otherwise see everything the same but is a quality of the object: a sunset, a tree, a woman's body.

That ethical and aesthetic values can be properties of matter seems strange simply because the spiritual has been separated from the material, and while it has been freely acknowledged that the human individual has his spiritual nature, the ethical and aesthetic have been considered to belong exclusively to the spiritual. Then again, they have been considered exclusively human. Goodness was human goodness, beauty an exclusively human creation or apprehension.

But there are now reasons for supposing that neither goodness nor beauty can be excluded from matter simply because they are qualitative. We have noted that matter is not exclusively a simple, inert affair of energy relations. In the new understanding of matter there is room for quality, as Bohm often writes of "the qualitative infinity of nature."

We conclude, then, that the spiritual values are not omitted but instead proved necessary by being shown to be incorporated in matter.

Both sets of the properties of matter, the physical and the spiritual, have been treated in the foregoing as though they were always present. But what about the absent objects to which we referred earlier? The answer will lead us into an expansion of the theory of forms and of the role of the energy by means of which the forms are interchanged. We shall see in this way how the facts of existence, which the defenders of mind, consciousness, spirit, purpose, the good, the beautiful, and the immaterial and unknown generally, mean to cover, can be included in the domain of matter, with the inevitable consequence that a theory of man in relation to materialism is made possible.

Minds Are Immaterial

John Eccles and Daniel N. Robinson

Sir John Eccles (1903-) is a Nobel laureate in medicine and physiology whose work in brain science ranks him among the best in the twentieth century. He has collaborated with philosopher Karl Popper to write *The Self and Its Brain* and with psychologist and historian of psychology Daniel Robinson to write *The Wonder of Being Human: Our Brain and Our Mind*, from which the present selection is taken. Eccles and Robinson begin by noting that human consciousness, unlike other mammalian consciousness, includes an awareness of self or soul, which includes awareness of death and moral status. They argue that the data is best understood in terms of three worlds or realities, one of which is material and two of which are immaterial. Human self-consciousness progressively develops as the result

Excerpted from *The Wonder of Being Human* by John Eccles and Daniel N. Robinson. New York: The Free Press, 1984. Reprinted by permission.

of a culturally directed interaction between the two immaterial worlds of consciousness and objective knowledge. The best way to explain how human persons can be a part of these three worlds is to assume that human persons consist of material brains and immaterial souls. The brain is a kind of personal computer for use by the soul and genuine interaction takes place between these two different types of things. The authors argue that such interaction is plausible even though we do not yet know exactly how it takes place. They see no reason to abandon their dualistic position in favor of a materialism they consider completely inadequate.

QUESTIONS

1. How do Eccles and Robinson define "self-consciousness"?
2. In what way, according to the authors, does the World 2 of animals differ from that of humans?
3. How important, according to Eccles and Robinson, is culture in the development of personhood?
4. According to the authors, what two considerations invalidate the claim that materialist theories of brain-mind are in accord with natural law?
5. How do Eccles and Robinson distinguish between self, self-identity, and personal identity?
6. What results, according to the authors, when the nerve fibers connecting the two cerebral hemispheres are cut? What does this tell us about the brain and human personhood?
7. What do Eccles and Robinson claim is the true source of our experiential uniqueness?

■ ■ ■

The Emergence of Self-Consciousness

It is proposed to use the term "self-conscious mind" for the highest mental experiences. It implies knowing that one knows, which is of course initially a subjective or introspective criterion. However, by linguistic communication it can be authenticated that other human beings share in this experience of self-knowing. Dobzhansky expresses well the extraordinary emergence of human self-consciousness—of self-awareness, as he calls it:

> Self-awareness is, then, one of the fundamental, possibly the most fundamental, characteristic of the human species. This characteristic is an evolutionary novelty; the biological species from which mankind has descended had only rudiments of self-awareness, or perhaps lacked it altogether. Self-awareness has, however, brought in its train somber companions—fear, anxiety, and death awareness. . . . Man is burdened by death awareness. A being who knows that he will die arose from ancestors who did not know.

This state of ultimate concern devolving from self-awareness can first be identified by the ceremonial burial customs that were inaugurated by Neanderthal man about 80,000 years ago. Karl Popper recognized the unfathomable problem of its origin: "The emergence of all consciousness capable of self-reflection is indeed one of the greatest of miracles." And Konrad Lorenz refers to "that most mysterious of barriers, utterly impenetrable to the human understanding, that runs through the middle of what is the undeniable oneness of our personality—the barrier that divides our subjective experience from the objective, verifiable physiological events that occur in our body."

The progressive development from the consciousness of the baby to the self-consciousness in the child provides a good model for the emergent evolution of self-consciousness in the hominids. There is even evidence for a primitive knowledge of self with the chimpanzee (but not lower primates) that recognizes itself in a mirror, as shown by the use of the mirror to remove a colored mark on its face. It would seem that, in the evolutionary process, there was some primitive recognition of self long before it became traumatically experienced in death-awareness, which achieved expression in some religious beliefs manifested in the ceremonial burials. Similarly, with the child knowledge of the self usually antedates by years the first experience of death-awareness.

It may be helpful to attempt some diagrammatic representation of the emergence of self-consciousness. In the formal information-flow diagram of brain-mind interaction (Figure 1) are three major components of World 2, which is the world of conscious experiences (cf. Figure 3). The "outer sense" and "inner sense" compartments are integrated in the central compartment, which may be labeled psyche, self, or soul according to the kind of discourse—psychological, philosophical, or religious. It was conjectured that higher animals are conscious, but not self-conscious. Thus the information-flow diagram would be simplified by elimination of the central core as shown in Figure 2 with the representation of only the outer sense and inner sense components. The language training of apes has revealed that feelings are dominant in their concentration on the pragmatic use of language for obtaining desirables. In the evolutionary emergence of self-consciousness David Lack and Konrad Lorenz speak of the unbridgeable gap or gulf between soul and body. Yet we must envisage the creation and development of the central core to give eventually the full emergence of psyche or soul as illustrated in Figure 1. It can be conjectured that in the phylogenetic process of hominid evolution were all transitions between the situations illustrated in Figures 2 and 1, just as occurs ontogenetically from human baby to human child to human adult; yet it remains a miracle.

The Human Person

Each of us continually has the experience of being a person with a self-consciousness not just conscious, but knowing that we know. In defining "person" I shall quote two admirable statements by Immanuel Kant: "A person is a subject who is responsible for his actions" and "A person is something that is conscious at different times of the numerical identity of its self." These statements are minimal and basic, and they should be enormously expanded. For example Popper and Eccles have published a six-hundred-page book on *The Self and Its Brain*. On page 144 Popper refers to "that greatest of miracles: the human consciousness of self."

We are not able to go much farther than Kant in defining the relations of the person to its brain. We are apt to regard the person as identical with the ensemble of face, body, limbs, and the rest that constitute each of us. It is easy to show that this is a mistake. Amputation of limbs or loss of eyes, for example, though crippling, leaves the human person with its essential identity. This is also the case with the removal of internal or-

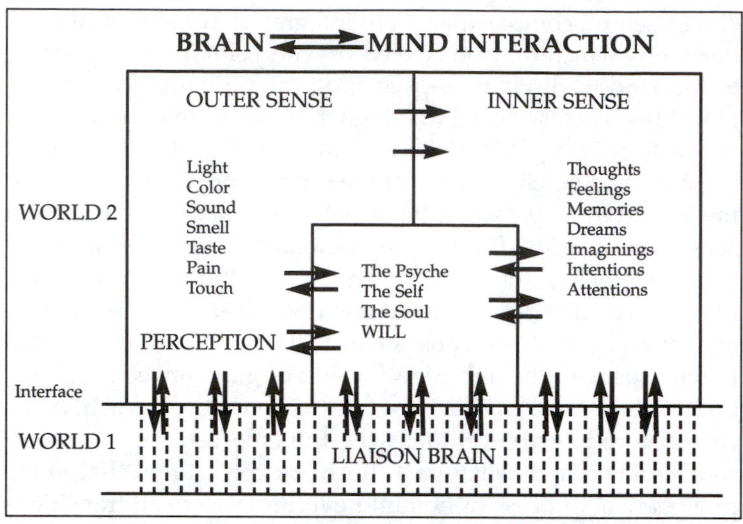

FIGURE 1 Information Flow Diagram for Brain-Mind Interaction in Human Brain. The three components of World 2—outer sense, inner sense, and the psyche, self, or soul—are diagrammed, with their communications shown by arrows. Also shown are the lines of communication across the interface between World 1 and World 2, that is, from the liaison brain to and from these World 2 components. The liaison brain has the columnar arrangement indicated by the vertical broken lines. It must be imagined that the area of the liaison brain is enormous, with open or active modules numbering over a million, not just the two score here depicted.

gans. Many can be excised in whole or in part. The human person survives unchanged after kidney transplants or even heart transplants. You may ask what happens with brain transplants. Mercifully this is not feasible surgically, but even now it would be possible successfully to accomplish a head transplant. Who can doubt that the person "owning" the transplanted head would now "own" the acquired body, and not vice versa! We can hope that with human persons this will remain a Gedanken experiment, but it has already been successfully done in mammals. We can recognize that all structures of the head extraneous to the brain are not involved in this transplanted ownership. For example eyes, nose, jaws, scalp, and so forth are no more concerned than are other parts of the body. So we can conclude that it is the brain and the brain alone that

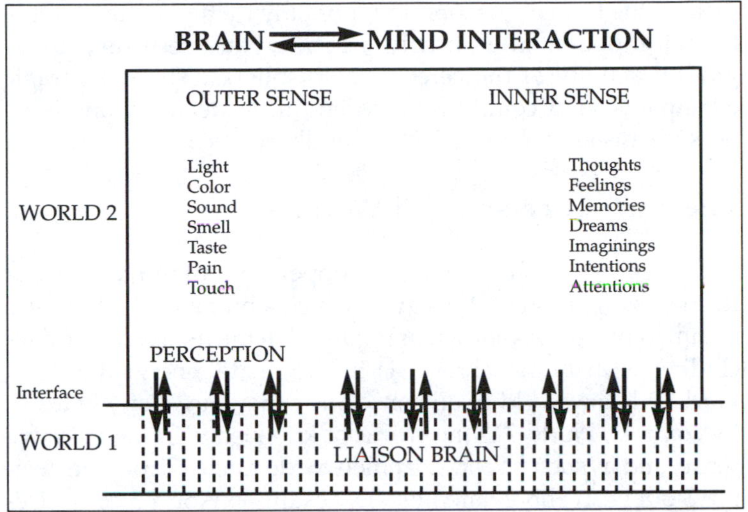

FIGURE 2 Information Flow Diagram for Brain-Mind Interaction for a Mammalian Brain. The two components of World 2, outer sense and inner sense, are diagrammed, with communications shown by arrows to the liaison brain in World 1. It will be noticed that mammals are given a World 2, corresponding to their consciousness, and that this World 2 has the same general features in outer sense and inner sense as with the human World 2 in Figure 1, but there is a complete absence of the central category of psyche, self, or soul.

provides the material basis of our personhood.

But when we come to consider the brain as the seat of the conscious personhood, we can also recognize that large parts of the brain are not essential. For example removal of the cerebellum gravely incapacitates movement, but the person is not otherwise affected. It is quite different with the main part of the brain, the cerebral hemispheres. They are intimately related to the consciousness of the person, but not equally. In 95 percent of persons there is dominance of the left hemisphere, which is the "speaking hemisphere." Except in infants its removal results in a most severe destruction of the human person, but not annihilation. On the other hand removal of the minor hemisphere (usually the right) is attended with loss of movement on the left side (hemiplegia) and blindness on the left side (hemianopia), but the person is otherwise not gravely disturbed. Damage to other parts of the brain can also greatly disturb the human personhood, possibly by the removal of the neural inputs that normally generate the necessary background activity of the cerebral hemispheres. The most tragic example is vigil coma in which enduring deep unconsciousness is caused by damage to the midbrain.

The Human Person and World 3

The three-world philosophy of Popper forms the basis of our further exploration of the way in which a human baby becomes a human person. As shown in Figure 3, all the material world including even human brains is in the matter-energy World 1. World 2 is the world of all conscious experiences (cf. Figure 1). By contrast, World 3 is the world of knowledge in the objective sense, and as such has an extremely wide range of contents. Figure 3 offers an abbreviated list. For example World 3 comprises the expressions of scientific, literary, and artistic ideas that have been preserved in codified form in libraries, in museums, and in all records of human culture. In their material composition of paper and ink, books are in World 1, but the knowledge encoded in the print is in World 3, and similarly for pictures, sculptures, and all other artifacts such as musical scores. Most important components of World 3 are languages for communicating thoughts and a system of values for regulating conduct and also arguments generated by discussion of these problems. In summary it can be stated that World 3 comprises the records of the intellectual efforts of all mankind through all ages up to the present—what we may call the cultural heritage.

At birth the human baby has a human brain, but its World 2 experiences are quite rudimentary, and World 3 is unknown to it. It, and even a human embryo, must be regarded as human beings, but not as human persons.* The emergence and development of self-consciousness (World 2) by continued interaction with World 3, the world of culture, is an utterly mysterious

* A being must be regarded as a *human* being when its genetic constitution (genotype) is formed from the gene pool of *Homo sapiens*. A human being graduates to be a *person* on less specific and more arguable grounds, e.g. when it displays certain social, moral, and intellectual attributes, or that of self-conscious reflection.

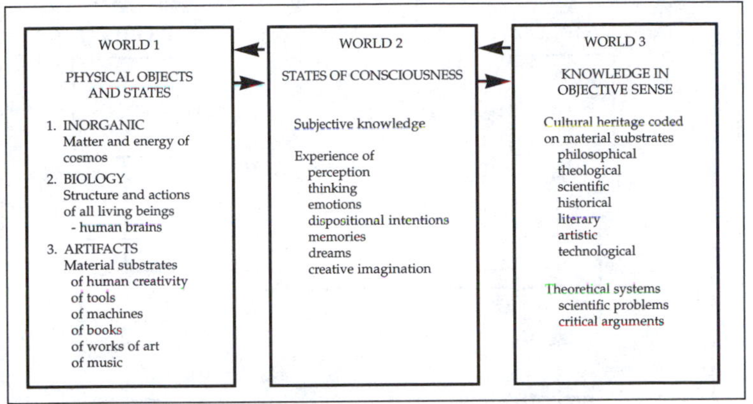

FIGURE 3 Tabular Representation of the Contents of the Three Worlds in Accordance with the Philosophy of Karl Popper. These three worlds are nonoverlapping but are intimately related, as indicated by the large open arrows at the top. They contain everything in existence and in experience. World 1 is material, Worlds 2 and 3 are immaterial.

process. It can be likened to a double structure (Figure 4) that ascends and grows by effective cross-linkage. The vertical arrow shows the passage of time from the earliest experiences of the child up to full human development. From each World 2 position an arrow leads through to World 3 at that level up to a higher, larger level, which illustrates symbolically a growth in the culture of that individual. Reciprocally the World 3 resources of the self act back to give a higher, expanded level of consciousness of that self (World 2). Figure 4 can be regarded symbolically as the ladder of personhood. And so each of us has developed progressively in self-creation, and this can go on throughout our whole lifetime. The more the World 3 resources of the human person, the more does it gain in the self-consciousness of World 2 by reciprocal enrichment. What we are is dependent on the World 3 that we have been immersed in and how effectively we have utilized our opportunities to make the most of our brain potentialities.

A recent tragic case is illustrative of Figure 4. A child, Genie, was deprived of all World 3 influences by her psychotic father. She was penned in isolation in a small room of his house in Los Angeles, never spoken to, and minimally serviced

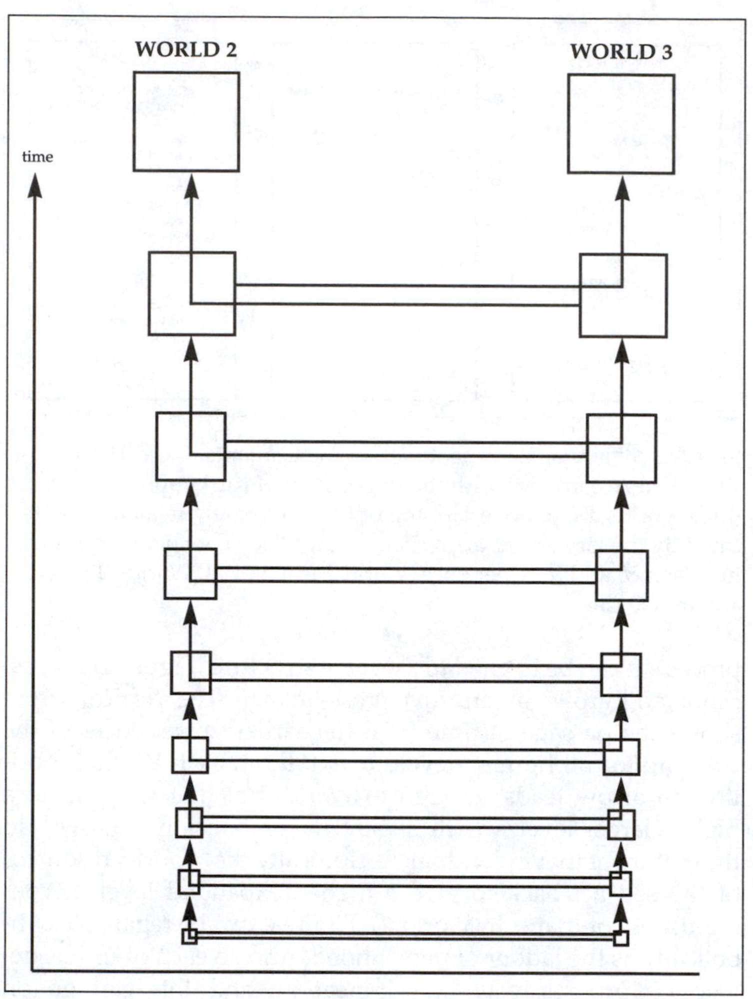

FIGURE 4 Diagrammatic Representation of the Postulated Interrelationships in the Developments of Self-Consciousness (World 2) and of Culture (World 3) of a Person in Time. Development is shown by the arrows; full description in text. We may call it the ladder of personhood that we can climb up throughout life.

from the age of twenty months up to thirteen years, eight months. On release from this terrible deprivation she was of course a human being, but not a human person. She was at the bottom rung of the ladder in Figure 4. Since then, with dedicated help by Dr. Susan Curtiss, she has been slowly climbing up that ladder of personhood for the last ten years. The linguistic deprivation seriously damaged her left hemisphere, but the right hemisphere stands in for a much-depleted language performance. Yet, despite this terribly delayed immersion in World 3, Genie has become a human person with self-consciousness, emotions, and excellent performances in manual dexterity and in visual recognition. We can recognize the necessity of World 3 for the development of the human person. The brain is built by genetic instructions (that is, Nature), but development of human personhood is dependent on World 3 environment (that is, Nurture). With Genie there was a gap of thirteen years between Nature and Nurture.

It may seem that a complete explanation of the development of the human person can be given in terms of the human brain. It is built anatomically by genetic instructions and subsequently developed functionally by learning from the environmental influences. A purely materialist explanation would seem to suffice with the conscious experiences as derivative from brain functioning. However, it is a mistake to think that the brain does everything and that our conscious experiences are simply a reflection of brain activities, which is a common philosophical view. If that were so, our conscious selves would be no more than passive spectators of the performances carried out by the neuronal mechanisms of the brain. Our beliefs that we can really make decisions and that we have some control over our actions would be nothing but illusions. There are, of course, all sorts of subtle coverups by philosophers from such a stark exposition, but they do not face up to the issue. In fact all people, even materialist philosophers, behave as if they had at least some responsibility for their own actions. It seems that their philosophy is for "the other people, not for themselves," as Schopenhauer wittily stated.

These considerations lead me to the alternative hypothesis of dualist-interactionism (cf. Figure 1), which has been expanded at length in *The Self and Its Brain*. It is really the commonsense view, namely, that we are a combination of two things or entities: our brains on the one hand; and our conscious selves on the other. The self is central to the totality of our conscious experiences as persons through our whole waking life. We link it in memory from our earliest conscious experiences. The self has a subconscious existence during sleep, except for dreams, and on waking the conscious self is resumed and linked with the past by the continuity of memory. But for memory we as experiencing persons would not exist. We have the extraordinary problem that was first recognized by Descartes: How can the conscious mind and the brain interact? . . .

Critical Evaluation of Brain-Mind Hypotheses

A great point is made by all varieties of materialists that their brain-mind theories (Figure 5) are in accord with natural law as it now stands. However, this claim is invalidated by two most weighty considerations.

First, nowhere in the laws of physics or in the laws of the derivative sciences, chemistry and biology, is there any reference to consciousness or mind. Regardless of the complexity of electrical, chemical, or biological machinery, there is no statement in the "natural laws" that there is an emergence of this strange nonmaterial entity, consciousness or mind. This is not to affirm that consciousness does not emerge in the evolutionary process, but merely to state that its emergence is not reconcilable with the natural laws as at present understood. For example such laws do not allow any statement that consciousness emerges at a specified level of complexity of systems, which is gratuitously assumed by all materialists except radical materialists and panpsychists. The panpsychist belief that some primordial consciousness attaches to all matter, presumably even to atoms and subatomic particles, finds no support whatsoever in physics. One can also recall the poignant questions by computer lovers: At what stage of complexity and performance can we agree to endow them with consciousness? Mercifully this emotionally charged question need not be answered. You can do what you like to computers without qualms of being cruel!

Second, all materialist theories of the mind are in conflict with biological evolution. Since they all (panpsychists, epiphenomenalists, and identity theorists) assert the causal ineffectiveness of consciousness *per se* (Figure 5), they fail completely to account for the evolutionary expansion of consciousness, which is an undeniable fact. There is first its emergence and then its progressive development with the growing complexity

World 1 = All of material or physical world including brains
World 2 = All subjective or mental experiences
World 1_P is all the material world that is without mental states
World 1_M is that minute fraction of the material world with associated mental states

Radical Materialism:	World 1 = World 1_P; World 1_M = 0; World 2 = 0.
Panpsychism:	All is World 1-2, World 1 or 2 does not exist alone.
Epiphenomenalism:	World 1 = World 1_P + World 1_M
	World $1_M \rightarrow$ World 2
Identity Theory:	World 1 = World 1_P + World 1_M
	World 1_M = World 2 (the identity)
Dualist-Interactionism:	World 1 = World 1_P + World 1_M
	World $1_M \rightleftharpoons$ World 2: this interaction occurs in the liaison brain, LB = World 1_M
	Thus World 1 = World 1_P + World 1_{LB}, and
	World $1_{LB} \rightleftharpoons$ World 2

FIGURE 5 Diagrammatic Representation of Brain-Mind Theories. Diagram incorporates the World 1 and World 2 of Figure 3. The essential features of the materialist theories of the mind are summarized for panpsychism, epiphenomenalism, and the identity theory. This last theory has a variety of names according to the whims of the creators of the minor varieties of what are essentially parallelist theories. The subdivision of World 1 into World 1_P and World 1_M helps in clarification of their specific features. World 1_M is assumed to be restricted to special states of the brain in epiphenominalism, the identity theory, and dualist-interactionism. The essential and unique feature of dualist-interactionism is shown by the reciprocal arrows between World 1_M and World 2 in the second line.

of the brain. Evolutionary theory holds that only those structures and processes that significantly aid in survival are developed in natural selection. If consciousness is causally impotent, its development cannot be accounted for by evolutionary theory. According to biological evolution, mental states and consciousness could have evolved and developed *only if they were causally effective* in bringing about changes in neural happenings in the brain with the consequent changes in behavior. That can occur only if the neural machinery of the brain is open to influences from the mental events of the world of conscious experiences, which is the basic postulate of dualist-interactionist theory.

Finally, the most telling criticism of all materialist theories of the mind is against its key postulate that the happenings in the neural machinery of the brain provide *a necessary and sufficient explanation of the totality both of the performance and of the conscious experience of a human being.* For example the willing of a voluntary movement is regarded as being *completely determined* by events in the neural machinery of the brain, as also are all other cognitive experiences. But as Popper states in his Compton Lecture:

> According to determinism, any such theory such as say determinism is held because of a certain physical structure of the holder—perhaps of his brain. Accordingly, we are deceiving ourselves and are physically so determined as to deceive ourselves whenever we believe that there are such things as *arguments or reasons* which make us accept determinism. Purely physical conditions, including our physical environment make us say or accept whatever we say or accept.

This is an effective *reductio ad absurdum.* This stricture applies to all of the materialist theories. So perforce we turn to dualist-interactionist explanations of the brain-mind problem, despite the extraordinary requirement that there be effective communication in both directions across the frontier shown in Figure 1.

Necessarily the dualist-interactionist theory is in conflict with present natural laws and so is in the same "unlawful" position as the materialist theories of the mind. The differences are that this conflict has always been admitted and that the neural machinery of the brain is assumed to operate in strict accordance to natural laws except for its openness to World 2 influences. . . .

The Human Brain

It is useful to think of the brain as an instrument, our computer, which has been a lifelong servant and companion. It provides us, as programmers, with the lines of communication from and to the material world (World 1) which comprises both our bodies and the external world. It does this by receiving information through the immense sensory system of millions of nerve fibers that fire impulses into the brain, where it is processed into the coded patterns of information that we read out from moment to moment in deriving all our experiences—our percepts, thoughts, ideas, memories. But we as experiencing persons do not slavishly accept all that is provided for us by our computer, the neuronal structures of our sensory system and of our brain. We select from all that is given according to interest and attention, and we modify the actions of the neuronal structures of our computer, for example to initiate some willed movement or in order to recall a memory or to concentrate our attention.

How then can we develop ideas with respect to the mode of operation of the brain? How can it provide the immense range of coded information that can be selected from by the mind in its activity of reading our conscious experiences? It is now possible to give much more informative answers because of very recent work on the essential mode of operation of the neocortex. By the use of radiotracer techniques it has been shown that the great brain mantle, the neocortex, is built up of units or modules. This modular organization has provided most valuable simplification of the enterprise of trying to understand how this tremendously complex structure works. The potential performance of a network of ten thousand million individual nerve cells is beyond all comprehension. The arrangement in modules of about four thousand nerve cells each reduces the number of functional units of the neocortex to between 2 and 3 million.

It can be asked, however, whether 2 to 3 million modules of the neocortex are adequate to generate the spatiotemporal patterns that encode the total cognitive performance of the human brain—all the sensing, all memories, all linguistic expression, all creativities, all aesthetic experiences—for our whole lifetime. The only answer I can give is to refer to the immense potentialities of the eighty-eight keys of a piano. Think of the creative performances of the great piano composers, Beethoven and Chopin for example. They could use only four parameters in their creation of piano music with the eighty-eight keys, each of which has an invariant pitch and tonal quality. And a comparable four parameters are used in creating the spatiotemporal patterns of activity in the 2 to 3 million modules of the human cerebral cortex.

I think it will be recognized that the enormous generation

of musical patterns using the eighty-eight keys of a piano points to a virtually infinite capacity of the 2 to 3 million modules to generate unique spatiotemporal patterns. Moreover it must be realized that these patterns giving the conscious experiences are dependent on the same four parameters as for the piano keys. We can imagine that the intensities of activation are signaled symbolically by the momentary lighting up of modules. So, if we could see the surface of our neocortex, it would present illuminated patterns of 50 cm by 50 cm in area composed at any moment of modules 0.3 mm across that have all ranges of "openness" from dark to dim to lighter to brilliant. And this pattern would be changing in a scintillating manner from moment to moment, giving a sparkling spatiotemporal pattern of the millions of modules that would appear exactly as on a TV screen. This symbolism gives some idea of the immense task confronting the mind in generating conscious experiences. The dark or dim modules would be neglected. Moreover it is an important feature of the hypothesis of mind-brain interaction that neither the mind nor the brain is passive in the transaction. There must be an active interchange of information across the frontier (Figure 1) between the material brain—the liaison brain—and the nonmaterial mind. The mind is not in the matter-energy world, so there can be no energy exchange in the transaction, merely a flow of information. Yet the mind must be able to change the pattern of energy operations in the modules of the brain, else it would be forever impotent.

It is difficult to understand how the self-conscious mind can relate to such an enormous complexity of spatiotemporal modular patterns. This difficulty is mitigated by three considerations. First, we must realize that our self-conscious mind has been learning to accomplish such tasks from our babyhood onward, a process that is colloquially called "learning to use one's brain." Second, by the process of attention the self-conscious mind selects from the total ensemble of modular patterns those features that are in accord with its present interests. Third, the self-conscious mind is engaged in extracting "meaning" from all that it reads out. This is well illustrated by the many ambiguous figures, for example a drawing that can be seen either as a staircase or an overhanging cornice. The switch from one interpretation to the other is instantaneous and holistic. There is never any transitional phase in the reading out by the mind of the modular pattern in the brain.

A key component of the hypothesis of brain-mind interaction is that the unity of conscious experience is provided by the self-conscious mind and not by the neuronal mechanism of the neocortex. Hitherto it has been impossible to develop any theory of brain function that would explain how the immense diversity of brain events comes to be synthesized so that there is a unity of conscious experience. The brain events remain disparate, being essentially the individual actions of countless modules.

The Unity of the Self

It is a universal human experience that subjectively there is a mental unity recognized as a continuity from one's earliest memories. It is the basis of the concept of the self. Experimental investigations on the unity of the self have been discussed in the book *The Human Psyche* (Eccles, 1980).

As Robinson has shown elsewhere,* there are insuperable objections to equating the self with memory or the continuity of memories. A total amnesic may not know *who* he is (or anything about his previous life) but he surely knows *that* he is and, therefore, that he is in possession of selfhood. It is, moreover, not the fact that a person recalls having done something that establishes that he, in fact, did it, for memories can be defective and even illusory. Thus the self is certainly not identical with memory. It becomes necessary, then, to make distinctions among three different concepts: *self, self-identity,* and *personal identity*. The self and its unity arise from the irreducible awareness of being. One is aware *that* he is and knows directly that all his experiences, memories, thoughts, and desires inhere in this very self. *Self-identity,* however, refers to the knowledge one has of *who* he is and arises chiefly from memory. Thus, a given (amnesic) self can be lacking in self-identity. *Personal identity*, on the other hand, refers to the knowledge others have of who a given person is. We may say, for example, that a total

* Daniel N. Robinson, "Cerebral Plurality and the Unity of Self," *American Psychologist*, August 1982.

stranger has no personal identity (as far as we know) although he may well have self-identity. The totally amnesic person who is also a total stranger thus lacks both personal identity and self-identity but possesses selfhood nonetheless. Accordingly, such striking conditions as those popularized in *The Three Faces of Eve* pertain not to the existence of three *selves* in one person but to three distinct *self-identities* possessed by one otherwise unique and irreducible *self*.

By far the most important experimental evidence relating to the unity of consciousness comes from the study by Roger Sperry and his associates on commissurotomized patients. In the operation for the relief of intractable epilepsy there was a section of the corpus callosum, the great tract of nerve fibers, about 200 million, that links the two cerebral hemispheres. With the most sophisticated investigations, allowing up to two hours of continual testing, it became clear that the right hemisphere, the so-called minor hemisphere, was correlated with conscious responses at a level superior to those exhibited by any nonhuman primates. The patient's consciousness was indubitable. The perplexing question is whether the right hemisphere mediates self-consciousness, meaning that it permits the knowledge of selfhood. In the most searching investigations of Sperry and associates there was testing of the ability of the patient to identify photographs projected to the right hemisphere alone. A considerable ability was displayed, but it was handicapped by the lack of verbal expression.

The tests for the existence of self-consciousness were at a relatively simple pictorial and emotional level. We can doubt if the right hemisphere with associated consciousness has a full self-conscious existence. For example, do planning and worrying about the future take place there? Are there decisions and judgments based on some value system? These are essential qualifications for personhood as ordinarily understood and for the existence of a psyche or soul. It can be concluded that a limited self-consciousness is associated with the right hemisphere, but the person remains apparently unscathed by the commissurotomy with mental unity intact in its now exclusive left hemisphere association. After commissurotomy the right hemisphere appears to mediate a self-awareness resembling that of a very young child. The information flow diagram for the right hemisphere would resemble Figure 2, except that there would be a small central core at a primitive level of self or ego, but with no representation of soul or psyche or personhood. It is generally agreed that the human person is not split by the commissurotomy but remains in liaison with the left (speaking) hemisphere.

The Uniqueness of Each Self

It is not in doubt that each human person recognizes its own uniqueness, and this is accepted as the basis of social life and of law. When we inquire into the grounds for this belief, modern neuroscience eliminates an explanation in terms of the body. There remain two possible alternatives, the brain and the psyche. Materialists must subscribe to the former, but dualist-interactionists have to regard the self of World 2 (cf. Figure 1) as the entity with the experienced uniqueness. It is important to disclaim a solipsistic solution of the uniqueness of the self. Our direct experiences are of course subjective, being derived entirely from our brain and self. The existence of other selves is established by intersubjective communication.

If one's experienced uniqueness is attributed to the uniqueness of our brain, built by the unique genetic instructions provided by one's genome, one is confronted by the infinitely improbable genetic lottery (even $10^{10,000}$ against) from which one's genome was derived,* as has been argued by Jennings, by Ec-

* This probability argument has been criticized by Willem Kuijik in *An Outline of a Complementarial Philosophy of Science with Special Reference to Mathematics*, forthcoming. His argument is simply that *after* a particular event the chance of its occurrence is 100 percent, and this holds true for one's own unique existence despite the odds that could be calculated, $10^{10,000}$ against, before that existence was realized. We reply that this refutation is inapplicable. We are not arguing about "myself" as *observed objectively* with "my body" and its behavior including verbal utterances as witnessed by an observer. We are in a completely different logical world when it is *self-experienced uniqueness* that is at issue, as can be gathered from the arguments presented in *The Human Psyche* on pages 237 to 241. This uniqueness is not objectively recognized by an observer. On the contrary, the argument is for the existence of myself known only to myself. One can imagine the extreme improbability of one's existence if it was dependent on the genetic code. *Before* it came to pass it would be $10^{10,000}$ against.

cles, and by Thorpe. There is further the impossibility of accounting for the experienced uniqueness of each identical twin despite the identical genome. A frequent and superficially plausible answer to this enigma is the assertion that the determining factor is the uniqueness of the accumulated experiences of a self throughout its lifetime. It is readily agreed that our behavior and memories, and in fact the whole content of our inner conscious life, are dependent on the accumulated experiences of our lives, but no matter how extreme the change at some particular decision point produced by the exigencies of circumstances, one would still be the same self able to trace back one's continuity in memory to the earliest remembrances at the age of one year or so, the same self in a quite other guise. There could be no elimination of a self and creation of a new self!

Since materialist solutions fail to account for our experienced uniqueness, we are constrained to attribute the uniqueness of the psyche or soul to a supernatural spiritual creation. To give the explanation in theological terms: Each soul is a Divine creation, which is "attached" to the growing fetus at some time between conception and birth. It is the certainty of the inner core of unique individuality that necessitates the "Divine creation." We submit that no other explanation is tenable; neither the genetic uniqueness with its fantastically impossible lottery nor the environmental differentiations, which do not *determine* one's uniqueness but merely modify it.

An appealing analogy is to regard the body and brain as a superb computer built by genetic coding that has been created by the wonderful process of biological evolution. On the analogy, the soul or psyche is the programmer of the computer. Each of us as a programmer is born with our computer in its initial embryonic state. We develop it throughout life, as is indicated in Figure 4. It is our lifelong intimate companion in all transactions. It receives from and gives to the world, which includes other selves. The great mysteries are in our creation as programmers or experiencing selves and in our association throughout life, each person with its own computer, as is diagrammed in Figure 1 across the frontier between World 2 and World 1.

Yet even in saying this perhaps we give too much away to the biological or scientific perspective and say too little of the striking dilemmas and confusions that stalk even the most modest of materialistic accounts.

Particulars Are Ultimately Real

DAVID HUME

David Hume (1711-1766) was a leading British empiricist who made major contributions to epistemology, metaphysics, political philosophy, ethics, and religious skepticism. Contemporary positivist and analytic philosophies take much of their inspiration from Hume. Hume was a nominalist concerning universals. Nominalists do not believe that universals are things that exist or have being. There is no need for a universal like *red* or *redness* to group things together, nominalists argue. All that are needed are individual abstract ideas like "red," which directs the mind to group many particular red things together. The only realities are the particular abstract idea red and the particular red things. This means that a *particular* idea or word can somehow paradoxically refer *generally* to numerous individual things without itself being a universal or general sort of thing. As an empiricist Hume believed that all human ideas are

From *A Treatise of Human Nature* by David Hume. New York: Doubleday, Doran and Co., 1935.

copies of sensory impressions. Because these impressions are particular things, copies of them must also be particular things. Abstract ideas like "red" or "line" are therefore particulars even though they can be applied generally to various shades of red things or lines of different lengths. Hume argues that this is possible because, when we form the idea of any quality like "red" or quantity like "length" (as in the length of a line), notions of degrees of red or lengths of lines come packaged with the original ideas. These notions of degree allow us to apply the ideas to numerous objects that are similar to one another in that they are "red things" or "lines with a length," but which have different *degrees* of red or length. Similarity plus degrees are all that the mind needs to group things together according to a common idea or name.

QUESTIONS

1. According to Hume, what was Berkeley's great discovery?
2. How does Hume attempt to prove that an idea must have a determinate quantity and quality?
3. In what sense does the author believe that abstract ideas are individual and in what sense are they general?
4. According to the author, what does habit constrain the mind to do when a universal term is used?
5. How does similarity or resemblance guide the mind, according to Hume?
6. Does Hume believe that we can understand the innermost workings of the mind?
7. What point does Hume make when he uses the examples of marble globes and cubes which can be either black or white?

■ ■ ■

Of Abstract Ideas

A very material question has been started concerning *abstract* or *general* ideas: *whether they be general or particular in the mind's conception of them*. A great philosopher[1] has disputed the received opinion in this particular, and has asserted that all general ideas are nothing but particular ones, annexed to a certain term which gives them a more extensive signification and makes them recall upon occasion other individuals which are similar to them. As I look upon this to be one of the greatest and most valuable discoveries that has been made of late years in the republic of letters, I shall here endeavor to confirm it by some arguments which I hope will put it beyond all doubt and controversy.

'Tis evident that in forming most of our general ideas, if not all of them, we abstract from every particular degree of quantity and quality, and that an object ceases not to be of any particular species on account of every small alteration in its extension, duration, and other properties. It may therefore be thought that here is a plain dilemma, that decides concerning the nature of those abstract ideas which have afforded so much speculation to philosophers. The abstract idea of a man represents men of all sizes and all qualities, which 'tis concluded it cannot do but either by representing at once all possible sizes and all possible qualities or by representing no particular one at all. Now it having been esteemed absurd to defend the former proposition, as implying an infinite capacity in the mind, it has been commonly inferred in favor of the latter; and our abstract ideas have been supposed to represent no particular degree either of quantity or quality. But that this inference is erroneous I shall endeavor to make appear: *first*, by proving that 'tis utterly impossible to conceive any quantity or quality without forming a precise notion of its degrees; and *secondly* by showing that though the capacity of the mind be not infinite, yet we can at once form a notion of all possible degrees of quantity and quality, in such a manner at least as, however imperfect, may serve all the purposes of reflection and conversation.

To begin with the first proposition, *that the mind cannot form any notion of quantity or quality without forming a precise notion of degrees of each*, we may prove this by the three following arguments. First, we have observed that whatever objects are different are distinguishable, and that whatever objects are distin-

[1] Dr. Berkeley. [See the Introduction to his *Principles:* Secs. 18 ff.]

guishable are separable by the thought and imagination. And we may here add that these propositions are equally true in the *inverse,* and that whatever objects are separable are also distinguishable, and that whatever objects are distinguishable are also different. For how is it possible we can separate what is not distinguishable, or distinguish what is not different? In order therefore to know whether abstraction implies a separation, we need only consider it in this view, and examine whether all the circumstances which we abstract from in our general ideas be such as are distinguishable and different from those which we retain as essential parts of them. But 'tis evident at first sight that the precise length of a line is not different nor distinguishable from the line itself, nor the precise degree of any quality from the quality. These ideas, therefore, admit no more of separation than they do of distinction and difference. They are consequently conjoined with each other in the conception; and the general idea of a line, notwithstanding all our abstractions and refinements, has in its appearance in the mind a precise degree of quantity and quality, however it may be made to represent others which have different degrees of both.

Secondly, 'tis confessed that no object can appear to the senses, or in other words that no impression can become present to the mind, without being determined in its degrees both of quantity and quality. The confusion in which impressions are sometimes involved proceeds only from their faintness and unsteadiness, not from any capacity in the mind to receive any impression which in its real existence has no particular degree nor proportion. That is a contradiction in terms, and even implies the flattest of all contradictions, *viz.,* that 'tis possible for the same thing both to be and not to be.

Now since all ideas are derived from impressions, and are nothing but copies and representations of them, whatever is true of the one must be acknowledged concerning the other. Impressions and ideas differ only in their strength and vivacity. The foregoing conclusion is not founded on any particular degree of vivacity. It cannot therefore be affected by any variation in that particular. An idea is a weaker impression; and as a strong impression must necessarily have a determinate quantity and quality, the case must be the same with its copy or representative.

Thirdly, 'tis a principle generally received in philosophy that everything in nature is individual, and that 'tis utterly absurd to suppose a triangle really existent which has no precise proportion of sides and angles. If this therefore be absurd in *fact and reality* it must also be absurd *in idea,* since nothing of which we can form a clear and distinct idea is absurd and impossible. But to form the idea of an object and to form an idea simply is the same thing; the reference of the idea to an object being an extraneous denomination, of which in itself it bears no mark or character. Now as 'tis impossible to form an idea of an object that is possessed of quantity and quality and yet is possessed of no precise degree of either, it follows that there is an equal impossibility of forming an idea that is not limited and confined in both these particulars. Abstract ideas are therefore in themselves individual, however they may become general in their representation. The image in the mind is only that of a particular object, though the application of it in our reasoning be the same as if it were universal.

This application of ideas beyond their nature proceeds from our collecting all their possible degrees of quantity and quality in such an imperfect manner as may serve the purposes of life, which is the second proposition I proposed to explain. When we have found a resemblance[1] among several objects that often occur to us, we apply the same name to all of them, whatever differences we may observe in the degrees of their quantity and quality, and whatever other differences may appear among them. After we have acquired a custom of this kind, the hearing of that name revives the idea of one of these

[1]'Tis evident that even different simple ideas may have a similarity or resemblance to each other, nor is it necessary that the point or circumstance of resemblance should be distinct or separable from that in which they differ. *Blue* and *green* are different simple ideas, but are more resembling than *blue* and *scarlet;* though their perfect simplicity excludes all possibility of separation or distinction. 'Tis the same case with particular sounds and tastes and smells. These admit of infinite resemblances upon the general appearance and comparison, without having any common circumstance the same. And of this we may be certain even from the very abstract terms 'simple idea.' They comprehend all simple ideas under them. These resemble each other in their simplicity. And yet from their very nature, which excludes all composition, this circumstance in which they resemble is not distinguishable nor separable from the rest. 'Tis the same case with all the degrees in any quality. They are all resembling, and yet the quality in any individual is not distinct from the degree. [Added by Hume in the Appendix.]

objects and makes the imagination conceive it with all its particular circumstances and proportions. But as the same word is supposed to have been frequently applied to other individuals that are different in many respects from that idea which is immediately present to the mind, the word, not being able to revive the idea of all these individuals, only touches the soul, if I may be allowed so to speak, and revives that custom which we have acquired by surveying them. They are not really and in fact present to the mind, but only in power; nor do we draw them all out distinctly in the imagination, but keep ourselves in a readiness to survey any of them as we may be prompted by a present design or necessity. The word raises up an individual idea along with a certain custom, and that custom produces any other individual one for which we may have occasion. But as the production of all the ideas to which the name may be applied is in most cases impossible, we abridge that work by a more partial consideration and find but few inconveniences to arise in our reasoning from that abridgement.

For this is one of the most extraordinary circumstances in the present affair, that after the mind has produced an individual idea upon which we reason, the attendant custom, revived by the general or abstract term, readily suggests any other individual, if by chance we form any reasoning that agrees not with it. Thus should we mention the word 'triangle' and form the idea of a particular equilateral one to correspond to it, and should we afterwards assert *that the three angles of a triangle are equal to* each other, the other individuals of a scalenum and isosceles, which we overlook at first, immediately crowd in upon us and make us perceive the falsehood of this proposition, though it be true with relation to that idea which we had formed. If the mind suggests not always these ideas upon occasion, it proceeds from some imperfection in its faculties; and such a one as is often the source of false reasoning and sophistry. But this is principally the case with those ideas which are abstruse and compounded. On other occasions the custom is more entire, and 'tis seldom we run into such errors.

Nay so entire is the custom, that the very same idea may be annexed to several different words, and may be employed in different reasonings without any danger of mistake. Thus the idea of an equilateral triangle of an inch perpendicular may serve us in talking of a figure, of a rectilinear figure, of a regular figure, of a triangle, and of an equilateral triangle. All these terms, therefore, are in this case attended with the same idea; but as they are wont to be applied in a greater or lesser compass, they excite their particular habits, and thereby keep the mind in a readiness to observe that no conclusion be formed to any ideas which are usually comprised under them.

Before those habits have become entirely perfect, perhaps the mind may not be content with forming the idea of only one individual, but may run over several, in order to make itself comprehend its own meaning and the compass of that collection which it intends to express by the general term. That we may fix the meaning of the word 'figure,' we may revolve in our mind the ideas of circles, squares, parallelograms, triangles of different sizes and proportions, and may not rest on one image or idea. However this may be, 'tis certain that we form the idea of individuals whenever we use any general term, that we seldom or never can exhaust these individuals, and that those which remain are only represented by means of that habit by which we recall them whenever any present occasion requires it. This then is the nature of our abstract ideas and general terms; and 'tis after this manner we account for the foregoing paradox, *that some ideas are particular in their nature but general in their representation.* A particular idea becomes general by being annexed to a general term; that is, to a term which from a customary conjunction has a relation to many other particular ideas and readily recalls them in the imagination.

The only difficulty that can remain on this subject must be with regard to that custom which so readily recalls every particular idea for which we may have occasion, and is excited by any word or sound to which we commonly annex it. The most proper method, in my opinion, of giving a satisfactory explication of this act of the mind, is by producing other instances which are analogous to it, and other principles which facilitate its operation. To explain the ultimate causes of our mental actions is impossible. 'Tis sufficient if we can give any satisfactory account of them from experience and analogy.

First, then, I observe that when we mention any great number, such as a thousand, the mind has generally no adequate idea of it, but only a power of producing such an idea by its adequate idea of the decimals under which the number is comprehended. This imperfection however in our ideas is never felt in our reasonings; which seems to be an instance parallel to the present one of universal ideas.

Secondly, we have several instances of habits which may be revived by one single word; as when a person who has by rote any periods of a discourse, or any number of verses, will be put in remembrance of the whole, which he is at a loss to recollect, by that single word or expression with which they begin.

Thirdly, I believe every one who examines the situation of his mind in reasoning will agree with me that we do not annex distinct and complete ideas to every term we make use of, and that in talking of *government, church, negotiation, conquest,* we seldom spread out in our minds all the simple ideas of which these complex ones are composed. 'Tis however observable that notwithstanding this imperfection we may avoid talking nonsense on these subjects and may perceive any repugnance among the ideas as well as if we had a full comprehension of them. Thus if instead of saying *that in war the weaker have always recourse to negotiation,* we should say *that they have always recourse to conquest,* the custom which we have acquired of attributing certain relations to ideas still follows the words and makes us immediately perceive the absurdity of that proposition, in the same manner as one particular idea may serve us in reasoning concerning other ideas, however different from it in several circumstances.

Fourthly, as the individuals are collected together, and placed under a general term with a view to that resemblance which they bear to each other, this relation must facilitate their entrance in the imagination and make them be suggested more readily upon occasion. And indeed if we consider the common progress of the thought, either in reflection or conversation, we shall find great reason to be satisfied in this particular. Nothing is more admirable than the readiness with which the imagination suggests its ideas and presents them at the very instant in which they become necessary or useful. The fancy runs from one end of the universe to the other in collecting those ideas which belong to any subject. One would think the whole intellectual world of ideas was at once subjected to our view, and that we did nothing but pick out such as were most proper for our purpose. There may not, however, be any present beside those very ideas that are thus collected by a kind of magical faculty in the soul, which, though it be always most perfect in the greatest geniuses, and is properly what we call a genius, is however inexplicable by the utmost efforts of human understanding.

Perhaps these four reflections may help to remove all difficulties to the hypothesis I have proposed concerning abstract ideas, so contrary to that which has hitherto prevailed in philosophy. But to tell the truth I place my chief confidence in what I have already proved concerning the impossibility of general ideas, according to the common method of explaining them. We must certainly seek some new system on this head, and there plainly is none beside what I have proposed. If ideas be particular in their nature, and at the same time finite in their number, 'tis only by custom they can become general in their representation and contain an infinite number of other ideas under them.

Before I leave this subject I shall employ the same principles to explain that *distinction of reason* which is so much talked of, and is so little understood, in the schools. Of this kind is the distinction betwixt figure and the body figured, motion and the body moved. The difficulty of explaining this distinction arises from the principle above explained, *that all ideas which are different are separable*. For it follows from thence that if the figure be different from the body their ideas must be separable as well as distinguishable; if they be not different their ideas can neither be separable nor distinguishable. What then is meant by a distinction of reason, since it implies neither a difference nor separation?

To remove this difficulty we must have recourse to the foregoing explication of abstract ideas. 'Tis certain that the mind would never have dreamed of distinguishing a figure from the body figured, as being in reality neither distinguishable nor different nor separable, did it not observe that even in this simplicity there might be contained many different resemblances and relations. Thus when a globe of white marble is presented, we receive only the impression of a white color disposed in a certain form, nor are we able to separate and distinguish the color from the form. But observing afterwards a globe of black marble and a cube of white and comparing them with our former objects, we find two separate resemblances in what formerly seemed and really is, perfectly inseparable. After a little more practice of this kind, we begin to distinguish the figure from the color by a *distinction of reason*; that is, we consider the figure and color together, since they are in effect the same and undistinguishable; but still view them in different aspects, according to the resemblances of which they are susceptible. When we would consider only the figure of the globe of white marble, we form in reality an idea both of the figure and color, but tacitly carry our eye to its resemblance with the globe of black marble; and in the same manner when we would consider its color only, we turn our view to its resemblance with the cube of white marble. By this means we accompany our ideas with a kind of reflection, of which custom renders us, in a great measure, insensible. A person who desires us to consider the figure of a globe of white marble without thinking of its color, desires an impossibility; but his meaning is that we should consider the color and figure together, but still keep in our eye the resemblance to the globe of black marble, or that to any other globe of whatever color or substance.

Universals Are Ultimately Real

BERTRAND RUSSELL

Bertrand Russell (1872-1970) was one of the most popular and influential philosophers of the twentieth century. He made significant contributions to logic, mathematics, epistemology, metaphysics, ethics, religion, and social and political philosophy. Russell changed his views on a variety of topics several times during his lifetime. In the following reading he expresses some of his early views on universals. Following the tradition begun by the Greek philosopher Plato, Russell argues that universals are necessary to explain the sorts of things that are shared by different particular things. Individual white particulars, for example, share a universal *whiteness*. He believes that logic and language point to the reality for universals because it is impossible to even express a truth without using some words which refer to universals, like verbs and prepositions. The relation "north of," for example,

From *The Problems of Philosophy* by Bertrand Russell. New York: Henry Holt & Co., n.d.

is certainly real when it refers to the relationship between Edinburgh and London, but the relation does not exist like a particular material thing or even a particular mental thing such as thought. Russell concludes that universals are real and that they exist independently of minds. Unlike particular things, which exist in time, universals subsist in a timeless world of being that is not accessible to the senses.

QUESTIONS

1. According to Russell, how do ideas or essences differ from the things of sense?
2. How does Russell define a universal?
3. Which kinds of universals does Russell think are the easiest to deny?
4. Why is resemblance so important for Russell's argument?
5. What does Russell mean when he says that something is not merely mental?
6. In what important ways does Russell think the word "idea" is ambiguous?
7. What does Russell mean by "subsist" and "exist"?

■ ■ ■

The problem with which we are now concerned is a very old one, since it was brought into philosophy by Plato. Plato's 'theory of ideas' is an attempt to solve this very problem, and in my opinion it is one of the most successful attempts hitherto made. The theory to be advocated in what follows is largely Plato's, with merely such modifications as time has shown to be necessary.

The way the problem arose for Plato was more or less as follows. Let us consider, say, such a notion as *justice*. If we ask ourselves what justice is, it is natural to proceed by considering this, that, and the other just act, with a view to discovering what they have in common. They must all, in some sense, partake of a common nature, which will be found in whatever is just and in nothing else. This common nature, in virtue of which they are all just, will be justice itself, the pure essence the admixture of which with facts of ordinary life produces the multiplicity of just acts. Similarly with any other word which may be applicable to common facts, such as 'whiteness' for example. The word will be applicable to a number of particular things because they all participate in a common nature or essence. This pure essence is what Plato calls an 'idea' or 'form.' (It must not be supposed that 'ideas', in his sense, exist in minds, though they may be apprehended by minds.) The 'idea' *justice* is not identical with anything that is just: it is something other than particular things, which particular things partake of. Not being particular, it cannot itself exist in the world of sense. Moreover it is not fleeting or changeable like the things of sense: it is eternally itself, immutable and indestructible.

Thus Plato is led to a supra-sensible world, more real than the common world of sense, the unchangeable world of ideas, which alone gives to the world of sense whatever pale reflection of reality may belong to it. The truly real world, for Plato, is the world of ideas; for whatever we may attempt to say about things in the world of sense, we can only succeed in saying that they participate in such and such ideas, which, therefore, constitute all their character. Hence it is easy to pass on into a mysticism. We may hope, in a mystic illumination, to *see* the ideas as we see objects of sense; and we may imagine that the ideas exist in heaven. These mystical developments are very natural, but the basis of the theory is in logic, and it is as based in logic that we have to consider it.

The word 'idea' has acquired, in the course of time, many associations which are quite misleading when applied to Plato's 'ideas'. We shall therefore use the word 'universal' instead of the word 'idea', to describe what Plato meant. The essence of the sort of entity that Plato meant is that it is opposed to the particular things that are given in sensation. We speak of whatever is given in sensation, or is of the same nature as things given in sensation, as a *particular*; by opposition to this, a *universal* will be anything which may be shared by many particulars, and has those characteristics which, as we saw, distinguish justice and whiteness from just acts and white things.

When we examine common words, we find that, broadly speaking, proper names stand for particulars, while other substantives, adjectives, prepositions, and verbs stand for universals. Pronouns stand for particulars, but are ambiguous: it is only by the context or the circumstances that we know what particulars they stand for. The word 'now' stands for a particular, namely the present moment; but like pronouns, it stands for an ambiguous particular, because the present is always changing.

It will be seen that no sentence can be made up without at least one word which denotes a universal. The nearest approach would be some such statement as 'I like this'. But even here the word 'like' denotes a universal, for I may like other things, and other people may like things. Thus all truths involve universals, and all knowledge of truths involves acquaintance with universals.

Seeing that nearly all the words to be found in the dictionary stand for universals, it is strange that hardly anybody except students of philosophy ever realizes that there are such entities as universals. We do not naturally dwell upon those words in a sentence which do not stand for particulars; and if we are forced to dwell upon a word which stands for a universal, we naturally think of it as standing for some one of the particulars that come under the universal. When, for example, we hear the sentence, 'Charles I's head was cut off', we may naturally enough think of Charles I, of Charles I's head, and of the operation of cutting off *his* head, which are all particulars; but we do not naturally dwell upon what is meant by the word 'head' or the word 'cut', which is a universal. We feel such words to be incomplete and insubstantial; they seem to demand a context before anything can be done with them. Hence we succeed in avoiding all notice of universals as such, until the study of philosophy forces them upon our attention.

Even among philosophers, we may say, broadly, that only those universals which are named by adjectives or substantives have been much or often recognized, while those named by verbs and prepositions have been usually overlooked. This omission has had a very great effect upon philosophy; it is hardly too much to say that most metaphysics, since Spinoza, has been largely determined by it. The way this has occurred is, in outline, as follows: Speaking generally, adjectives and common nouns express qualities or properties of single things, whereas prepositions and verbs tend to express relations between two or more things. Thus the neglect of prepositions and verbs led to the belief that every proposition can be regarded as attributing a property to a single thing, rather than as expressing a relation between two or more things. Hence it was supposed that, ultimately, there can be no such entities as relations between things. Hence either there can be only one thing in the universe, or, if there are many things, they cannot possibly interact in any way, since any interaction would be a relation, and relations are impossible.

The first of these views, advocated by Spinoza and held in our own day by Bradley and many other philosophers, is called *monism*; the second, advocated by Leibniz but not very common nowadays, is called *monadism*, because each of the isolated things is called a *monad*. Both these opposing philosophies, interesting as they are, result, in my opinion, from an undue attention to one sort of universals, namely the sort represented by adjectives and substantives rather than by verbs and prepositions.

As a matter of fact, if any one were anxious to deny altogether that there are such things as universals, we should find that we cannot strictly prove that there are such entities as *qualities*, i.e. the universals represented by adjectives and substantives, whereas we can prove that there must be *relations*, i.e. the sort of universals generally represented by verbs and prepositions. Let us take in illustration the universal *whiteness*. If we believe that there is such a universal, we shall say that things are white because they have the quality of whiteness. This view, however, was strenuously denied by Berkeley and Hume, who have been followed in this by later empiricists. The form which their denial took was to deny that there are such things as 'abstract ideas'. When we want to think of whiteness, they said, we form an image of some particular white thing, and reason concerning this particular, taking care not to deduce anything concerning it which we cannot see to be equally true of any other white thing. As an account of our actual mental processes, this is no doubt largely true. In geometry, for example, when we wish to prove something about all triangles, we draw a particular triangle and reason about it, taking care not to use any characteristic which it does not share with other triangles. The beginner, in order to avoid error, often finds it useful to draw several triangles, as unlike each other as possible, in order to make sure that his reasoning is equally applicable to all of them. But a difficulty emerges as soon as we ask ourselves how we know that a thing is white or a triangle. If we wish to avoid the universals *whiteness* and *tri-*

angularity, we shall choose some particular patch of white or some particular triangle, and say that anything is white or a triangle if it has the right sort of resemblance to our chosen particular. But then the resemblance required will have to be universal. Since there are many white things, the resemblance must hold between many pairs of particular white things; and this is the characteristic of a universal. It will be useless to say that there is a different resemblance for each pair, for then we shall have to say that these resemblances resemble each other, and thus at last we shall be forced to admit resemblance as a universal. The relation of resemblance, therefore, must be a true universal. And having been forced to admit this universal, we find that it is no longer worth while to invent difficult and unplausible theories to avoid the admission of such universals as whiteness and triangularity.

Berkeley and Hume failed to perceive this refutation of their rejection of 'abstract ideas', because, like their adversaries, they only thought of *qualities*, and altogether ignored *relations* as universals. We have therefore here another respect in which the rationalists appear to have been in the right as against the empiricists, although, owing to the neglect or denial of relations, the deductions made by rationalists were, if anything, more apt to be mistaken than those made by empiricists.

Having now seen that there must be such entities as universals, the next point to be proved is that their being is not merely mental. By this is meant that whatever being belongs to them is independent of their being thought of or in any way apprehended by minds. We must now consider more fully what sort of being it is that belongs to universals.

Consider such a proposition as 'Edinburgh is north of London'. Here we have a relation between two places, and it seems plain that the relation subsists independently of our knowledge of it. When we come to know that Edinburgh is north of London, we come to know something which has to do only with Edinburgh and London: we do not cause the truth of the proposition by coming to know it, on the contrary we merely apprehend a fact which was there before we knew it. The part of the earth's surface where Edinburgh stands would be north of the part where London stands, even if there were no human being to know about north and south, and even if there were no minds at all in the universe. This is, of course, denied by many philosophers, either for Berkeley's reasons or for Kant's. But we have already considered these reasons, and decided that they are inadequate. We may therefore now assume it to be true that nothing mental is presupposed in the fact that Edinburgh is north of London. But this fact involves the relation 'north of', which is a universal; and it would be impossible for the whole fact to involve nothing mental if the relation 'north of', which is a constituent part of the fact, did involve anything mental. Hence we must admit that the relation, like the terms it relates, is not dependent upon thought, but belongs to the independent world which thought apprehends but does not create.

This conclusion, however, is met by the difficulty that the relation 'north of' does not seem to *exist* in the same sense in which Edinburgh and London exist. If we ask 'Where and when does this relation exist?' the answer must be 'Nowhere and nowhen'. There is no place or time where we can find the relation 'north of'. It does not exist in Edinburgh any more than in London, for it relates the two and is neutral as between them. Nor can we say that it exists at any particular time. Now everything that can be apprehended by the senses or by introspection exists at some particular time. Hence the relation 'north of' is radically different from such things. It is neither in space nor in time, neither material nor mental; yet it is something.

It is largely the very peculiar kind of being that belongs to universals which has led many people to suppose that they are really mental. We can think *of* a universal, and our thinking then exists in a perfectly ordinary sense, like any other mental act. Suppose, for example, that we are thinking of whiteness. Then *in one sense* it may be said that whiteness is 'in our mind'. We have here the same ambiguity as in discussing Berkeley. In the strict sense, it is not whiteness that is in our mind, but the act of thinking of whiteness. The connected ambiguity in the word 'idea', which we noted at the same time, also causes confusion here. In one sense of this word, namely the sense in which it denotes the *object* of an act of thought, whiteness is an 'idea'. Hence, if the ambiguity is not guarded against, we may come to think that whiteness is an 'idea' in the other sense, i.e. an act of thought; and thus we come to think that whiteness is mental. But in so thinking, we rob it of its essential quality of universality. One man's act of thought is necessarily a different thing from another man's; one man's act of thought at one time is necessarily a different thing from the same man's act of thought at another time. Hence, if whiteness were the thought as opposed to its object, no two different men could think of it, and no one man could think of it twice. That which many different thoughts of whiteness have in common is their *object*, and this object is different from all of them. Thus universals are not thoughts, though when known they are the objects of thoughts.

We shall find it convenient only to speak of things *existing* when they are in time, that is to say, when we can point to some time *at* which they exist (not excluding the possibility of their existing at all times). Thus thoughts and feelings, minds and physical objects *exist*. But universals do not exist in this sense; we shall say that they *subsist* or *have being*, where 'being' is opposed to 'existence' as being timeless. The world of universals, therefore, may also be described as the world of being. The world of being is unchangeable, rigid, exact, delightful to the mathematician, the logician, the builder of metaphysical systems, and all who love perfection more than life. The world of existence is fleeting, vague, without sharp boundaries, without any clear plan or arrangement, but it contains all thoughts and feelings, all the data of sense, and all physical objects, everything that can do either good or harm, everything that makes any difference to the value of life and the world. According to our temperaments, we shall prefer the contemplation of the one or of the other. The one we do not prefer will probably seem to us a pale shadow of the one we prefer, and hardly worthy to be regarded as in any sense real. But the truth is that both have the same claim on our impartial attention, both are real, and both are important to the metaphysician. Indeed no sooner have we distinguished the two worlds than it becomes necessary to consider their relations.

Does God Exist?

CHAPTER PREFACE

At some point every reflective person in our society confronts the question of God's existence. Although there are several competing understandings of Absolute or Ultimate Reality, in Western cultures the question has been framed as one of two alternate explanations for the universe. Either the universe has its source in some being that resembles a person or intelligence, or the universe is the result of something totally impersonal. The question is not whether there are gods or super beings greater than humans, but whether there is a supreme God and Creator. This is, perhaps, the ultimate metaphysical question. Related to this question are other questions, including whether the beauty and order of the world was designed by someone. Or whether any God could be good considering the amount of suffering in the world. Philosophers begin with these sorts of questions and attempt to draw out their consequences.

Perhaps the most fundamental intuition we have is that the world or universe must have been caused by something. The existence of the world seems to us to be a fact in need of an explanation. This intuition is addressed in the Jewish, Christian, and Islamic religions in the form of God, who is revealed as the Creator of the universe. Whenever religious thinkers have acquired philosophical tools, they have quickly applied them to their own religious beliefs. The great Christian theologian St. Thomas Aquinas argued that the existence of God could be proved by carefully examining the world and discovering that certain processes were at work which required explanations outside of and beyond the world itself. Arguments that claim God can be deduced as the cause of the world are called "cosmological arguments."

Other theologians, like William Paley, argue that what appears to be design and purpose in the workings of the world is exactly that, and that it is possible to prove the existence of a Designer if we look carefully and logically at the magnitude and implications of this design. The world not only tells us that it has a Designer, but the design tells us much about the nature of the Designer. This important proof is contested by the skeptical philosopher David Hume, who points out that the world looks not only like something that has been designed like a machine, but also like something that may have grown like a plant or animal. Hume does not think there is any reason to conclude that the world is more likely to be caused by an intelligent Designer than by some sort of organic principle. In fact, he doubts that it makes sense to talk about the world being caused at all, since we have no experience of things like worlds being caused. The theory of evolution has recently given a new twist to the argument for design, with both sides claiming that it supports their positions.

Some people are fascinated by the question, "Why is there not nothing?" If God is the cause of the universe, then perhaps God's nature is somehow the answer to this question. One common philosophical approach to God's nature is to define God as a "necessary being," a being which cannot not exist. St. Anselm considered necessary being from several perspectives. One approach was through a definition of God as "that than which no greater can be conceived." Anselm believed that such a being must be conceived of as existing, and so the very idea of God shows that God must exist. Anselm immediately met opposition in the person of a fellow monk, Gaunilo, who gave an example which he thought refuted Anselm. Anselm answered him and the debate continues to the present. Can we prove God's existence from the definition or idea of God? This proof is called the "ontological argument." Some contemporary philosophers argue that only statements like "A is A" can be truly necessary and that beings just are. Others point out that some beings like "square circles" are impossible beings, so why not the opposite, a necessary being?

Even if we find good reason to believe that there is a God, the sheer magnitude of evil and suffering in the world raises the question of whether God can be both good and all-powerful. This is the well-known "problem of evil." It is a favorite contemporary refutation of God's existence among atheists, who try to show that every attempt believers make to explain how God can be good is vain. Theists like John Hick argue that real evil and real suffering are a necessary part of a world which is designed for developing souls exercising free choice. Hick does not believe that the world is simply meant to be a place of pleasure. The problem of evil has been an especially active topic in the philosophy of religion since the suffering caused by the Holocaust in World War II.

In addition to considering particular arguments for and

against God's existence, it is possible to ask the more general question, "Is belief in God purely a matter of rationality?" The popular Christian writer and lay theologian C.S. Lewis argues that Christian theism is a personal relationship, not merely a speculative hypothesis. In the end, it is possible for philosophers with equally astute minds to disagree.

God Must Exist Because the World Exists

ST. THOMAS AQUINAS

St. Thomas Aquinas (1225-1274) was a Dominican monk born in Roccasicca, Italy. He studied in Naples, Cologne, and Paris. He taught in Paris and Rome and his major works are *Summa Theologica* and *Summa Contra Gentiles*. Aquinas was heavily influenced by the Greek philosopher Aristotle. Through St. Thomas several of Aristotle's major metaphysical ideas were incorporated into Christian thought. The resulting philosophical and theological system is often considered the "synthesis of ideas" which marks the high point of medieval thought. Following Aristotle, Aquinas divided the universe into things which are possibilities and things which are actualities. For example, an acorn is a possible oak tree and a full-grown tree is an actual oak tree. A possible tree does not just sponta-

From St. Thomas Aquinas, *Summa Theologiae,* vol. 2, "Existence and Nature of God," question 2, articles 2, 3, translated by Timothy McDermott, O.P. London: Spottiswood, 1964.

neously become an actual tree. A variety of causes must work together to make that actual tree. Since mere possibilities can not make anything happen, these causes must be actual things themselves. A pile of wood, for example, is a possible fire, but some cause which is actually hot, like a spark or a lighted match, is necessary to start it burning. St. Thomas did not believe that anything just happens. He thought that all events have reasons or explanations. Put another way, the things in the world are all effects which require causes. The need for explanations extends beyond the things in the world to include the world itself. The fact that the world exists, that there is something rather than nothing, requires an explanation. The world Aquinas observed appeared to be perishable, something that might not have been at all. Consequently the world is not a good candidate for explaining existence, but a mere effect which itself requires a cause to explain its dynamic nature and its sheer existence. Only God, the necessary being, can serve as the needed explanation or cause.

QUESTIONS

1. What two kinds of demonstration does St. Thomas identify? Which kind is used to demonstrate the existence of God?
2. Does St. Thomas believe that our arguments can tell us everything about what God is like? Why?
3. According to St. Thomas, would anything change if there were no first cause to start the process of change?
4. Why is it important for the author's second argument that causes precede their effects? Can you think of any causes that follow their effects?
5. Given St. Thomas's third proof, do you think that eventually there would be nothing at all if each thing in the universe had some real chance of popping out of existence?
6. What point is St. Thomas trying to make when he compares fire to God in the fourth proof?
7. Given the author's fifth proof, do you think that he could argue that modern evolutionary biology simply shows the need for God since the process itself is without purpose? Why or why not?

■ ■ ■

Reply: There are two types of demonstration. One, showing 'why', follows the natural order of things among themselves, arguing from cause to effect; the other, showing 'that', follows the order in which we know things, arguing from effect to cause (for when an effect is more apparent to us than its cause, we come to know the cause through the effect). Now any effect of a cause demonstrates that that cause exists, in cases where the effect is better known to us, since effects are dependent upon causes, and can only occur if the causes already exist. From effects evident to us, therefore, we can demonstrate what in itself is not evident to us, namely, that God exists.

Hence: **1.** The truths about God which St. Paul says we can know by our natural powers of reasoning—that God exists, for example—are not numbered among the articles of faith, but are presupposed to them. For faith presupposes natural knowledge, just as grace does nature and all perfections that which they perfect. However, there is nothing to stop a man accepting on faith some truth which he personally cannot demonstrate, even if that truth in itself is such that demonstration could make it evident.

2. When we argue from effect to cause, the effect will take the place of a definition of the cause in the proof that the cause exists; and this especially if the cause is God. For when proving anything to exist, the central link is not what that thing is (we cannot even ask what it is until we know that it exists), but rather what we are using the name of the thing to mean. Now when demonstrating from effects that God exists, we are able to start from what the word 'God' means, for, as we shall see, the names of God are derived from these effects.

3. Effects can give comprehensive knowledge of their cause only when commensurate with it: but, as we have said, any effect whatever can make it clear that a cause exists. God's effects, therefore, can serve to demonstrate that God exists, even though they cannot help us to know him comprehensively for what he is. . . .

Reply: There are five ways in which one can prove that there is a God. The first and most obvious way is based on change. Some things in the world are certainly in process of change: this we plainly see. Now anything in process of change is being changed by something else. This is so because it is characteristic of things in process of change that they do not yet have the perfection towards which they move, though able to have it; whereas it is characteristic of something causing change to have that perfection already. For to cause change is to bring into being what was previously only able to be, and this can only be done by something that already is: thus fire, which is actually hot, causes wood, which is able to be hot, to become actually hot, and in this way causes change in the wood. Now the same thing cannot at the same time be both actually x and potentially x, though it can be actually x and potentially y: the actually hot cannot at the same time be potentially hot, though it can be potentially cold. Consequently, a thing in process of change cannot itself cause that same change; it cannot change itself. Of necessity therefore anything in process of change is being changed by something else. Moreover, this something else, if in process of change, is itself being changed by yet another thing; and this last by another. Now we must stop somewhere, otherwise there will be no first cause of the change, and, as a result, no subsequent causes. For it is only when acted upon by the first cause that the intermediate causes will produce the change: if the hand does not move the stick, the stick will not move anything else. Hence one is bound to arrive at some first cause of change not itself being changed by anything, and this is what everybody understands by God.

The second way is based on the nature of causation. In the observable world causes are found to be ordered in series; we never observe, nor ever could, something causing itself, for this would mean it preceded itself, and this is not possible. Such a series of causes must however stop somewhere; for in it an earlier member causes an intermediate and the intermediate a last (whether the intermediate be one or many). Now if you eliminate a cause you also eliminate its effects, so that you cannot have a last cause, nor an intermediate one, unless you have a first. Given therefore no stop in the series of causes, and hence no first cause, there would be no intermediate causes either, and no last effect, and this would be an open mistake. One is therefore forced to suppose some first cause, to which everyone gives the name 'God'.

The third way is based on what need not be and on what must be, and runs as follows. Some of the things we come across can be but need not be, for we find them springing up and dying away, thus sometimes in being and sometimes not. Now everything cannot be like this, for a thing that need not be, once was not; and if everything need not be, once upon a time there was nothing. But if that were true there would be nothing even now, because something that does not exist can only be brought into being by something already existing. So that if nothing was in being nothing could be brought into being, and nothing would be in being now, which contradicts observation. Not everything therefore is the sort of thing that need not be; there has got to be something that must be. Now a thing that must be, may or may not owe this necessity to something else. But just as we must stop somewhere in a series of causes, so also in the series of things which must be and owe this to other things. One is forced therefore to suppose something which must be, and owes this to no other thing than itself; indeed it itself is the cause that other things must be.

The fourth way is based on the gradation observed in things. Some things are found to be more good, more true, more noble, and so on, and other things less. But such comparative terms describe varying degrees of approximation to a superlative; for example, things are hotter and hotter the nearer they approach what is hottest. Something therefore is the truest and best and most noble of things, and hence the most fully in being; for Aristotle says that the truest things are the things most fully in being. Now *when many things possess some property in common, the one most fully possessing it causes it in the others: fire,* to use Aristotle's example, *the hottest of all things, causes all other things to be hot*. There is something therefore which causes in all other things their being, their goodness, and whatever other perfection they have. And this we call 'God'.

The fifth way is based on the guidedness of nature. An orderedness of actions to an end is observed in all bodies obeying natural laws, even when they lack awareness. For their behaviour hardly ever varies, and will practically always turn out well; which shows that they truly tend to a goal, and do not merely hit it by accident. Nothing however that lacks awareness tends to a goal, except under the direction of someone with awareness and with understanding; the arrow, for example, requires an archer. Everything in nature, therefore, is directed to its goal by someone with understanding, and this we call 'God'.

Hence: **1.** As Augustine says, *Since God is supremely good, he would not permit any evil at all in his works, unless he were sufficiently almighty and good to bring good even from evil.* It is therefore a mark of the limitless goodness of God that he permits evils to exist, and draws from them good.

2. Natural causes act for definite purposes under the direction of some higher cause, so that their effects must also be referred to God as the first of all causes. In the same manner contrived effects must likewise be referred back to a higher cause than human reasoning and will, for these are changeable and can cease to be, and, as we have seen, all changeable things and things that can cease to be require some first cause which cannot change and of itself must be.

God Necessarily Exists

ST. ANSELM

St. Anselm (c.1033-1109) was born in Aosta, Italy, and entered a monastery in Bec in Normandy where he became abbot. He was later elevated to archbishop of Canterbury. Anselm distinguished himself as a scholar and theologian and wrote several important treatises including the *Proslogium* or *Discourse* which he dedicated to proving the existence of God. The present selection is taken from the *Proslogium* and from a response by Gaunilo, a monk who is otherwise not well known. The reading concludes with Anselm's response to Gaunilo. Anselm begins by defining God as "that than which no greater can be conceived." He believes that it is greater to exist than not to exist. This means that any being that only exists as an idea in the mind is less than a being which also ex-

Excerpts of St. Anselm, *Basic Writings*, translated by S.N. Deane, The Open Court Publishing Co., 1903.

ists outside the mind. In fact, any being which can even be conceived of as not existing is less than one which cannot be conceived of as not existing. Anselm believes that once we clearly understand what he means by this being, we will recognize that it must exist. Any being which either does not exist or which could even be thought not to exist is not the being Anselm is talking about. Gaunilo replies that he is not convinced that an island which surpasses all other islands exists just because he can conceive of it. He believes that this analogy refutes Anselm's argument for God's existence. Anselm replies that, if the island fit his definition and form of reasoning, he could prove that it exists! Anselm does not believe, of course, that the island fits his reasoning. It is easy to conceive of something greater than Gaunilo's greatest island, but one cannot conceive of something greater than the greatest conceivable being, God! That would be a contradiction. So, God must, and therefore does, exist.

QUESTIONS

1. Why is it important for Anselm to assert that even the fool who denies God understands what Anselm means by God?
2. How, according to the author, does a being which can be conceived *not* to exist compare to a being that cannot be conceived not to exist?
3. What two types or levels of understanding or conceiving does Anselm identify? Why is this important for his argument? On which level is it possible, according to Anselm, to deny God's existence?
4. What kind of existence does Anselm believe God has? Does this make sense in light of his argument?
5. How does Gaunilo define the lost island whose existence he can doubt? What analogy is Gaunilo making?
6. Does Anselm think Gaunilo has successfully made his case? How does Gaunilo's definition of the island differ from Anselm's definition of God?
7. What does Anselm mean when he says that it is "greater" to exist in reality than just to exist in the mind? Does this make sense to you?

■ ■ ■

St. Anselm's Presentation

Truly there is a God, although the fool hath said in his heart, There is no God.

And so, Lord, do thou, who dost give understanding to faith, give me, so far as thou knowest it to be profitable, to understand that thou art as we believe; and that thou art that which we believe. And, indeed, we believe that thou art a being than which nothing greater can be conceived. Or is there no such nature, since the fool hath said in his heart, there is no God? (Psalms xiii, 1). But, at any rate, this very fool, when he hears of this being of which I speak—a being than which nothing greater can be conceived—understands what he hears, and what he understands is in his understanding; although he does not understand it to exist.

For, it is one thing for an object to be in the understanding, and another to understand that the object exists. When a painter first conceives of what he will afterwards perform, he has it in his understanding, but he does not yet understand it to be, because he has not yet performed it. But after he has made the painting, he both has it in his understanding, and he understands that it exists, because he has made it.

Hence, even the fool is convinced that something exists in the understanding, at least, than which nothing greater can be conceived. For, when he hears of this, he understands it. And whatever is understood, exists in the understanding. And assuredly that, than which nothing greater can be conceived, cannot exist in the understanding alone. For, suppose it exists in the understanding alone: then it can be conceived to exist in reality; which is greater.

Therefore, if that, than which nothing greater can be conceived, exists in the understanding alone, the very being, than which nothing greater can be conceived, is one, than which a greater can be conceived. But obviously this is impossible. Hence, there is no doubt that there exists a being, than which nothing greater can be conceived, and it exists both in the understanding and in reality.

God cannot be conceived not to exist.—God is that, than which nothing greater can be conceived.—That which can be conceived not to exist is not God.

And it assuredly exists so truly, that it cannot be conceived not to exist. For, it is possible to conceive of a being which cannot be conceived not to exist; and this is greater than one which can be conceived not to exist. Hence, if that, than which nothing greater can be conceived, can be conceived not to exist, it is not that, than which nothing greater can be conceived. But this is an irreconcilable contradiction. There is, then, so truly a being than which nothing greater can be conceived to exist, that it cannot even be conceived not to exist; and this being thou art, O Lord, our God.

So truly, therefore, dost thou exist, O Lord, my God, that thou canst not be conceived not to exist; and rightly. For, if a mind could conceive of a being better than thee, the creature would rise above the Creator; and this is most absurd. And, indeed, whatever else there is, except thee alone, can be conceived not to exist. To thee alone, therefore, it belongs to exist more truly than all other beings, and hence in a higher degree than all others. For, whatever else exists does not exist so truly, and hence in a less degree it belongs to it to exist. Why, then, has the fool said in his heart, there is no God (Psalms xiii, 1), since it is so evident, to a rational mind, that thou dost exist in the highest degree of all? Why, except that he is dull and a fool?

How the fool has said in his heart what cannot be conceived.—A thing may be conceived in two ways: (1) when the word signifying it is conceived; (2) when the thing itself is understood. As far as the word goes, God can be conceived not to exist; in reality he cannot.

But how has the fool said in his heart what he could not conceive; or how is it that he could not conceive what he said in his heart? since it is the same to say in the heart, and to conceive.

But, if really, nay, since really, he both conceived, because he said in his heart; and did not say in his heart, because he could not conceive; there is more than one way in which a thing is said in the heart or conceived. For, in one sense, an object is conceived, when the word signifying it is conceived; and in another, when the very entity, which the object is, is understood.

In the former sense, then, God can be conceived not to exist;

but in the latter, not at all. For no one who understands what fire and water are can conceive fire to be water, in accordance with the nature of the facts themselves, although this is possible according to the words. So, then, no one who understands what God is can conceive that God does not exist; although he says these words in his heart, either without any or with some foreign, signification. For, God is that than which a greater cannot be conceived. And he who thoroughly understands this, assuredly understands that this being so truly exists, that not even in concept can it be nonexistent. Therefore, he who understands that God so exists, cannot conceive that he does not exist.

I thank thee, Gracious Lord, I thank thee; because what I formerly believed by thy bounty, I now so understand by thine illumination, that if I were unwilling to believe that thou dost exist, I should not be able not to understand this to be true.

Gaunilo's Criticism

For example: it is said that somewhere in the ocean is an island, which, because of the difficulty, or rather the impossibility, of discovering what does not exist, is called the lost island. And they say that this island has an inestimable wealth of all manner of riches and delicacies in greater abundance than is told of the Islands of the Blest; and that having no owner or inhabitant, it is more excellent than all other countries, which are inhabited by mankind, in the abundance with which it is stored.

Now if some one should tell me that there is such an island, I should easily understand his words, in which there is no difficulty. But suppose that he went on to say, as if by a logical inference: "You can no longer doubt that this island which is more excellent than all lands exists somewhere, since you have no doubt that it is in your understanding. And since it is more excellent not to be in the understanding alone, but to exist both in the understanding and in reality, for this reason it must exist. For if it does not exist, any land which really exists will be more excellent than it; and so the island already understood by you to be more excellent will not be more excellent."

If a man should try to prove to me by such reasoning that this island truly exists, and that its existence should no longer be doubted, either I should believe that he was jesting, or I know not which I ought to regard as the greater fool: myself, supposing that I should allow this proof; or him, if he should suppose that he had established with any certainty the existence of this island. For he ought to show first that the hypothetical excellence of this island exists as a real and indubitable fact, and in no wise as any unreal object, or one whose existence is uncertain, in my understanding.

St. Anselm's Rejoinder

But, you say, it is as if one should suppose an island in the ocean, which surpasses all lands in its fertility, and which, because of the difficulty, or rather the impossibility, of discovering what does not exist, is called a lost island; and should say that there can be no doubt that this island truly exists in reality, for this reason, that one who hears it described easily understands what he hears.

Now I promise confidently that if any man shall devise anything existing either in reality or in concept alone (except that than which a greater cannot be conceived) to which he can adapt the sequence of my reasoning, I will discover that thing, and will give him his lost island, not to be lost again.

But it now appears that this being than which a greater is inconceivable cannot be conceived not to be, because it exists on so assured a ground of truth; for otherwise it would not exist at all.

Hence, if any one says that he conceives this being not to exist, I say that at the time when he conceives of this either he conceives of a being than which a greater is inconceivable, or he does not conceive at all. If he does not conceive, he does not conceive of the non-existence of that of which he does not conceive. But if he does conceive, he certainly conceives of a being which cannot be even conceived not to exist. For if it could be conceived not to exist, it could be conceived to have a beginning and an end. But this is impossible.

He, then, who conceives of this being conceives of a being which cannot be even conceived not to exist; but he who conceives of this being does not conceive that it does not exist; else he conceives what is inconceivable. The non-existence then, of that than which a greater cannot be conceived is inconceivable.

Evil Proves That God Cannot Be All Good

B.C. Johnson

B.C. Johnson is a pen name for an author who wishes to remain anonymous. The current selection is taken from *The Atheist Debater's Handbook*, published by Prometheus Books, which specializes in books attacking religion, parapsychology, miraculous claims, and other perspectives which are considered inconsistent with atheistic humanism. Johnson argues that God has no excuse for inaction when God fails to prevent much of the suffering and disaster in the world. Because God has no excuse, it is not reasonable to assume that God is completely good, even if there is a God. Johnson appeals to moral intuitions we have concerning what we would expect capable human beings to do when confronted with suffering and tragedy, such as babies burning to death. He argues that

From B.C. Johnson, *The Atheist Debater's Handbook*. Buffalo: Prometheus Books, 1981.

good humans would be obligated to intervene to prevent the suffering. God, being even more powerful, is also obligated, but does nothing. Johnson argues against several major defenses of God, which he considers merely poor excuses. He believes, for example, that there is more suffering in the world than is necessary for persons to develop "virtue" through suffering. God could constantly intervene with subtle unnoticed miracles without destroying the regular natural order of the world if he existed and was caring. He concludes by arguing that the world is the same, whether one perceives God to be evil or good.

QUESTIONS

1. How do you think Johnson would define a good God? What exactly does he expect from God?
2. Why does the author compare God with physicians and firefighters? Do you think this is a good comparison?
3. What does "moral urgency" mean? What is Johnson's argument against a defense of God based upon this urgency?
4. How does Johnson argue against the "virtue building" defense of God?
5. In what sense does the author think that God's morality is the opposite of human morality?
6. What does Johnson mean by "knowing" God? Do you think this is what religious people mean when they say that they know God?
7. Why, according to the author, are we not justified in faith that God is good?
8. What fact about the world does Johnson cite to show that the world can be made consistent with an evil God?

■ ■ ■

Here is a common situation: a house catches on fire and a six-month-old baby is painfully burned to death. Could we possibly describe as "good" any person who had the power to save this child and yet refused to do so? God undoubtedly has this power and yet in many cases of this sort he has refused to help. Can we call God "good"? Are there adequate excuses for his behavior?

First, it will not do to claim that the baby will go to heaven. It was either necessary for the baby to suffer or it was not. If it was not, then it was wrong to allow it. The child's ascent to heaven does not change this fact. If it was necessary, the fact that the baby will go to heaven does not explain why it was necessary, and we are still left without an excuse for God's inaction. It is not enough to say that the baby's painful death would in the long run have good results and therefore should have happened, otherwise God would not have permitted it. For if we know this to be true, then we know—just as God knows—that every action successfully performed must in the end be good and therefore the right thing to do, otherwise God would not have allowed it to happen. We could deliberately set houses ablaze to kill innocent people and if successful we would then know we had a duty to do it. A defense of God's goodness which takes as its foundation duties known only after the fact would result in a morality unworthy of the name. Furthermore, this argument does not explain why God allowed the child to burn to death. It merely claims that there is some reason discoverable in the long run. But the belief that such a reason is within our grasp must rest upon the additional belief that God is good. This is just to counter evidence against such a belief by assuming the belief to be true. It is not unlike a lawyer defending his client by claiming that the client is innocent and therefore the evidence against him must be misleading—that proof vindicating the defendant will be found in the long run. No jury of reasonable men and women would accept such a defense and the theist cannot expect a more favorable outcome.

The theist often claims that man has been given free will so that if he accidentally or purposefully causes fires, killing small children, it is his fault alone. Consider a bystander who had nothing to do with starting the fire but who refused to help even though he could have saved the child with no harm to himself. Could such a bystander be called good? Certainly not. If we would not consider a mortal human being good under these circumstances, what grounds could we possibly have for continuing to assert the goodness of an all-powerful God?

The suggestion is sometimes made that it is best for us to face disasters without assistance, otherwise we would become dependent on an outside power for aid. Should we then abolish modern medical care or do away with efficient fire departments? Are we not dependent on their help? Is it not the case that their presence transforms us into soft, dependent creatures? The vast majority are not physicians or firemen. These people help in their capacity as professional outside sources of aid in much the same way that we would expect God to be helpful. Theists refer to aid from firemen and physicians as cases of man helping himself. In reality, it is a tiny minority of men helping a great many. We can become just as dependent on them as we can on God. Now the existence of this kind of outside help is either wrong or right. If it is right, then God should assist those areas of the world which do not have this kind of help. In fact, throughout history, such help has not been available. If aid ought to have been provided, then God should have provided it. On the other hand, if it is wrong to provide this kind of assistance, then we should abolish the aid altogether. But we obviously do not believe it is wrong.

Similar considerations apply to the claim that if God interferes in disasters, he would destroy a considerable amount of moral urgency to make things right. Once again, note that such institutions as modern medicine and fire departments are relatively recent. They function irrespective of whether we as individuals feel any moral urgency to support them. To the extent that they help others, opportunities to feel moral urgency are destroyed because they reduce the number of cases which appeal to us for help. Since we have not always had such institutions, there must have been a time when there was greater moral urgency than there is now. If such a situation is morally desirable, then we should abolish modern medical care and fire departments. If the situation is not morally desirable, then God should have remedied it.

Besides this point, we should note that God is represented as one who tolerates disasters, such as infants burning to death, in order to create moral urgency. It follows that God approves of these disasters as a means to encourage the creation of moral urgency. Furthermore, if there were no such disasters occurring, God would have to see to it that they occur. If it so happened that we lived in a world in which babies never perished in burning houses, God would be morally obliged to take an active hand in setting fire to houses with infants in them. In fact, if the frequency of infant mortality due to fire should happen to fall below a level necessary for the creation of maximum moral urgency in our real world, God would be justified in setting a few fires of his own. This may well be happening right now, for there is no guarantee that the maximum number of infant deaths necessary for moral urgency are occurring.

All of this is of course absurd. If I see an opportunity to create otherwise nonexistent opportunities for moral urgency by burning an infant or two, then I should *not* do so. But if it is good to maximize moral urgency, then I *should* do so. Therefore, it is not good to maximize moral urgency. Plainly we do not in general believe that it is a good thing to maximize moral urgency. The fact that we approve of modern medical care and applaud medical advances is proof enough of this.

The theist may point out that in a world without suffering there would be no occasion for the production of such virtues as courage, sympathy, and the like. This may be true, but the atheist need not demand a world without suffering. He need only claim that there is suffering which is in excess of that needed for the production of various virtues. For example, God's active attempts to save six-month-old infants from fires would not in itself create a world without suffering. But no one could sincerely doubt that it would improve the world.

The two arguments against the previous theistic excuse apply here also. "Moral urgency" and "building virtue" are susceptible to the same criticisms. It is worthwhile to emphasize, however, that we encourage efforts to eliminate evils; we approve of efforts to promote peace, prevent famine, and wipe out disease. In other words, we do value a world with fewer or (if possible) no opportunities for the development of virtue (when "virtue" is understood to mean the reduction of suffering). If we produce such a world for succeeding generations, how will they develop virtues? Without war, disease, and famine, they will not be virtuous. Should we then cease our attempts to wipe out war, disease, and famine? If we do not believe that it is right to cease attempts at improving the world, then by implication we admit that virtue-building is not an excuse for God to permit disasters. For we admit that the development of virtue is no excuse for permitting disasters.

It might be said that God allows innocent people to suffer in order to deflate man's ego so that the latter will not be proud of his apparently deserved good fortune. But this excuse succumbs to the arguments used against the preceding excuses and we need discuss them no further.

Theists may claim that evil is a necessary by-product of the laws of nature and therefore it is irrational for God to interfere every time a disaster happens. Such a state of affairs would alter the whole causal order and we would then find it impossible to predict anything. But the death of a child caused by an electrical fire could have been prevented by a miracle and no one would ever have known. Only a minor alteration in electrical equipment would have been necessary. A very large disaster could have been avoided simply by producing in Hitler a miraculous heart attack—and no one would have known it was a miracle. To argue that continued miraculous intervention by God would be wrong is like insisting that one should never use salt because ingesting five pounds of it would be fatal. No one is requesting that God interfere all of the time. He should, however, intervene to prevent especially horrible disasters. Of course, the question arises: where does one draw the line? Well, certainly the line should be drawn somewhere this side of infants burning to death. To argue that we do not know where the line should be drawn is no excuse for failing to interfere in those instances that would be called clear cases of evil.

It will not do to claim that evil exists as a necessary contrast to good so that we might know what good is. A very small amount of evil, such as a toothache, would allow that. It is not necessary to destroy innocent human beings.

The claim could be made that God has a "higher morality" by which his actions are to be judged. But it is a strange "higher morality" which claims that what we call "bad" is good and what we call "good" is bad. Such a morality can have no meaning to us. It would be like calling black "white" and white "black." In reply the theist may say that God is the wise Father and we are ignorant children. How can we judge God any more than a child is able to judge his parent? It is true that a child may be puzzled by his parents' conduct, but his basis for deciding that their conduct is nevertheless good would be the many instances of good behavior he has observed. Even so, this could be misleading. Hitler, by all accounts, loved animals and children of the proper race; but if Hitler had had a child, this offspring would hardly have been justified in arguing that his father was a good man. At any rate, God's "higher morality," being the opposite of ours, cannot offer any grounds for deciding that he is somehow good.

Perhaps the main problem with the solutions to the problem of evil we have thus far considered is that no matter how convincing they may be in the abstract, they are implausible in certain particular cases. Picture an infant dying in a burning house and then imagine God simply observing from afar. Perhaps God is reciting excuses in his own behalf. As the child succumbs to the smoke and flames, God may be pictured as saying: "Sorry, but if I helped you I would have considerable trouble deflating the ego of your parents. And don't forget I have to keep those laws of nature consistent. And anyway if you weren't dying in that fire, a lot of moral urgency would just go down the drain. Besides, I didn't start this fire, so you can't blame *me*."

It does no good to assert that God may not be all-powerful and thus not able to prevent evil. He can create a universe and yet is conveniently unable to do what the fire department can do—rescue a baby from a burning building. God should at least be as powerful as a man. A man, if he had been at the right place and time, could have killed Hitler. Was this beyond God's abilities? If God knew in 1910 how to produce polio vaccine and if he was able to communicate with somebody, he should have communicated this knowledge. He must be incredibly limited if he could not have managed this modest accomplishment. Such a God if not dead is the next thing to it. And a person who believes in such a ghost of a God is practically an atheist. To call such a thing a god would be to strain the meaning of the word.

The theist, as usual, may retreat to faith. He may say that he has faith in God's goodness and therefore the Christian Deity's existence has not been disproved. "Faith" is here understood as being much like confidence in a friend's innocence despite the evidence against him. Now in order to have confidence in a friend one must know him well enough to justify faith in his goodness. We cannot have justifiable faith in the supreme goodness of strangers. Moreover, such confidence must come not just from a speaking acquaintance. The friend may continually assure us with his words that he is good but if he does not act like a good person, we would have no reason to trust him. A person who says he has faith in God's goodness is speaking as if he had known God for a long time and during that time had never seen Him do any serious evil. But we know that throughout history God has allowed numerous atrocities to occur. No one can have justifiable faith in the goodness of such a God. This faith would have to be based on a close friendship wherein God was never found to do anything wrong. But a person would have to be blind and deaf to have had such a relationship with God. Suppose a friend of yours had always claimed to be good yet refused to help people when he was in a position to render aid. Could you have justifiable faith in his goodness?

You can of course say that you trust God anyway—that no arguments can undermine your faith. But this is just a statement describing how stubborn you are; it has no bearing whatsoever on the question of God's goodness.

The various excuses theists offer for why God has allowed evil to exist have been demonstrated to be inadequate. However, the conclusive objection to these excuses does not depend on their inadequacy.

First, we should note that every possible excuse making the actual world consistent with the existence of a good God could be used in reverse to make that same world consistent with an evil God. For example, we could say that God is evil and that he allows free will so that we can freely do evil things, which would make us more truly evil than we would be if forced to perform evil acts. Or we could say that natural disasters occur in order to make people more selfish and bitter, for most people tend to have a "me-first" attitude in a disaster (note, for example, stampedes to leave burning buildings). Even though some people achieve virtue from disasters, this outcome is necessary if persons are to react freely to disaster—necessary if the development of moral degeneracy is to continue freely. But, enough; the point is made. Every excuse we could provide to make the world consistent with a good God can be paralleled by an excuse to make the world consistent with an evil God. This is so because the world is a mixture of both good and bad.

Now there are only three possibilities concerning God's moral character. Considering the world as it actually is, we may believe: (*a*) that God is more likely to be all evil than he is to be all good; (*b*) that God is less likely to be all evil than he is to be all good; or (*c*) that God is equally as likely to be all evil as he is to be all good. In case (*a*) it would be admitted that God is unlikely to be all good. Case (*b*) cannot be true at all, since—as we have seen—the belief that God is all evil can be justified to precisely the same extent as the belief that God is all good. Case (*c*) leaves us with no reasonable excuses for a good God to permit evil. The reason is as follows: if an excuse is to be a reasonable excuse, the circumstances it identifies as excusing conditions must be actual. For example, if I run over a pedestrian and my excuse is that the brakes failed because someone tampered with them, then the facts had better bear this out. Otherwise the excuse will not hold. Now if case (*c*) is correct and, given the facts of the actual world, God is as likely to be all evil as he is to be all good, then these facts do not support the excuses which could be made for a good God permitting evil. Consider an analogous example. If my excuse for running over the pedestrian is that my brakes were tampered with, and if the actual facts lead us to believe that it is no more likely that they were tampered with than that they were not, the excuse is no longer reasonable. To make good my excuse, I must show that it is a fact or at least highly probable that my brakes were tampered with—not that it is just a possibility. The same point holds for God. His excuse must not be a possible excuse, but an actual one. But case (*c*), in maintaining that it is just as likely that God is all evil as that he is all good, rules this out. For if case (*c*) is true, then the facts of the actual world do not make it any more likely that God is all good than that he is all evil. Therefore, they do not make it any more likely that his excuses are good than that they are not. But, as we have seen, good excuses have a higher probability of being true.

Cases (*a*) and (*c*) conclude that it is unlikely that God is all good, and case (*b*) cannot be true. Since these are the only possible cases, there is no escape from the conclusion that it is unlikely that God is all good. Thus the problem of evil triumphs over traditional theism.

Evil Is Compatible with a Good God

JOHN HICK

John Hick (1922-) is former professor of Christian philosophy at Princeton Theological Seminary and lecturer in divinity at Cambridge University. Hick, who received his Ph.D. from Oxford University, has written extensively on theological and philosophical topics. His approach to the problem of evil has been highly influential in philosophical circles. Hicks begins by defining the problem in terms of the dilemma of a perfectly loving all-powerful God who allows evil to exist. He rejects solutions that either reject the reality of evil or reject the traditional understanding of God by defining God as either less than omnipotent or less than perfectly loving and good. Hick follows Augustine in explaining the reality of evil in terms of a real distortion or perversion of something inherently good. He believes that the suffering that is inherent in the system of the physical universe is an inevitable conse-

From John Hick, *Philosophy of Religion*, 4th ed., pp. 39-47, © 1990. Reprinted by permission of Prentice Hall, Englewood Cliffs, New Jersey.

quence of the fact that the universe is a place of soul making. Such a place must contain real choices and real consequences. Things like risk, reward, pain, and pleasure are necessary if souls are to develop certain important characteristics. Hick thinks the suffering that results from evil human choices is inevitable because even an all-powerful God cannot create a logical contradiction like a race of free beings who will never choose evil. Short of creating only robots, God must accept the consequences of real, free humans. Hick thinks the process of soul making is worth the suffering and must continue after death to make any ultimate sense.

QUESTIONS

1. Why does Hick reject the solution to evil given by the Christian Science Church?
2. In what sense, according to Augustine, is the world good? How does Augustine explain evil?
3. What, according to Hick, is the purpose of theodicy? What is it that theodicy cannot do?
4. According to Hick, what two kinds of evil need to be explained?
5. Why does Hick reject the notion that God could have created free beings that always choose good?
6. What does the author mean by "omnipotence" as it applies to God?
7. What kind of evil does Hick think the soul making argument explains?
8. What kinds of personal characteristics does Hick think it is important for God to promote?
9. How, according to Hick, can good come from evil?

■ ■ ■

To many, the most powerful positive objection to belief in God is the fact of evil. Probably for most agnostics it is the appalling depth and extent of human suffering, more than anything else, that makes the idea of a loving Creator seem so implausible and disposes them toward one or another of the various naturalistic theories of religion.

As a challenge to theism, the problem of evil has traditionally been posed in the form of a dilemma; if God is perfectly loving, he must wish to abolish evil; and if he is all-powerful, he must be able to abolish evil. But evil exists; therefore God cannot be both omnipotent and perfectly loving.

Certain solutions, which at once suggest themselves, have to be ruled out so far as the Judaic-Christian faith is concerned.

To say, for example (with contemporary Christian Science), that evil is an illusion of the human mind, is impossible within a religion based upon the stark realism of the Bible. Its pages faithfully reflect the characteristic mixture of good and evil in human experience. They record every kind of sorrow and suffering, every mode of man's inhumanity to man and of his painfully insecure existence in the world. There is no attempt to regard evil as anything but dark, menacingly ugly, heart-rending, and crushing. In the Christian scriptures, the climax of this history of evil is the crucifixion of Jesus, which is presented not only as a case of utterly unjust suffering, but as the violent and murderous rejection of God's Messiah. There can be no doubt, then, that for biblical faith, evil is unambiguously evil, and stands in direct opposition to God's will.

Again, to solve the problem of evil by means of the theory (sponsored, for example, by the Boston "Personalist" School)[1] of a finite deity who does the best he can with a material, intractable and co-eternal with himself, is to have abandoned the basic premise of Hebrew-Christian monotheism; for the theory amounts to rejecting belief in the infinity and sovereignty of God.

Indeed, any theory which would avoid the problem of the origin of evil by depicting it as an ultimate constituent of the universe, coordinate with good, has been repudiated in advance by the classic Christian teaching, first developed by Augustine, that evil represents the going wrong of something which in itself is good.[2] Augustine holds firmly to the Hebrew-Christian conviction that the universe is *good*—that is to say, it

[1]Edgar Brightman's *A Philosophy of Religion* (Englewood Cliffs, N.J.: Prentice-Hall, Inc., 1940). Chaps. 8-10 are a classic exposition of one form of this view.

[2]See Augustine's *Confessions*, Book VII, Chap. 12; *City of God*, Book XII, Chap. 3; *Enchiridion*, Chap. 4.

is the creation of a good God for a good purpose. He completely rejects the ancient prejudice, widespread in his day, that matter is evil. There are, according to Augustine, higher and lower, greater and lesser goods in immense abundance and variety; but everything which has being is good in its own way and degree, except in so far as it may have become spoiled or corrupted. Evil—whether it be an evil will, an instance of pain, or some disorder or decay in nature—has not been set there by God, but represents the distortion of something that is inherently valuable. Whatever exists is, as such, and in its proper place, good; evil is essentially parasitic upon good, being disorder and perversion in a fundamentally good creation. This understanding of evil as something negative means that it is not willed and created by God; but it does not mean (as some have supposed) that evil is unreal and can be disregarded. Clearly, the first effect of this doctrine is to accentuate even more the question of the origin of evil.

Theodicy,[3] as many modern Christian thinkers see it, is a modest enterprise, negative rather than positive in its conclusions. It does not claim to explain, nor to explain away, every instance of evil in human experience, but only to point to certain considerations which prevent the fact of evil (largely incomprehensible though it remains) from constituting a final and insuperable bar to rational belief in God.

In indicating these considerations it will be useful to follow the traditional division of the subject. There is the problem of *moral evil* or wickedness; why does an all-good and all-powerful God permit this? And there is the problem of the *non-moral evil* of suffering or pain, both physical and mental: why has an all-good and all powerful God created a world in which this occurs?

Christian thought has always considered moral evil in its relation to human freedom and responsibility. To be a person is to be a finite center of freedom, a (relatively) free and self-directing agent responsible for one's own decisions. This involves being free to act wrongly as well as to act rightly. The idea of a person who can be infallibly guaranteed always to act

[3] The word "theodicy" from the Greek *theos* (God) and *dike* (righteous) means the justification of God's goodness in face of the fact of evil.

rightly is self-contradictory. There can be no guarantee in advance that a genuinely free moral agent will never choose amiss. Consequently, the possibility of wrongdoing or sin is logically inseparable from the creation of finite persons, and to say that God should not have created beings who might sin amounts to saying that he should not have created people.

This thesis has been challenged in some recent philosophical discussions of the problem of evil, in which it is claimed that no contradiction is involved in saying that God might have made people who would be genuinely free and who could yet be guaranteed always to act rightly. A quotation from one of these discussions follows:

> If there is no logical impossibility in a man's freely choosing the good on one, or on several occasions, there cannot be a logical impossibility in his freely choosing the good on every occasion. God was not, then, faced with a choice between making innocent automata and making beings who, in acting freely, would sometimes go wrong: there was open to him the obviously better possibility of making beings who would act freely but always go right. Clearly, his failure to avail himself of this possibility is inconsistent with his being both omnipotent and wholly good.[4]

A reply to this argument is suggested in another recent contribution to the discussion.[5] If by a free action we mean an action which is not externally compelled but which flows from the nature of the agent as he reacts to the circumstances in which he finds himself, there is, indeed, no contradiction between our being free and our actions being "caused" (by our own nature) and therefore being in principle predictable. There is a contradiction, however, in saying that God is the cause of our acting as we do but that we are free beings in relation to God. There is, in other words, a contradiction in saying that

---

[4] J.L. Mackie, "Evil and Omnipotence," *Mind* (April, 1995), p. 209. A similar point is made by Antony Flew in "Divine Omnipotence and Human Freedom," *New Essays in Philosophical Theology*. An important critical comment on these arguments is offered by Ninian Smart in "Omnipotence, Evil and Supermen," *Philosophy* (April, 1961), with replies by Flew (January, 1962) and Mackie (April, 1962).

[5] Flew, in *New Essays in Philosophical Theology.*

God has made us so that we shall of necessity act in a certain way, and that we are genuinely independent persons in relation to him. If all our thoughts and actions are divinely predestined, however free and morally responsible we may seem to be to ourselves, we cannot be free and morally responsible in the sight of God, but must instead be his helpless puppets. Such "freedom" is like that of a patient acting out a series of posthypnotic suggestions: he appears, even to himself, to be free, but his volitions have actually been predetermined by another will, that of the hypnotist, in relation to whom the patient is not a free agent.

A different objector might raise the question of whether or not we deny God's omnipotence if we admit that he is unable to create persons who are free from the risks inherent in personal freedom. The answer that has always been given is that to create such beings is logically impossible. It is no limitation upon God's power that he cannot accomplish the logically impossible, since there is nothing here to accomplish, but only a meaningless conjunction of words[6]— in this case "person who is not a person." God is able to create beings of any and every conceivable kind; but creatures who lack moral freedom, however superior they might be to human beings in other respects, would not be what we mean by persons. They would constitute a different form of life which God might have brought into existence instead of persons. When we ask why God did not create such beings in place of persons, the traditional answer is that only persons could, in any meaningful sense, become "children of God," capable of entering into a personal relationship with their Creator by a free and uncompelled response to his love.

When we turn from the possibility of moral evil as a correlate of man's personal freedom to its actuality, we face something which must remain inexplicable even when it can be seen to be possible. For we can never provide a complete causal explanation of a free act; if we could, it would not be a free act. The origin of moral evil lies forever concealed within the mystery of human freedom.

---

[6] As Aquinas said, ". . . nothing that implies a contradiction falls under the scope of God's omnipotence." *Summa Theologica*, Part I, Question 25, article 4.

The necessary connection between moral freedom and the possibility, now actualized, of sin throws light upon a great deal of the suffering which afflicts mankind. For an enormous amount of human pain arises either from the inhumanity or the culpable incompetence of mankind. This includes such major scourges as poverty, oppression and persecution, war, and all the injustice, indignity, and inequity which occur even in the most advanced societies. These evils are manifestations of human sin. Even disease is fostered to an extent, the limits of which have not yet been determined by psychosomatic medicine, by moral and emotional factors seated both in the individual and in his social environment. To the extent that all of these evils stem from human failures and wrong decisions, their possibility is inherent in the creation of free persons inhabiting a world which presents them with real choices which are followed by real consequences.

We may now turn more directly to the problem of suffering. Even though the major bulk of actual human pain is traceable to man's misused freedom as a sole or part cause, there remain other sources of pain which are entirely independent of the human will, for example, earthquake, hurricane, storm, flood, drought, and blight. In practice, it is often impossible to trace a boundary between the suffering which results from human wickedness and folly and that which falls upon mankind from without. Both kinds of suffering are inextricably mingled together in human experience. For our present purpose, however, it is important to note that the latter category does exist and that it seems to be built into the very structure of our world. In response to it, theodicy, if it is wisely conducted, follows a negative path. It is not possible to show positively that each item of human pain serves the divine purpose of good; but, on the other hand, it does seem possible to show that the divine purpose as it is understood in Judaism and Christianity could not be forwarded in a world which was designed as a permanent hedonistic paradise.

An essential premise of this argument concerns the nature of the divine purpose in creating the world. The skeptic's assumption is that man is to be viewed as a completed creation and that God's purpose in making the world was to provide a suitable dwelling-place for this fully-formed creature. Since God is good and loving, the environment which he has created for human life to inhabit is naturally as pleasant and comfortable as possible. The problem is essentially similar to that of a man who builds a cage for some pet animal. Since our world, in fact, contains sources of hardship, inconvenience, and danger of innumerable kinds, the conclusion follows that this world cannot have been created by a perfectly benevolent and all-powerful deity.[7]

Christianity, however, has never supposed that God's purpose in the creation of the world was to construct a paradise whose inhabitants would experience a maximum of pleasure and a minimum of pain. The world is seen, instead, as a place of "soul-making" in which free beings grappling with the tasks and challenges of their existence in a common environment may become "children of God" and "heirs of eternal life." A way of thinking theologically of God's continuing creative purpose for man was suggested by some of the early Hellenistic Fathers of the Christian Church, especially Irenaeus. Following hints from St. Paul, Irenaeus taught that man has been made as a person in the image of God but has not yet been brought as a free and responsible agent into the finite likeness of God, which is revealed in Christ.[8] Our world, with all its rough edges, is the sphere in which this second and harder stage of the creative process is taking place.

This conception of the world (whether or not set in Irenaeus' theological framework) can be supported by the method of negative theodicy. Suppose, contrary to fact, that this world were a paradise from which all possibility of pain and suffering were excluded. The consequences would be very far-reaching. For example, no one could ever injure anyone else: the murderer's knife would turn to paper or his bullets to thin air, the bank safe, robbed of a million dollars, would miraculously become filled with another million dollars (without this device, on however large a scale, proving inflationary); fraud, deceit, conspiracy, and treason would somehow always leave the fabric of society undamaged. Again, no one would

[7]This is the nature of David Hume's argument in his discussion of the problem of evil in his *Dialogues*, Part XI. . . .

[8]See Irenaeus' *Against Heresies*, Book IV, Chaps. 37 and 38.

ever be injured by accident: the mountain-climber, steeplejack, or playing child falling from a height would float unharmed to the ground; the reckless driver would never meet with disaster. There would be no need to work, since no harm could result from avoiding work; there would be no call to be concerned for others in time of need or danger, for in such a world there could be no real needs or dangers.

To make possible this continual series of individual adjustments, nature would have to work by "special providences" instead of running according to general laws which men must learn to respect on penalty of pain or death. The laws of nature would have to be extremely flexible: sometimes gravity would operate, sometimes not; sometimes an object would be hard and solid, sometimes soft. There could be no sciences, for there would be no enduring world structure to investigate. In eliminating the problems and hardships of an objective environment, with its own laws, life would become like a dream in which, delightfully but aimlessly, we would float and drift at ease.

One can at least begin to imagine such a world. It is evident that our present ethical concepts would have no meaning in it. If, for example, the notion of harming someone is an essential element in the concept of a wrong action, in our hedonistic paradise there could be no wrong actions—nor any right actions in distinction from wrong. Courage and fortitude would have no point in an environment in which there is, by definition, no danger or difficulty. Generosity, kindness, the *agape* aspect of love, prudence, unselfishness, and all other ethical notions which presuppose life in a stable environment, could not even be formed. Consequently, such a world, however well it might promote pleasure, would be very ill adapted for the development of the moral qualities of human personality. In relation to this purpose it would be the worst of all possible worlds.

It would seem, then, that an environment intended to make possible the growth in free beings of the finest characteristics of personal life, must have a good deal in common with our present world. It must operate according to general and dependable laws; and it must involve real dangers, difficulties, problems, obstacles, and possibilities of pain, failure, sorrow, frustration, and defeat. If it did not contain the particular trials and perils which—subtracting man's own very considerable contribution—our world contains, it would have to contain others instead.

To realize this is not, by any means, to be in possession of a detailed theodicy. It is to understand that this world, with all its "heartaches and the thousand natural shocks that flesh is heir to," an environment so manifestly not designed for the maximization of human pleasure and the minimization of human pain, may be rather well adapted to the quite different purpose of "soul-making."[9]

These considerations are related to theism as such. Specifically, Christian theism goes further in the light of the death of Christ, which is seen paradoxically both (as the murder of the divine Son) as the worst thing that has ever happened and (as the occasion of Man's salvation) as the best thing that has ever happened. As the supreme evil turned to supreme good, it provides the paradigm for the distinctively Christian reaction to evil. Viewed from the standpoint of Christian faith, evils do not cease to be evils; and certainly, in view of Christ's healing work, they cannot be said to have been sent by God. Yet, it has been the persistent claim of those seriously and wholeheartedly committed to Christian discipleship that tragedy, though truly tragic, may nevertheless be turned, through a man's reaction to it, from a cause of despair and alienation from God to a stage in the fulfillment of God's loving purpose for that individual. As the greatest of all evils, the crucifixion of Christ, was made the occasion of man's redemption, so good can be won from other evils. As Jesus saw his execution by the Romans as an experience which God desired him to accept, an experience which was to be brought within the sphere of the divine purpose and made to serve the divine ends, so the Christian response to calamity is to accept the adversities, pains, and af-

[9]This brief discussion has been confined to the problem of human suffering. The large and intractable problem of animal pain is not taken up here. For a discussion of it, see, for example, Nels Ferré, *Evil and the Christian Faith* (New York: Harper & Row, Publishers, Inc., 1947), Chap. 7; and Austin Farrer, *Love Almighty and Ills Unlimited* (New York: Doubleday & Company, Inc., 1961), Chap. 5.

flictions which life brings, in order that they can be turned to a positive spiritual use.[10]

At this point, theodicy points forward in two ways to the subject of life after death.

First, although there are many striking instances of good being triumphantly brought out of evil through a man's or a woman's reaction to it, there are many other cases in which the opposite has happened. Sometimes obstacles breed strength of character, dangers evoke courage and unselfishness, and calamities produce patience and moral steadfastness. But sometimes they lead, instead, to resentment, fear, grasping selfishness, and disintegration of character. Therefore, it would seem that any divine purpose of soul-making which is at work in earthly history must continue beyond this life if it is ever to achieve more than a very partial and fragmentary success.

Second, if we ask whether the business of soul-making is worth all the toil and sorrow of human life, the Christian answer must be in terms of a future good which is great enough to justify all that has happened on the way to it.

---

[10]This conception of providence is stated more fully in John Hick, *Faith and Knowledge* (Ithaca: Cornell University Press, 1957), Chap. 7, from which some sentences are incorporated in this paragraph.

The World Was Designed by a Higher Being

WILLIAM PALEY

William Paley (1743-1805) was the archdeacon of Carlisle and a leading apologist for Christianity. In his most important work, *Natural Theology, or Evidences of the Existence and Attributes of the Deity Collected from the Appearances of Nature,* he argues that a careful look at the world shows that it must have an intelligent designer. Our viewpoint is taken from the first three chapters of that book. He begins by comparing the world to a watch with parts finely attuned to one another. Since a mechanism like a watch must have a designer, Paley argues, so must a similar mechanism like the world. He rejects the explanation that some law or principle can be used to explain the order of the world since it takes some agent, like a person, to make something happen according to a law or principle. The fact that animals, which appear to be designed, produce other animals is even stronger evidence for a grand overall design and

William Paley, *Natural Theology*, chapters 1-3. Boston: Gould and Lincoln, 1856.

Designer. Watches that make other watches are more amazing than mere watches. It does no good, according to Paley, to explain something that appears to be designed by referring to any series, even an infinite series, of causes or mechanisms that supposedly explain why the thing appears designed. The series itself requires a Designer. He concludes that, just as nature surpasses the products of human design, so the Designer of nature surpasses humanity.

QUESTIONS

1. Why, according to Paley, would we give different answers when questioned about the origin of a stone and a watch?
2. In order to understand Paley's argument, do we need to have seen a watch being made?
3. Does Paley limit agency to human agency?
4. What would the author say to someone who claimed that some "principle of order" had formed the watch?
5. Does Paley believe that phenomena can be explained by reference to things like the laws of vegetative nature or animal nature? Why or why not?
6. If one watch produced another, would Paley say that the first watch was in every sense the maker of the second?
7. What is the point of the author's chain argument?
8. How does Paley compare nature to the watch? Why does he think that this comparison refutes atheism?
9. Do you think that Paley would consider the existence of an evolutionary process a strong argument for design? Why or why not?

■ ■ ■

State of the Argument

In crossing a heath, suppose I pitched my foot against a stone, and were asked how the stone came to be there; I might possibly answer, that, for anything I knew to the contrary, it had lain there forever: nor would it perhaps be very easy to show the absurdity of this answer. But suppose I had found a *watch* upon the ground, and it should be inquired how the watch happened to be in that place; I should hardly think of the answer which I had before given, that, for anything I knew, the watch might have always been there. Yet why should not this answer serve for the watch as well as for the stone? Why is it not as admissible in the second case, as in the first? For this reason, and for no other, viz. that, when we come to inspect the watch, we perceive (what we could not discover in the stone) that its several parts are framed and put together for a purpose, *e.g.* that they are so formed and adjusted as to produce motion, and that motion so regulated as to point out the hour of the day; that if the different parts had been differently shaped from what they are, of a different size from what they are, or placed after any other manner, or in any other order, than that in which they are placed, either no motion at all would have been carried on in the machine, or none which would have answered the use that is now served by it. To reckon up a few of the plainest of these parts, and of their offices, all tending to one result: We see a cylindrical box containing a coiled elastic spring, which, by its endeavor to relax itself, turns round the box. We next observe a flexible chain (artificially wrought for the sake of flexure) communicating the action of the spring from the box to the fusee. We then find a series of wheels, the teeth of which catch in, and apply to each other, conducting the motion from the fusee to the balance, and from the balance to the pointer; and at the same time, by the size and shape of those wheels, so regulating that motion, as to terminate in causing an index, by an equable and measured progression, to pass over a given space in a given time. We take notice that the wheels are made of brass in order to keep them from rust; the springs of steel, no other metal being so elastic; that over the face of the watch there is place a glass, a material employed in no other part of the work; but in the room of which, if there had been any other than a transparent substance, the hour could not be seen without opening the case. This mechanism being observed (it requires indeed an examination of the instrument, and perhaps some previous knowledge of the subject, to perceive and understand it; but being once, as we have said, observed and understood,) the inference, we think, is inevitable; that the watch must have had a maker; that there must have existed, at sometime, and at some place or other, an artificer or artificers, who formed it for the purpose which we find it actually to answer; who comprehended its construction, and designed its use.

I. Nor would it, I apprehend, weaken the conclusion, that we had never seen a watch made: that we had never known an artist capable of making one; that we were altogether incapable of executing such a piece of workmanship ourselves, or of understanding in what manner it was performed; all this being no more than what is true of some exquisite remains of ancient art, of some lost arts, and, to the generality of mankind, of the more curious productions of modern manufacture. Does one man in a million know how oval frames are turned? Ignorance of this kind exalts our opinion of the unseen and unknown artist's skill, if he be unseen and unknown, but raises no doubt in our minds of the existence and agency of such an artist, at some former time, and in some place or other. Nor can I perceive that it varies at all the inference, whether the question arise concerning a human agent, or concerning an agent of a different species, or an agent possessing, in some respects, a different nature.

II. Neither, secondly, would it invalidate our conclusion, that the watch sometimes went wrong, or that it seldom went exactly right. The purpose of the machinery, the design and the designer, might be evident, and in the case supposed would be evident in whatever way we accounted for the irregularity of the movement, or whether we could account for it or not. It is not necessary that a machine be perfect, in order to show with what design it was made: still less necessary, where the only question is, whether it were made with any design at all.

III. Nor, thirdly, would it bring any uncertainty into the argument, if there were a few parts of the watch, concerning which we could not discover, or had not yet discovered, in what manner they conduced to the general effect; or even some parts, concerning which we could not ascertain whether they conduced to that effect in any matter whatever. For, as to the first branch of the case; if by the loss, or disorder, or decay of the parts in question, the movement of the watch were found in fact to be stopped, or disturbed, or retarded, no doubt would remain in our minds as to the utility or intention of these parts, although we should be unable to investigate the manner according to which, or the connexion by which, the ultimate effect depended upon their action or assistance; and the more complex is the machine, the more likely is this obscurity to arise. Then, as to the second thing supposed, namely, that there were parts which might be spared, without prejudice to the movement of the watch, and that we had proved this by experiment—these superfluous parts, even if we were completely assured that they were such, would not vacate the reasoning which we had instituted concerning other parts. The indication of contrivance remained, with respect to them, nearly as it was before.

IV. Nor, fourthly, would any man in his senses think the existence of the watch, with its various machinery, accounted for, by being told that it was one out of possible combinations of material forms; that whatever he had found in the place where he found the watch, must have contained some internal configuration or other; and that this configuration might be the structure now exhibited, viz. of the works of a watch, as well as a different structure.

V. Nor, fifthly, would it yield his inquiry more satisfaction to be answered, that there existed in things a principle of order, which had disposed the parts of the watch into their present form and situation. He never knew a watch made by the principle of order; nor can he even form to himself an idea of what is meant by a principle of order distinct from the intelligence of the watchmaker.

VI. Sixthly, he would be surprised to hear that the mechanism of the watch was no proof of contrivance, only a motive to induce the mind to think so.

VII. And not less surprised to be informed, that the watch in his hand was nothing more than the result of the laws of *metallic* nature. It is a perversion of language to assign any law as the efficient, operative cause of anything. A law presupposes an agent; for it is only the mode according to which an agent proceeds: it implies a power; for it is the order, according to which that power acts. Without this agent, without this power, which are both distinct from itself, the *law* does nothing; is nothing. The expression, "the law of metallic nature," may sound strange and harsh to a philosophic ear; but it seems quite as justifiable as some others which are more familiar to him, such as "the law of vegetable nature," "the law of animal nature," or indeed as "the law of nature" in general, when assigned as the cause of phenomena, in exclusion of agency and power; or when it is substituted into the place of these.

VIII. Neither, lastly, would our observer be driven out of his conclusion, or from his confidence in its truth, by being told that he knew nothing at all about the matter. He knows enough for his argument. He knows the utility of the end: he knows the subserviency and adaptation of the means to the end. These points being known, his ignorance of other points, his doubts concerning other points, affect not the certainty of his reasoning. The consciousness of knowing little need not beget a distrust of that which he does know.

State of the Argument Continued

Suppose, in the next place, that the person who found the watch, should, after sometime, discover, that, in addition to all the properties which he had hitherto observed in it, it possessed the unexpected property of producing, in the course of its movement, another watch like itself, (the thing is conceivable;) that it contained within it a mechanism, a system of parts, a mould for instance, or a complex adjustment of lathes, files, and other tools, evidently and separately calculated for this purpose; let us inquire, what effect ought such a discovery to have upon his former conclusion.

I. The first effect would be to increase his admiration of the contrivance, and his conviction of the consummate skill of the contriver. Whether he regarded the object of the contrivance, the distinct apparatus, the intricate, yet in many parts intelligible mechanism, by which it was carried on, he would perceive, in this new observation, nothing but an additional reason for doing what he had already done,—for referring the construction of the watch to design, and to supreme art. If that construction *without* this property, or, which is the same thing, before this property had been noticed, proved intention and art to have been employed about it, still more strong would the proof appear, when he came to the knowledge of this farther property, the crown and perfection of all the rest.

II. He would reflect, that though the watch before him were, *in some sense*, the maker of the watch which was fabricated in the course of its movements, yet it was in a very different sense from that in which a carpenter, for instance, is the maker of a chair; the author of its contrivance, the cause of the relation of its parts to their use. With respect to these, the first watch was no cause at all to the second: in no such sense as this was it the author of the constitution and order, either of the parts which the new watch contained, or of the parts by the aid and instrumentality of which it was produced. We might possibly say, but with great latitude of expression, that a stream of water ground corn; but no latitude of expression would allow us to say, no stretch of conjecture could lead us to think, that the stream of water built the mill, though it were too ancient for us to know who the builder was. What the stream of water does in the affair, is neither more nor less than this; by the application of an unintelligent impulse to a mechanism previously arranged, arranged independently of it, and arranged by intelligence, an effect is produced, viz. the corn is ground. But the effect results from the arrangement. The force of the stream cannot be said to be the cause or author of the effect, still less of the arrangement. Understanding and plan in the formation of the mill were not the less necessary, for any share which the water has in grinding the corn; yet is this share the same as that which the watch would have contributed to the production of the new watch, upon the supposition assumed in the last section. Therefore,

III. Though it be now no longer probable, that the individual watch which our observer had found was made immediately by the and of an artificer, yet doth not this alteration in any-wise affect the inference, than an artificer had been originally employed and concerned in the production. The argument from design remains as it was. Marks of design and contrivance are no more accounted for now than they were before. In the same thing, we may ask for the cause of different properties. We may ask for the cause of the color of a body, of its hardness, of its heat; and these causes may be all different. We are now asking for the cause of that subserviency to a use, that relation to an end, which we have remarked in the watch before us. No answer is given to this question by telling us that a preceding watch produced it. There cannot be design without a designer; contrivance, without a contriver; order, without choice; arrangement, without anything capable of arranging; subserviency and relation to a purpose, without that which could intend a purpose; means suitable to an end, and executing their office in accomplishing that end, without the end ever having been contemplated, or the means accommodated to it. Arrangement, disposition of part, subserviency of means to an end, relation of instruments to a use, imply the presence of intelligence and mind. No one, therefore, can rationally believe, that the insensible, inanimate watch, from which the watch before us issued, was the proper cause of the mechanism we so much admire in it;—could be truly said to have constructed the instrument, disposed its parts, assigned their office, determined their order, action, and mutual dependency, combined their several motions into one result, and that also a result connected with the utilities of other beings. All these properties, therefore, are as much unaccounted for as they were before.

IV. Nor is anything gained by running the difficulty farther back, *i.e.* by supposing the watch before us to have been produced from another watch, that from a former, and so on indefinitely. Our going back ever so far brings us no nearer to the least degree of satisfaction upon the subject. Contrivance is still unaccounted for. We still want a contriver. A designing mind is neither supplied by this supposition, nor dispensed with. If the difficulty were diminished the farther we went back, by going back indefinitely we might exhaust it. And this is the only case to which this sort of reasoning applies. Where there is a tendency, or, as we increase the number of terms, a continual approach towards a limit, *there*, by supposing the number of terms to be what is called infinite, we may conceive the limit to be attained: but where there is no such tendency, or approach, nothing is effected by lengthening the series. There is no difference, as to the point in question, (whatever there may be as to many points,) between one series and another; between a series which is finite, and a series which is infinite. A chain, composed of an infinite number of links, can no more support itself, than a chain composed of a finite number of links. And of this we are assured, (though we never *can* have tried the experiment,) because, by increasing the number of links, from ten, for instance, to a hundred, from a hundred to a thousand, &c. we make not the smallest approach, we observe not the smallest tendency, towards self-support. There is no difference in this respect (yet there may be a great difference in several respects) between a chain of a greater or lesser length, between one chain and another, between one that is finite and one that is infinite. This very much resembles the case before us. The machine which we are inspecting demonstrates, by its construction, contrivance and design. Contrivance must have had a contriver; design, a designer; whether the machine immediately proceeded from another machine or not. That circumstance alters not the case. That other machine may, in like manner, have proceeded from a former machine: nor does that alter the case; contrivance must have had a contriver. That former one from one preceding it: no alteration still; a contriver is still necessary. No tendency is perceived, no approach towards a diminution of this necessity. It is the same with any and every succession of these machines; a succession of ten, of a hundred, of a thousand; with one series as with another; a series which is finite, as with a series which is infinite. In whatever other respects they may differ, in this they do not. In all, equally, contrivance and design are unaccounted for.

The question is not simply, How came the first watch into existence? which question, it may be pretended, is done away by supposing the series of watches thus produced from one another to have been infinite, and consequently to have had no such *first*, for which it was necessary to provide a cause. This, perhaps, would have been nearly the state of the question, if nothing had been before us but an unorganized, unmechanized substance, without mark or indication of contrivance. It might be difficult to show that such substance could not have existed from eternity, either in succession (if it were possible, which I think it is not, for unorganized bodies to spring from one another) or by individual perpetuity. But that is not the question now. To suppose it to be so, is to suppose that it made no difference whether we had found a watch or a stone. As it is, the metaphysics of that question have no place; for, in the watch which we are examining, are seen contrivance, design; an end, a purpose; means for the end, adaptation to the purpose. And the question which irresistibly presses upon our thoughts, is, whence this contrivance and design? The thing required is the intending mind, the adapting hand, the intelligence by which that hand was directed. This question, this demand, is not shaken off, by increasing a number or succession of substances, destitute of these properties; nor the more, by increasing that number to infinity. If it be said, that, upon the supposition of one watch being produced from another in the course of that other's movements, and by means of the mechanism within it, we have a cause for the watch in my hand, viz. the watch from which it proceeded: I deny, that for the design, the contrivance, the suitableness of means to an end, the adaptation of instruments to a use, (all which we discover in a watch,) we have any cause whatever. It is in vain, therefore, to assign a series of such causes, or to allege that a series may be carried back to infinity; for I do not admit that we have yet any cause at all of the phenomena, still less any series of causes either finite or infinite. Here is the contrivance, but no contriver: proofs of design, but no designer.

V. Our observer would farther also reflect, that the maker of the watch before him, was, in truth and reality, the maker of every watch produced from it; there being no difference (except that the latter manifests a more exquisite skill) between the making of another watch with his own hands, by the mediation of files, lathes, chisels, &c. and the disposing, fixing, and inserting of these instruments, or of others equivalent to them, in the body of the watch already made, in such a manner as to form a new watch in the course of the movements which he had given to the old one. It is only working by one set of tools instead of another.

The conclusion which the *first* examination of the watch, of its works, construction, and movement, suggested, was, that it must have had, for the cause and author of that construction, an artificer, who understood its mechanism, and designed its use. This conclusion is invincible. A *second* examination presents us with a new discovery. The watch is found, in the course of its movement, to produce another watch, similar to itself: and not only so, but we perceive in it a system or organization, separately calculated for that purpose. What effect would this discovery have or ought it to have, upon our former inference? What, as hath already been said, but to increase, beyond measure, our admiration of the skill which had been employed in the formation of such a machine! Or shall it, instead of this, all at once turn us round to an opposite conclusion, viz that no art or skill whatever has been concerned in the business, although all other evidences of art and skill remain as they were, and this last and supreme piece of art be now added to the rest? Can this be maintained without absurdity? Yet this is atheism.

Application of the Argument

This is atheism: for every indication of contrivance, every manifestation of design, which existed in the watch, exists in the works of nature; with the difference, on the side of nature, of being greater and more, and that in a degree which exceeds all computation. I mean, that the contrivances of nature surpass the contrivances of art, in the complexity, subtilty, and curiosity of the mechanism; and still more, if possible, do they go beyond them in number and variety: yet, in a multitude of cases, are not less evidently mechanical, not less evidently contrivances, not less evidently accommodated to their end, or suited to their office, than are the most perfect productions of human ingenuity.

God Is Not the Designer of the World

DAVID HUME

David Hume (1711-1776) was a skeptic as well as an empiricist. In addition to his foundational work in epistemology and metaphysics, his *Dialogues Concerning Natural Religion* and essays on immortality and suicide were published posthumously. In his *Dialogues*, from which this viewpoint is taken, Hume sets up an imaginary dialogue between three persons to argue against the teleological argument for God's existence. The teleological argument begins with the observation that the world is a complex of interrelated parts which resembles a machine and concludes that the world, like a machine, requires an intelligent Designer because similar effects require similar causes. Hume argues that the world also resembles an organism, as well as other things, all of which have causes other than intelligent designers. He does not think we are justified in giving intelligence as we know it a privileged position

Excerpted from David Hume, *Dialogues Concerning Natural Religion*, edited by Richard H. Popkin. Reprinted with permission of Hackett Publishing Co.

as an explanation of the world. Furthermore, he points out that we know that things like machines have certain kinds of causes because we see machines repeatedly associated with these causes when they are created whereas we have no experience at all of worlds being created. In this viewpoint Cleanthes represents a natural theologian who argues for the teleological argument, Demea is an orthodox believer, and Philo is a skeptic representing Hume's position.

QUESTIONS

1. How does Cleanthes use cause and effect to argue for the existence of God?
2. When, according to Philo, does an argument from analogy become weak?
3. How does Philo argue for the importance of experience?
4. What does experience imply about order, according to Philo?
5. How does Philo argue against using human thought as a basis for explaining the universe?
6. When, according to Philo, can we infer the existence of one object from the existence of another? What does this have to do with the universe and God?
7. Why does Philo compare the world to an animal body or plant? What is his point?
8. Does Philo think there is a way of choosing between alternate explanations of the world?

■ ■ ■

Cleanthes: Look round the world: Contemplate the whole and every part of it: You will find it to be nothing but one great machine, subdivided into an infinite number of lesser machines, which again admit of subdivisions to a degree beyond what human senses and faculties can trace and explain. All these various machines, and even their most minute parts, are adjusted to each other with an accuracy which ravishes into admiration all men who have ever contemplated them. The curious adapting of means to ends, throughout all nature, resembles exactly, though it much exceeds, the productions of human contrivance; of human design, thought, wisdom, and intelligence. Since therefore the effects resemble each other, we are led to infer, by all the rules of analogy, that the causes also resemble, and that the Author of Nature is somewhat similar to the mind of man, though possessed of much larger faculties, proportioned to the grandeur of the work which he has executed. By this argument *a posteriori*, and by this argument alone, do we prove at once the existence of a Deity and his similarity to human mind and intelligence.

Demea: I shall be so free, *Cleanthes*, said *Demea*, as to tell you that from the beginning I could not approve of your conclusion concerning the similarity of the Deity to men; still less can I approve of the mediums by which you endeavor to establish it. What! No demonstration of the Being of God! No abstract arguments! No proofs *a priori*! Are these which have hitherto been so much insisted on by philosophers all fallacy, all sophism? Can we reach no farther in this subject than experience and probability? I will say not that this is betraying the cause of a Deity; but surely, by this affected candor, you give advantages to atheists which they never could obtain by the mere dint of argument and reasoning.

Philo: What I chiefly scruple in this subject, said *Philo*, is not so much that all religious arguments are by *Cleanthes* reduced to experience, as that they appear not to be even the most certain and irrefragable of that inferior kind. That a stone will fall, that fire will burn, that the earth has solidity, we have observed a thousand and a thousand times; and when any new instance of this nature is presented, we draw without hesitation the accustomed inference. The exact similarity of the cases gives us a perfect assurance of a similar event, and a stronger evidence is never desired nor sought after. But wherever you depart, in the least, from the similarity of the cases, you diminish proportionably the evidence; and may at last bring it to a very weak *analogy*, which is confessedly liable to error and uncertainty. After having experienced the circulation of the blood in human creatures, we make no doubt that it takes place in *Titius* and *Maevius*; but from its circulation in frogs and fishes it is only a presumption, though a strong one, from analogy that it takes place in men and other animals. The analogical reasoning is much weaker when we infer the circulation of the sap in vegetables from our experience that the blood circulates in animals; and those who hastily followed that imperfect analogy are found, by more accurate experiments, to have been mistaken.

If we see a house, *Cleanthes*, we conclude, with the greatest certainty, that it had an architect or builder because this is precisely that species of effect which we have experienced to proceed from that species of cause. But surely you will not affirm that the universe bears such a resemblance to a house that we can with the same certainty infer a similar cause, or that the analogy is here entire and perfect. The dissimilitude is so striking that the utmost you can here pretend to is a guess, a conjecture, a presumption concerning a similar cause; and how that pretension will be received in the world, I leave you to consider.

Cleanthes: It would surely be very ill received, replied *Cleanthes*; and I should be deservedly blamed and detested did I allow that the proofs of a Deity amounted to no more than a guess or conjecture. But is the whole adjustment of means to ends in a house and in the universe so slight a resemblance? The economy of final causes? The order, proportion, and arrangement of every part? Steps of a stair are plainly contrived that human legs may use them in mounting; and this inference is certain and infallible. Human legs are also contrived for walking and mounting; and this inference, I allow, is not altogether so certain because of the dissimilarity which you remark; but does it, therefore, deserve the name only of presumption or conjecture?

Demea: Good God! cried *Demea*, interrupting him, where are we? Zealous defenders of religion allow that the proofs of a Deity fall short of perfect evidence! And you, *Philo*, on whose assistance I depended in proving the adorable mysteriousness of the Divine Nature, do you assent to all these extravagant opinions of *Cleanthes*? For what other name can I give them? or, why spare my censure when such principles are advanced, supported by such an authority, before so young a man as *Pamphilus*?

Philo: You seem not to apprehend, replied *Philo*, that I argue with *Cleanthes* in his own way, and, by showing him the dangerous consequences of his tenets, hope at last to reduce him to our opinion. But what sticks most with you, I observe, is the representation which *Cleanthes* has made of the argument *a posteriori*; and, finding that that argument is likely to escape your hold and vanish into air, you think it so disguised that you can scarcely believe it to be set in its true light. Now, however much I may dissent, in other respects, from the dangerous principle of *Cleanthes,* I must allow that he has fairly represented that argument, and I shall endeavor so to state the matter to you that you will entertain no further scruples with regard to it.

Were a man to abstract from everything which he knows or has seen, he would be altogether incapable, merely from his own ideas, to determine what kind of scene the universe must be, or to give the preference to one state or situation of things above another. For as nothing which he clearly conceives could be esteemed impossible or implying a contradiction, every chimera of his fancy would be upon an equal footing; nor could he assign any just reason why he adheres to one idea or system, and rejects the others which are equally possible.

Again, after he opens his eyes and contemplates the world as it really is, it would be impossible for him at first to assign the cause of any one event, much less of the whole of things, or of the universe. He might set his fancy a rambling, and she might bring him in an infinite variety of reports and representations. These would all be possible; but, being all equally possible, he would never of himself give a satisfactory account for his preferring one of them to the rest. Experience alone can point out to him the true cause of any phenomenon.

Now, according to this method of reasoning, *Demea,* it follows (and is, indeed, tacitly allowed by *Cleanthes* himself) that order, arrangement, or the adjustment of final causes, is not of itself any proof of design, but only so far as it has been experienced to proceed from that principle. For aught we can know *a priori,* matter may contain the source or spring of order originally within itself, as well as mind does; and there is no more difficulty in conceiving that the several elements, from an internal unknown cause, may fall into the most exquisite arrangement, than to conceive that their ideas, in the great universal mind, from a like internal unknown cause, fall into that arrangement. The equal possibility of both these suppositions is allowed. But, by experience, we find, according to *Cleanthes,* that there is a difference between them. Throw several pieces of steel together, without shape or form; they will never arrange themselves so as to compose a watch. Stone and mortar and wood, without an architect, never erect a house. But the ideas in a human mind, we see, by an unknown, inexplicable economy, arrange themselves so as to form the plan of a watch or house. Experience, therefore, proves that there is an original principle of order in mind, not in matter. From similar effects we infer similar causes. The adjustment of means to ends is alike in the universe, as in a machine of human contrivance. The causes, therefore, must be resembling.

I was from the beginning scandalized, I must own, with this resemblance which is asserted between the Deity and human creatures, and must conceive it to imply such a degradation of the Supreme Being as no sound theist could endure. With your assistance, therefore, *Demea*, I shall endeavor to defend what you justly call the adorable mysteriousness of the Divine Nature, and shall refute this reasoning of *Cleanthes*, provided he allows that I have made a fair representation of it.

When *Cleanthes* had assented, *Philo*, after a short pause, proceeded in the following manner.

That all inferences, *Cleanthes*, concerning fact are founded on experience, and that all experimental reasonings are founded on the supposition that similar causes prove similar effects, and similar effects similar causes, I shall not at present much dispute with you. But observe, I entreat you, with what extreme caution all just reasoners proceed in the transferring of experiments to similar cases. Unless the cases be exactly similar, they repose no perfect confidence in applying their past observation to any particular phenomenon. Every alteration of circumstances occasions a doubt concerning the event; and it requires new experiments to prove certainly that the new circumstances are of no moment or importance. A change in bulk, situation, arrangement, age, disposition of the air, or surrounding bodies; any of these particulars may be attended with the most unexpected consequences. And unless the objects be quite familiar to us, it is the highest temerity to expect with assurance, after any of these changes, an event similar to that which before fell under our observation. The slow and deliberate steps of philosophers here, if anywhere, are distinguished from the precipitate march of the vulgar, who, hurried on by the smallest similitude, are incapable of all discernment or consideration.

But can you think, *Cleanthes*, that your usual phlegm and

philosophy have been preserved in so wide a step as you have taken when you compared to the universe houses, ships, furniture, machines; and, from their similarity in some circumstances, inferred a similarity in their causes? Thought, design, intelligence, such as we discover in men and other animals, is no more than one of the springs and principles of the universe, as well as heat or cold, attraction or repulsion, and a hundred others which fall under daily observation. It is an active cause by which some particular parts of nature, we find, produce alterations on other parts. But can a conclusion, with any propriety, be transferred from parts to the whole? Does not the great disproportion bar all comparison and inference? From observing the growth of a hair, can we learn anything concerning the generation of a man? Would the manner of a leaf's blowing, even though perfectly known, afford us any instruction concerning the vegetation of a tree?

But allowing that we were to take the *operations* of one part of nature upon another for the foundation of our judgment concerning the *origin* of the whole (which never can be admitted), yet why select so minute, so weak, so bounded a principle as the reason and design of animals is found to be upon this planet? What peculiar privilege has this little agitation of the brain which we call "thought", that we must thus make it the model of the whole universe? Our partiality in our own favor does indeed present it on all occasions, but sound philosophy ought carefully to guard against so natural an illusion.

So far from admitting, continued *Philo*, that the operations of a part can afford us any just conclusion concerning the origin of the whole, I will not allow any one part to form a rule for another part if the latter be very remote from the former. Is there any reasonable ground to conclude that the inhabitants of other planets possess thought, intelligence, reason, or anything similar to these faculties in men? When nature has so extremely diversified her manner of operation in this small globe, can we imagine that she incessantly copies herself throughout so immense a universe? And if thought, as we may well suppose, be confined merely to this narrow corner, and has even there so limited a sphere of action, with what propriety can we assign it for the original cause of all things? The narrow views of a peasant who makes his domestic economy the rule for the government of kingdoms is in comparison a pardonable sophism.

But were we ever so much assured that a thought and reason resembling the human were to be found throughout the whole universe, and were its activity elsewhere vastly greater and more commanding than it appears in this globe; yet I cannot see why the operations of a world constituted, arranged, adjusted, can with any propriety be extended to a world which is in its embryo-state, and is advancing towards that constitution and arrangement. By observation we know somewhat of the economy, action, and nourishment of a finished animal; but we must transfer with great caution that observation to the growth of a foetus in the womb, and still more to the formation of an animalcule in the loins of its male parent. Nature, we find, even from our limited experience, possesses an infinite number of springs and principles which incessantly discover themselves on every change of her position and situation. And what new and unknown principles would actuate her in so new and unknown a situation as that of the formation of a universe, we cannot, without the utmost temerity, pretend to determine.

A very small part of this great system, during a very short time, is very imperfectly discovered to us; and do we thence pronounce decisively concerning the origin of the whole?

Admirable conclusion! Stone, wood, brick, iron, brass, have not, at this time, in this minute globe of earth, an order or arrangement without human art and contrivance; therefore, the universe could not originally attain its order and arrangement without something similar to human art. But is a part of nature a rule for another part very wide of the former? Is it a rule for the whole? Is a very small part a rule for the universe? Is nature in one situation a certain rule for nature in another situation vastly different from the former?

And can you blame me, *Cleanthes*, if I here imitate the prudent reserve of *Simonides*, who, according to the noted story, being asked by *Hiero, What God was?* desired a day to think of it, and then two days more; and after that manner continually prolonged the term, without ever bringing in his definition or description? Could you even blame me if I had answered, at first, *that I did not know*, and was sensible that this subject lay vastly beyond the reach of my faculties? You might cry out skeptic and raillier, as much as you pleased; but, having found in so many other subjects much more familiar the imperfections and even contradictions of human reason, I never should expect any success from its feeble conjectures in a subject so sublime and so remote from the sphere of our observation. When two *species* of objects have always been observed to be conjoined together, I can *infer*, by custom, the existence of one wherever I *see* the existence of the other; and this I call an argument from experience. But how this argument can have place where the objects, as in the present case, are single, individual, without parallel or specific resemblance, may be difficult to explain. And will any man tell me with a serious countenance that an orderly universe must arise from some thought and art like the human because we have experience of it? To ascertain this reasoning it were requisite that we had experience of the origin of worlds; and it is not sufficient, surely, that we have seen ships and cities arise from human art and contrivance. . . .

If the universe bears a greater likeness to animal bodies and to vegetables than to the works of human art, it is more probable that its cause resembles the cause of the former than that of the latter, and its origin ought rather to be abscribed to generation or vegetation than to reason or design. Your conclusion, even according to your own principles, is therefore lame and defective.

Demea: Pray open up this argument a little farther, said *Demea*, for I do not rightly apprehend it in that concise manner in which you have expressed it.

Philo: Our friend *Cleanthes*, replied *Philo*, as you have heard, asserts that since no question of fact can be proved otherwise than by experience, the existence of a Deity admits not of proof from any other medium. The world, says he, resembles the works of human contrivance; therefore its cause must also resemble that of the other. Here we may remark that the operation of one very small part of nature, to wit, man, upon another very small part, to wit, that inanimate matter lying within his reach, is the rule by which *Cleanthes* judges of the origin of the whole; and he measures objects, so widely disproportioned, by the same individual standard. But to waive all objections drawn from this topic, I affirm that there are other parts of the universe (besides the machines of human invention) which bear still a greater resemblance to the fabric of the world, and which, therefore, afford a better conjecture concerning the universal origin of this system. These parts are animals and vegetables. The world plainly resembles more an animal or a vegetable than it does a watch or a knitting-loom. Its cause, therefore, it is more probable, resembles the cause of the former. The cause of the former is generation or vegetation. The cause, therefore, of the world we may infer to be something similar or analogous to generation or vegetation.

Demea: But how is it conceivable, said *Demea,* that the world can arise from anything similar to vegetation or generation?

Philo: Very easily, replied *Philo*. In like manner as a tree sheds its seed into the neighboring fields and produces other trees; so the great vegetable, the world, or this planetary system, produces within itself certain seeds which, being scattered into the surrounding chaos, vegetate into new worlds. A comet, for instance, is the seed of a world; and after it has been fully ripened, by passing from sun to sun, and star to star, it is at last tossed into the unformed elements which everywhere surround this universe, and immediately sprouts up into a new system.

Or if, for the sake of variety (for I see no other advantage) we should suppose this world to be an animal; a comet is the egg of this animal; and in like manner as an ostrich lays its egg in the sand, which, without any further care, hatches the egg and produces a new animal, so. . . .

Demea: I understand you, says *Demea*: But what wild, arbitrary suppositions are these? What *data* have you for such extraordinary conclusions? And is the slight, imaginary resemblance of the world to a vegetable or an animal sufficient to establish the same inference with regard to both? Objects which are in general so widely different; ought they to be a standard for each other?

Philo: Right, cries *Philo*: This is the topic on which I have all along insisted. I have still asserted that we have no *data* to establish any system of cosmogony. Our experience, so imperfect in itself and so limited both in extent and duration, can afford us no probable conjecture concerning the whole of things. But if we must needs fix on some hypothesis, by what rule, pray, ought we to determine our choice? Is there any other rule than the great similarity of the objects compared? And does not a plant or an animal, which springs from vegetation or generation, bear a stronger resemblance to the world than does any artificial machine, which arises from reason and design?

Demea: But what is this vegetation and generation of which you talk? said *Demea*. Can you explain their operations, and anatomize that fine internal structure on which they depend?

Philo: As much, at least, replied *Philo*, as *Cleanthes* can explain the operations of reason, or anatomize that internal structure on which *it* depends. But without any such elaborate disquisitions, when I see an animal, I infer that it sprang from generation; and that with as great certainty as you conclude a house to have been reared by design. These words *generation, reason* mark only certain powers and energies in nature whose effects are known, but whose essence is incomprehensible; and one of these principles, more than the other, has no privilege for being made a standard to the whole of nature.

In reality, *Demea*, it may reasonably be expected that the larger the views are which we take of things, the better will they conduct us in our conclusions concerning such extraordinary and such magnificent subjects. In this little corner of the world alone, there are four principles, *reason*, *instinct*, *generation*, *vegetation*, which are similar to each other, and are the causes of similar effects. What a number of other principles may we naturally suppose in the immense extent and variety of the universe could we travel from planet to planet, and from system to system, in order to examine each part of this mighty fabric? Any one of these four principles above mentioned (and a hundred others which lie open to our conjecture) may afford us a theory by which to judge of the origin of the world; and it is a palpable and egregious partiality to confine our view entirely to that principle by which our own minds operate. Were this principle more intelligible on that account, such a partiality might be somewhat excusable: But reason, in its internal fabric and structure, is really as little known to us as instinct or vegetation; and, perhaps even that vague, undeterminate word "nature" to which the vulgar refer everything is not at the bottom more inexplicable. The effects of these principles are all known to us from experience; but the principles themselves and their manner of operation are totally unknown: Nor is it less intelligible or less conformable to experience to say that the world arose by vegetation, from a seed shed by another world, than to say that it arose from a divine reason or contrivance, according to the sense in which *Cleanthes* understands it.

Demea: But methinks, said *Demea*, if the world had a vegetative quality and could sow the seeds of new worlds into the infinite chaos, this power would be still an additional argument for design in its author. For whence could arise so wonderful a faculty but from design? Or how can order spring from anything which perceives not that order which it bestows?

Philo: You need only look around you, replied *Philo*, to satisfy yourself with regard to this question. A tree bestows order and organization on that tree which springs from it, without knowing the order: An animal in the same manner on its offspring: A bird on its nest; and instances of this kind are even more frequent in the world than those of order which arise from reason and contrivance. To say that all this order in animals and vegetables proceeds ultimately from design is begging the question; nor can that great point be ascertained otherwise than by proving, *a priori*, both that order is, from its nature, inseparably attached to thought, and that it can never of itself or from original unknown principles belong to matter.

But further, *Demea*, this objection which you urge can never be made use of by *Cleanthes*, without renouncing a defence which he has already made against one of my objections. When I inquired concerning the cause of that supreme reason and intelligence into which he resolves everything, he told me that the impossibility of satisfying such inquiries could never be admitted as an objection in any species of philosophy. *We must stop somewhere*, says he; *nor is it ever within the reach of human capacity to explain ultimate causes or show the last connections of any objects. It is sufficient if any steps, so far as we go, are supported by experience and observation.* Now, that vegetation and generation, as well as reason, are experienced to be principles of order in nature is undeniable. If I rest my system of cosmogony on the former, preferably to the latter, it is at my choice. The matter seems entirely arbitrary. And when *Cleanthes* asks me what is the cause of my great vegetative or generative faculty, I am equally entitled to ask him the cause of his great reasoning principle. These questions we have agreed to forbear on both sides; and it is chiefly his interest on the present occasion to stick to this agreement. Judging by our limited and imperfect experience, generation has some privileges above reason: For we see every day the latter arise from the former, never the former from the latter.

Compare, I beseech you, the consequences on both sides. The world, say I, resembles an animal; therefore it is an animal, therefore it arose from generation. The steps, I confess, are wide; yet there is some small appearance of analogy in each step. The world, says *Cleanthes*, resembles a machine; therefore it is a machine, therefore it arose from design. The steps are here equally wide, and the analogy less striking. And if he pretends to carry on *my* hypothesis a step further, and to infer design or reason from the great principle of generation on which I insist, I may, with better authority, use the same freedom to push further his hypothesis, and infer a divine generation or theogony from his principle of reason. I have at least some faint shadow of experience, which is the utmost that can ever be attained in the present subject. Reason, in innumerable instances, is observed to arise from the principle of generation, and never to arise from any other principle.

Hesiod and all the ancient mythologists were so struck with this analogy that they universally explained the origin of nature from an animal birth, and copulation. *Plato*, too, so far as he is intelligible, seems to have adopted some such notion in his *Timaeus*.

The *Brahmins* assert that the world arose from an infinite spider, who spun this whole complicated mass from his bowels, and annihilates afterwards the whole or any part of it, by absorbing it again and resolving it into his own essence. Here is a species of cosmogony which appears to us ridiculous because a spider is a little contemptible animal whose operations we are never likely to take for a model of the whole universe. But still here is a new species of analogy, even in our globe. And were there a planet wholly inhabited by spiders (which is very possible), this inference would there appear as natural and irrefragable as that which in our planet ascribes the origin of all things to design and intelligence, as explained by *Cleanthes*. Why an orderly system may not be spun from the belly as well as from the brain, it will be difficult for him to give a satisfactory reason.

Faith Proves God's Existence to the Believer

C.S. Lewis

C.S. Lewis (1898-1963) was a British literary scholar and lay theologian who held appointments at both Oxford and Cambridge Universities. He is probably the best-read author among English-speaking Christians and his books continue to be highly influential in diverse circles. His works include *Mere Christianity*, an exposition of his understanding of the Christian faith, *The Screwtape Letters*, *The Problem of Pain*, *Miracles*, a series of science fiction books, and the children's *Narnia* series. In this viewpoint Lewis addresses the obstinacy or tenacity with which Christians hold to their faith even when confronted with evidence which casts doubts on their beliefs. Atheistic scientists accuse these Christians of irrationality because it appears that they believe more than they are justified in believing given available evidence. Lewis begins by explaining what Christians really mean by "belief" and by claiming that, outside their specialized disciplines, scientists have the same belief patterns as Christians. For example, the atheistic beliefs of some scientists are held with a subjective certainty which far exceeds what is justified by the evidence they have to disprove the existence of God. Lewis goes on to argue that, once a person becomes a Christian, the existence of God is no longer a matter of speculation, but a matter of relationship. This changes the rules so that it is no longer a matter of justified belief, but a process of growth worked out in the context of a relationship with God who is trusted in all sorts of circumstances. In such a relational context loyalty and obstinacy are virtues, not defects.

QUESTIONS

1. Describe the stereotypes of scientists and Christians that Lewis encountered at Oxford.
2. How does the author define the "belief" of Christians? In what sense do atheists also "believe"?
3. According to Lewis, what kinds of people rely upon authority as a kind of "evidence"?
4. What makes Lewis think that religion is considered a serious opponent by its adversaries?
5. How much does the author think wish fulfillment can explain?
6. According to Lewis, how is a scientist's attitude towards his wife like a Christian's belief?
7. When, according to the author, is it necessary and good for belief to go beyond the evidence?
8. How, according to Lewis, does the Christian faith logically demand a measure of trust even in the face of contrary evidence?
9. According to the author, what situation is a person suddenly thrust into when he or she accepts as fact the existence of God? What change takes place?
10. Do you agree with Lewis that the logic of personal relations rather than the logic of speculative thought applies after someone becomes a Christian? What are your reasons?

■ ■ ■

Papers have more than once been read to the Socratic Club at Oxford in which a contrast was drawn between a supposedly Christian attitude and a supposedly scientific attitude to belief. We have been told that the scientist thinks it his duty to proportion the strength of his belief exactly to the evidence; to believe less as there is less evidence and to withdraw belief altogether when reliable adverse evidence turns up. We have been told that, on the contrary, the Christian regards it as positively praiseworthy to believe without evidence, or in excess of the evidence, or to maintain his belief unmodified in the teeth of steadily increasing evidence against it. Thus a "faith that has stood firm," which appears to mean a belief immune from all the assaults of reality, is commended.

If this were a fair statement of the case, then the co-existence within the same species of such scientists and such Christians, would be a very staggering phenomenon. The fact that the two classes appear to overlap, as they do, would be quite inexplicable. Certainly all discussion between creatures so different would be hopeless. The purpose of this essay is to show that things are really not quite so bad as that. The sense in which scientists proportion their belief to the evidence and the sense in which Christians do not, both need to be defined more closely. My hope is that when this has been done, though disagreement between the two parties may remain, they will not be left staring at one another in wholly dumb and desperate incomprehension.

And first, a word about belief in general. I do not see that the state of "proportioning belief to evidence" is anything like so common in the scientific life as has been claimed. Scientists are mainly concerned not with believing things but with finding things out. And no one, to the best of my knowledge, uses the word "believe" about things he has found out. The doctor says he "believes" a man was poisoned before he has examined the body; after the examination, he says the man was poisoned. No one says that he believes the multiplication table. No one who catches a thief red-handed says he believes that man was stealing. The scientist, when at work, that is, when he is a scientist, is labouring to escape from belief and unbelief into knowledge. Of course he uses hypotheses or supposals. I do not think these are beliefs. We must look, then, for the scientist's behaviour about belief not to his scientific life but to his leisure hours.

In actual modern English usage the verb "believes," except for two special usages, generally expresses a very weak degree of opinion. "Where is Tom?" "Gone to London, I believe." The speaker would be only mildly surprised if Tom had not gone to London after all. "What was the date?" "430 B.C., I believe." The speaker means that he is far from sure. It is the same with the negative if it is put in the form "I believe not." ("Is Jones coming up this term?" "I believe not.") But if the negative is put in a different form it then becomes one of the special usages I mentioned a moment ago. This is of course the form "I don't believe it," or the still stronger "I don't believe you." "I don't believe it" is far stronger on the negative side than "I believe" is on the positive. "Where is Mrs. Jones?" "Eloped with the butler, I believe." "I don't believe it." This, especially if said with anger, may imply a conviction which in subjective certitude might be hard to distinguish from knowledge by experience. The other special usage is "I believe" as uttered by a Christian. There is no great difficulty in making the hardened materialist understand, however little he approves, the sort of mental attitude which this "I believe" expresses. The materialist need only picture himself replying, to some report of a miracle, "I don't believe it," and then imagine this same degree of conviction on the opposite side. He knows that he cannot, there and then, produce a refutation of the miracle which would have the certainty of mathematical demonstration; but the formal possibility that the miracle might after all have occurred does not really trouble him any more than a fear that water might not be H and O. Similarly, the Christian does not necessarily claim to have demonstrative proof; but the formal possibility that God might not exist is not necessarily present in the form of the least actual doubt. Of course there are Christians who hold that such demonstrative proof exists, just as there may be materialists who hold that there is demonstrative disproof. But then, whichever of them is right (if either is) while he retained the proof or disproof would be not believing or disbelieving but knowing. We are speaking of belief and disbelief in the strongest degree but not of knowledge. Belief, in this sense, seems to me to be assent to a proposition which we think so overwhelmingly probable that there is a psychological exclusion of doubt, though not a logical exclusion of dispute.

It may be asked whether belief (and of course disbelief) of this sort ever attaches to any but theological propositions. I think that many beliefs approximate to it; that is, many probabilities seem to us so strong that the absence of logical certainty does not induce in us the least shade of doubt. The scientific beliefs of those who are not themselves scientists often have this character, especially among the uneducated. Most of our beliefs about other people are of the same sort. The scientist himself, or he who was a scientist in the laboratory, has beliefs about his wife and friends which he holds, not indeed without evidence, but with more certitude than the evidence, if weighed in a laboratory manner, would justify. Most of my generation had a belief in the reality of the external world and of other people—if you prefer it, a disbelief in solipsism—far in excess of our strongest arguments. It may be true, as they now say, that the whole thing arose from category mistakes and was a pseudo-problem; but then we didn't know that in the twenties. Yet we managed to disbelieve in solipsism all the same.

There is, of course, no question so far of belief without evidence. We must beware of confusion between the way in which a Christian first assents to certain propositions and the way in which he afterwards adheres to them. These must be carefully distinguished. Of the second it is true, in a sense, to say that Christians do recommend a certain discounting of apparent contrary evidence, and I will later attempt to explain why. But so far as I know it is not expected that a man should assent to these propositions in the first place without evidence or in the teeth of the evidence. At any rate, if anyone expects that, I certainly do not. And in fact, the man who accepts Christianity always thinks he had good evidence; whether, like Dante, *fisici e metafisici argomenti*, or historical evidence, or the evidence of religious experience, or authority, or all these together. For of course authority, however we may value it in this or that particular instance, is a kind of evidence. All of our historical beliefs, most of our geographical beliefs, many of our beliefs about matters that concern us in daily life, are accepted on the authority of other human beings, whether we are Christians, Atheists, Scientists, or Men-in-the-Street.

It is not the purpose of this essay to weigh the evidence, of whatever kind, on which Christians base their belief. To do that would be to write a full-dress *apologia*. All that I need do here is to point out that, at the very worst, this evidence cannot be so weak as to warrant the view that all whom it convinces are indifferent to evidence. The history of thought seems to make this quite plain. We know, in fact, that believers are not cut off from unbelievers by any portentous inferiority of intelligence or any perverse refusal to think. Many of them have been people of powerful minds. Many of them have been scientists. We may suppose them to have been mistaken, but we must suppose their error was at least plausible. We might indeed, conclude that it was, merely from the multitude and diversity of the arguments against it. For there is not one case against religion, but many. Some say, like Capaneus in Statius, that it is a projection of our primitive fears, *primus in orbe deos fecit timor:* others, with Euhemerus, that it is all a "plant" put up by wicked kings, priests, or capitalists; others, with Tylor, that it comes from dreams about the dead; others, with Frazer, that it is a by-product of agriculture; others, like Freud, that it is a complex; the moderns that it is a category mistake. I will never believe that an error against which so many and various defensive weapons have been found necessary was, from the outset, wholly lacking in plausibility. All this "post haste and rummage in the land" obviously implies a respectable enemy.

There are of course people in our own day to whom the whole situation seems altered by the doctrine of the concealed wish. They will admit that men, otherwise apparently rational, have been deceived by the arguments for religion. But they will say that they have been deceived first by their own desires and produced the arguments afterwards as a rationalisation: that these arguments have never been intrinsically even plausible, but have seemed so because they were secretly weighted by our wishes. Now I do not doubt that this sort of thing happens in thinking about religion as in thinking about other things: but as a general explanation of religious assent it seems to me quite useless. On that issue our wishes may favour either side or both. The assumption that every man would be pleased, and nothing but pleased, if only he could conclude that Christianity is true, appears to me to be simply preposterous. If Freud is right about the Oedipus complex, the universal pressure of the wish that God should not exist must be enormous, and atheism must be an admirable gratification to one of our strongest suppressed impulses. This argument, in fact, could be used on the theistic side. But I have no intention of so using it. It will not really help either party. It is fatally ambivalent. Men wish on both sides: and again, there is fear-fulfillment as well as wish-fulfillment, and hypochondriac temperaments will always tend to think true what they most wish to be false. Thus instead of the one predicament on which our opponents sometimes concentrate there are in fact four. A man may be a Christian because he wants Christianity to be true. He may be an atheist because he wants atheism to be true. He may be an atheist because he wants Christianity to be true. He may be a Christian because he wants atheism to be true. Surely these possibilities cancel one another out? They may be of some use in analysing a particular instance of belief or disbelief, where we know the case history, but as a general explanation of either they will not help us. I do not think they overthrow the view that there is evidence both for and against the Christian propositions which fully rational minds, working honestly, can assess differently.

I therefore ask you to substitute a different and less tidy picture for that with which we began. In it, you remember, two different kinds of men, scientists, who proportioned their belief to the evidence, and Christians, who did not, were left facing one another across a chasm. The picture I should prefer is like this. All men alike, on questions which interest them, escape from the region of belief into that of knowledge when they can, and if they succeed in knowing, they no longer say they believe. The questions in which mathematicians are interested admit of treatment by a particularly clear and strict technique. Those of the scientists have their own technique, which is not quite the same. Those of the historian and the judge are different again. The mathematician's proof (at least so we laymen suppose) is by reasoning, the scientist's by experiment, the historian's by documents, the judge's by concurring sworn testimony. But all these men, as men, on questions outside their own disciplines, have numerous beliefs to which they do not normally apply the methods of their own disciplines. It would indeed carry some suspicion of morbidity and even of insanity if they did. These beliefs vary in strength from weak opinion to complete subjective certitude. Specimens of such beliefs at their strongest are the Christian's "I believe" and the convinced atheist's "I don't believe a word of it." The particular subject-matter on which these two disagree does not, of course, necessarily involve such strength of belief and disbelief. There are some who moderately opine that there is, or is not, a God. But there are others whose belief or disbelief is free from doubt. And all these beliefs, weak or strong, are based on what appears to the holders to be evidence; but the strong believers or disbelievers of course think they have very strong evidence. There is no need to suppose stark unreason on either side. We need only suppose error. One side has estimated the evidence wrongly. And even so, the mistake cannot be supposed to be of a flagrant nature; otherwise the debate would not continue.

So much, then, for the way in which Christians come to assent to certain propositions. But we have now to consider something quite different; their adherence to their belief after it has once been formed. It is here that the charge of irrationality and resistance to evidence becomes really important. For it must be admitted at once that Christians do praise such an adherence as if it were meritorious; and even, in a sense, more meritorious the stronger the apparent evidence against their faith becomes. They even warn one another that such apparent contrary evidence—such "trials to faith" or "temptations to doubt"—may be expected to occur, and determine in advance to resist them. And this is certainly shockingly unlike the behaviour we all demand of the scientist or the historian in their own disciplines. There, to slur over or ignore the faintest evidence against a favourite hypothesis, is admittedly foolish and shameful. It must be exposed to every test; every doubt must be invited. But then I do not admit that a hypothesis is a belief. And if we consider the scientist not among his hypotheses in the laboratory but among the beliefs in his ordinary life, I think the contrast between him and the Christian would be weakened. If, for the first time, a doubt of his wife's fidelity crosses the scientist's mind, does he consider it his duty at once to entertain this doubt with complete impartiality, at once to evolve a series of experiments by which it can be tested, and to await the result with pure neutrality of mind? No doubt it may come to that in the end. There are unfaithful wives; there are experimental husbands. But is such a course what his brother scientists would recommend to him (all of them, I suppose, except one) as the first step he should take and the only one consistent with his honour as a scientist? Or would they, like us, blame him for a moral flaw rather than praise him for an intellectual virtue if he did so?

This is intended, however, merely as a precaution against exaggerating the difference between Christian obstinacy in belief and the behaviour of normal people about their non-theological beliefs. I am far from suggesting that the case I have supposed is exactly parallel to the Christian obstinacy. For of course evidence of the wife's infidelity might accumulate, and presently reach a point at which the scientist would be pitiably foolish to disbelieve it. But the Christians seems to praise an adherence to the original belief which holds out against any evidence whatever. I must now try to show why such praise is in fact a logical conclusion from the original belief itself.

This can be done best by thinking for a moment of situations in which the thing is reversed. In Christianity such faith is demanded of us; but there are situations in which we demand it of others. There are times when we can do all that a fellow creature needs if only he will trust us. In getting a dog out of a trap, in extracting a thorn from a child's finger, in teaching a boy to swim or rescuing one who can't, in getting a frightened beginner over a nasty place on a mountain, the one fatal obstacle may be their distrust. We are asking them to trust us in the teeth of their senses, their imagination, and their intelligence. We ask them to believe that what is painful will relieve their pain and that what looks dangerous is their only safety. We ask them to accept apparent impossibilities: that moving the paw farther back into the trap is the way to get it out—that hurting the finger very much more will stop the finger hurting—that water which is obviously permeable will resist and support the body—that holding on to the only support within reach is not the way to avoid sinking—that to go higher and on to a more exposed ledge is the way not to fall. To support all these *incredibilia* we can rely only on the other party's confidence in us—a confidence certainly not based on demonstration, admittedly shot through with emotion, and perhaps, if we are strangers, resting on nothing but such assurance as the look of our face and the tone of our voice can supply, or even, for the dog, on our smell. Sometimes, because of their unbelief, we can do no mighty works. But if we succeed, we do so because they have maintained their faith in us against apparently contrary evidence. No one blames us for demanding such faith. No one blames them for giving it. No one says afterwards what an unintelligent dog or child or boy that must have been to trust us. If the young mountaineer were a scientist, it would not be held against him, when he came up for a fellowship, that he had once departed from Clifford's rule of evidence by entertaining a belief with strength greater than the evidence logically obliged him to.

Now to accept the Christian propositions is *ipso facto* to believe that we are to God, always, as that dog or child or bather or mountain climber was to us, only very much more so. From this it is a strictly logical conclusion that the behaviour which was appropriate to them will be appropriate to us, only very much more so. Mark: I am not saying that the strength of our original belief must by psychological necessity produce such behaviour. I am saying that the content of our original belief by logical necessity entails the proposition that such behaviour is appropriate. If human life is in fact ordered by a beneficent being whose knowledge of our real needs and of the way in which they can be satisfied infinitely exceeds our own, we must expect *a priori* that His operations will often appear to us far from beneficent and far from wise, and that it will be our highest prudence to give Him our confidence in spite of this. This expectation is increased by the fact that when we accept Christianity we are warned that apparent evidence against it will occur—evidence strong enough "to deceive if possible the very elect." Our situation is rendered tolerable by two facts. One is that we seem to ourselves, besides the apparently contrary evidence, to receive favourable evidence. Some of it is in the form of external events: as when I go to see a man, moved by what I felt to be a whim, and find he has been praying that I should come to him that day. Some of it is more like the evidence on which the mountaineer or the dog might trust his rescuer—the rescuer's voice, look, and smell. For it seems to us (though you, on your premises, must believe us deluded) that we have something like a knowledge-by-acquaintance of the Person we believe in, however imperfect and intermittent it may be. We trust not because "a God" exists, but because *this* God exists. Or if we ourselves dare not claim to "know" Him,

Christendom does, and we trust at least some of its representatives in the same way: because of the sort of people they are. The second fact is this. We think we can see already why, if our original belief is true, such trust beyond the evidence, against much apparent evidence, has to be demanded of us. For the question is not about being helped out of one trap or over one difficult place in a climb. We believe that His intention is to create a certain personal relation between Himself and us, a relation really *sui generis* but analogically describable in terms of filial or of erotic love. Complete trust is an ingredient in that relation—such trust as could have no room to grow except where there is also room for doubt. To love involves trusting the beloved beyond the evidence, even against much evidence. No man is our friend who believes in our good intentions only when they are proved. No man is our friend who will not be very slow to accept evidence against them. Such confidence, between one man and another, is in fact almost universally praised as a moral beauty, not blamed as a logical error. And the suspicious man is blamed for a meanness of character, not admired for the excellence of his logic.

There is, you see, no real parallel between Christian obstinacy in faith and the obstinacy of a bad scientist trying to preserve a hypothesis although the evidence has turned against it. Unbelievers very pardonably get the impression that an adherence to our faith is like that, because they meet Christianity, if at all, mainly in apologetic works. And there, of course, the existence and beneficence of God must appear as a speculative question like any other. Indeed, it is a speculative question as long as it is a question at all. But once it has been answered in the affirmative, you get quite a new situation. To believe that God—at least *this* God—exists is to believe that you as a person now stand in the presence of God as a Person. What would, a moment before, have been variations in opinion, now becomes variations in your personal attitude to a Person. You are no longer faced with an argument which demands your assent, but with a Person who demands your confidence. A faint analogy would be this. It is one thing to discuss *in vacuo* whether So-and-So will join us tonight, and another to discuss this when So-and-So's honour is pledged to come and some great matter depends on his coming. In the first case it would be merely reasonable, as the clock ticked on, to expect him less and less. In the second, a continued expectation far into the night would be due to our friend's character if we had found him reliable before. Which of us would not feel slightly ashamed if one moment after we had given him up he arrived with a full explanation of his delay? We should feel that we ought to have known him better.

Now of course we see, quite as clearly as you, how agonisingly two-edged all this is. A faith of this sort, if it happens to be true, is obviously what we need, and it is infinitely ruinous to lack it. But there can be faith of this sort where it is wholly ungrounded. The dog may lick the face of the man who comes to take it out of the trap; but the man may only mean to vivisect it in South Parks Road when he has done so. The ducks who come to the call "Dilly, dilly, come and be killed" have confidence in the farmer's wife, and she wrings their necks for their pains. There is that famous French story of the fire in the theatre. Panic was spreading, the spectators were just turning from an audience into a mob. At that moment a huge bearded man leaped through the orchestra on to the stage, raised his hand with a gesture full of nobility, and cried, "*Que chacun regagne sa place.*" Such was the authority of his voice and bearing that everyone obeyed him. As a result they were all burned to death, while the bearded man walked quietly out through the wings to the stage door, took a cab which was waiting for someone else, and went home to bed.

That demand for our confidence which a true friend makes of us is exactly the same that a confidence trickster would make. That refusal to trust, which is sensible in reply to a confidence trickster, is ungenerous and ignoble to a friend, and deeply damaging to our relation with him. To be forewarned and therefore forearmed against apparently contrary appearance is eminently rational if our belief is true; but if our belief is a delusion, this same forewarning and forearming would obviously be the method whereby the delusion rendered itself incurable. And yet again, to be aware of these possibilities and still to reject them is clearly the precise mode, and the only mode, in which our personal response to God can establish itself. In that sense the ambiguity is not something that conflicts with faith so much as a condition which makes faith possible. When you are asked for trust you may give it or withhold it; it is senseless to say that you will trust if you are given demonstrative certainty. There would be no room for trust if demonstration were given. When demonstration is given what will be left will be simply the sort of relation which results from having trusted, or not having trusted, before it was given.

The saying "Blessed are those that have not seen and have believed" has nothing to do with our original assent to the Christian propositions. It was not addressed to a philosopher inquiring whether God exists. It was addressed to a man who already believed that, who already had long acquaintance with a particular Person, and evidence that that Person could do very odd things, and who then refused to believe one odd thing more, often predicted by that Person and vouched for by all his closest friends. It is a rebuke not to scepticism in the philosophic sense but to the psychological quality of being "suspicious." It says in effect, "You should have known me better." There are cases between man and man where we should all, in our different way, bless those who have not seen and have believed. Our relation to those who trusted us only after we were proved innocent in court cannot be the same as our relation to those who trusted us all through.

Our opponents, then, have a perfect right to dispute with us about the grounds of our original assent. But they must not accuse us of sheer insanity if, after the assent has been given, our adherence to it is no longer proportioned to every fluctuation of the apparent evidence. They cannot of course be expected to know on what our assurance feeds, and how it revives and is always rising from its ashes. They cannot be expected to see how the *quality* of the object which we think we are beginning to know by acquaintance drives us to the view that if this were a delusion then we should have to say that the universe had produced no real thing of comparable value and that all explanations of the delusion seemed somehow less important than the thing explained. That is knowledge we cannot communicate. But they can see how the assent, of necessity, moves us from the logic of speculative thought into what might perhaps be called the logic of personal relations. What would, up till then, have been variations simply of opinion become variations of conduct by a person to a Person. *Credere Deum esse* turns into *Credere in Deum*. And *Deum* here is this God, the increasingly knowable lord.

What Is Morality?

Chapter Preface

What makes an action right or wrong? What makes a person good? Are moral rules objective and absolute, or are they just personal opinions or opinions of different cultural groups? Do I have to believe in God to be moral? Why should I be moral at all? When moral situations are simple and straightforward we are not usually motivated to think critically about morality. When situations are complicated and responsible people disagree, however, we are forced to look deeper. Unfortunately, most of the important issues that confront us, like abortion, capital punishment, and use of the environment, are complicated. In these cases philosophical reflection can give us a great deal of insight into the merits and demerits of different approaches.

There are several standard answers to the question, "What makes an action right or wrong?" Each of these answers has a certain intuitive appeal. One answer is that the consequences of an action make it right or wrong. An action which produces good consequences is good and one which produces bad consequences is evil. Philosophers who believe this are called "consequentialists." Consequentialists do not all agree about what sorts of things constitute good consequences. Different candidates include power, knowledge, self-actualization, satisfaction, pleasure, and life, or some combination of these. Some consequentialists, the ethical egoists, believe we ought to be concerned only about our own good. Others disagree and argue that we must seek the good for others as well as for ourselves. John Stuart Mill argues that the good is pleasure or satisfaction and that pain or dissatisfaction is evil. He claims that we ought to seek to maximize this good, which he calls "utility," and minimize evil, for everybody concerned, not just ourselves. This position is called "utilitarianism."

Not everyone agrees that only consequences count. They argue that motives rather than consequences are important and that the quest for mere satisfaction or any other good thing, while acceptable, leaves something fundamental to human morality out of the picture. Immanuel Kant asserts that the only truly good thing is a good will, a will which acts according to duty and does the right thing because it is right. Kant and others who share this perspective, the deontologists, look for rules which describe actions themselves rather than the consequences of the actions. Actions which conform to certain rules are thought to be morally right and obligatory. Other approaches to morality also consider things other than consequences. Adherents of virtue theory, for example, focus not on what makes actions right or wrong, but on what makes a person good and virtuous. Aristotle argues that a major moral concern is the development of people who have certain virtues that dispose them to act in wise and moral ways. He identifies several of these virtues and asserts that a good moral education, one which encourages habits of moderation and avoidance of extremes, can result in individuals who have these characteristics.

To what extent are the judgments we make about good and bad actions and virtuous people universal? Anthropologists and sociologists have revealed a bewildering variety of human moral behavior. In different cultures, for example, different numbers of husbands or wives are allowed. Does this mean that morality is relative to culture, or even to personal opinion, or is there some sense in which moral rules and standards are objective and binding on people regardless of culture? Social scientist Ruth Benedict, for example, is a cultural relativist. She believes that moral values reflect ways of life in different cultures and that they cannot be taken out of one cultural context and applied to another. A person who is virtuous in one culture, for example, might be anything but virtuous in another. Philosopher W.T. Stace recognizes that there are different moral practices in different cultures, but he explains these differences in terms of different understandings of the world and different stages of cultural development. He argues that the principle of altruism, which is fundamental to all human moral behavior, can be identified in all cultures even though its application is determined by the different circumstances which prevail in different cultures.

Religion and morality are thought to go together in most or all cultures. How close is this connection? Is belief in God necessary to make sense of morality? Atheist Bertrand Russell argues that true morality is not even possible until we accept the fact that there is no God. The world, Russell believes, is a terrible place which is indifferent to human life and value. It will eventually destroy not only individual humans, but the human race and all its works. This realization frees us from a religion and morality which hopes to please God by groveling before him and opens the door to ideals of truth and beauty and goodness which we follow for their own sake despite the hopelessness of life. Christian philosopher George Mavrodes does not think Russell's position takes obligation seriously enough. How can we be genuinely obligated to sacrifice what little good we have in an indifferent universe in which morality is not deeply grounded? This reasoning leads to the question, "Why be moral in the first place?" This question does not ask what makes an action or a person good, but rather asks why we should even be concerned with being good, especially if it involves going against our own self-interests.

Morality Is Governed by Consequences of Behavior

JOHN STUART MILL

John Stuart Mill (1806-1873) was a highly influential British philosopher who made major contributions to ethics, political philosophy, political theory, logic, the philosophy of science, and the philosophy of religion. His major works include *On Liberty, A System of Logic,* and *Utilitarianism*. Mill was a home-educated child prodigy who learned Greek at the age of three and eventually became the director of the East India Company and a member of Parliament. In this viewpoint, taken from the first two chapters of *Utilitarianism*, Mill argues for the need of a clear first or defining principle for morality. He believes that the consequences of actions are what ultimately make them right and wrong. In ethics, such a position is called a consequentialist or teleological theory, where "teleology" refers to the end or purpose of an action. The end that Mill believes is worth pursuing is utility, which includes both

From John Stuart Mill, *Utilitarianism*. London: Parker, Son, and Dourne, 1863.

positive pleasure and an absence of pain. He does not think any moral theory can function which does not recognize this. Mill's understanding of pleasure is anything but shallow. He distinguishes between levels of physical and intellectual pleasure and even discusses how we can decide which pleasures are best. Mill understands the good life for a human being to include a healthy concern for others and a wide variety of personal satisfactions. We are to seek the greatest happiness possible for all people, and not to live merely selfish lives.

QUESTIONS

1. How does Mill define "utility"?
2. According to Mill, in what two ways are things desirable?
3. How does the author distinguish between human and animal pleasures?
4. Why is a "sense of dignity" important for Mill's argument?
5. What reasons does Mill give to explain why some people choose lower rather than higher pleasures?
6. In what way are the judgments of people who have experienced many kinds of pleasures important for Mill's theory? Could we get along without these kinds of judgments?
7. How does Mill describe the happy life?

■ ■ ■

On the present occasion, I shall attempt to contribute something towards the understanding and appreciation of the Utilitarian or Happiness theory, and towards such proof as it is susceptible of. It is evident that this cannot be proof in the ordinary and popular meaning of the term. Questions of ultimate ends are not amenable to direct proof. Whatever can be proved to be good, must be so by being shown to be a means to something admitted to be good without proof. The medical art is proved to be good by its conducing to health; but how is it possible to prove that health is good? The art of music is good, for the reason, among others, that it produces pleasure; but what proof is it possible to give that pleasure is good? If, then, it is asserted that there is a comprehensive formula, including all things which are in themselves good, and that whatever else is good, is not so as an end, but as a mean, the formula may be accepted or rejected, but is not a subject of what is commonly understood by proof. We are not, however, to infer that its acceptance or rejection must depend on blind impulse, or arbitrary choice. There is a larger meaning of the word proof, in which this question is as amenable to it as any other of the disputed questions of philosophy. The subject is within the cognisance of the rational faculty; and neither does that faculty deal with it solely in the way of intuition. Considerations may be presented capable of determining the intellect either to give or withhold its assent to the doctrine; and this is equivalent to proof.

We shall examine presently of what nature are these considerations; in what manner they apply to the case, and what rational grounds, therefore, can be given for accepting or rejecting the utilitarian formula. But it is a preliminary condition of rational acceptance or rejection, that the formula should be correctly understood. I believe that the very imperfect notion ordinarily formed of its meaning, is the chief obstacle which impedes its reception; and that could it be cleared, even from only the grosser misconceptions, the question would be greatly simplified, and a large proportion of its difficulties removed. Before, therefore, I attempt to enter into the philosophical grounds which can be given for assenting to the utilitarian standard, I shall offer some illustrations of the doctrine itself; with the view of showing more clearly what it is, distinguishing it from what it is not, and disposing of such of the practical objections to it as either originate in, or are closely connected with, mistaken interpretations of its meaning. Having thus prepared the ground, I shall afterwards endeavour to throw such light as I can upon the question, considered as one of philosophical theory.

What Utilitarianism Is

A passing remark is all that needs be given to the ignorant blunder of supposing that those who stand up for utility as the test of right and wrong, use the term in that restricted and merely colloquial sense in which utility is opposed to pleasure. An apology is due to the philosophical opponents of utilitarianism, for even the momentary appearance of confounding them with any one capable of so absurd a misconception; which is the more extraordinary, inasmuch as the contrary accusation, of referring everything to pleasure, and that too in its grossest form, is another of the common charges against utilitarianism: and, as has been pointedly remarked by an able writer, the same sort of persons, and often the very same persons, denounce the theory "as impracticably dry when the word utility precedes the word pleasure, and as too practicably voluptuous when the word pleasure precedes the word utility." Those who know anything about the matter are aware that every writer, from Epicurus to Bentham, who maintained the theory of utility, meant by it, not something to be contradistinguished from pleasure, but pleasure itself, together with exemption from pain; and instead of opposing the useful to the agreeable or the ornamental, have always declared that the useful means these, among other things. Yet the common herd, including the herd of writers, not only in newspapers and periodicals, but in books of weight and pretension, are perpetually falling into this shallow mistake. Having caught up the word utilitarian, while knowing nothing whatever about it but its sound, they habitually express by it the rejection, or the neglect, of pleasure in some of its forms; of beauty, of ornament, or of amusement. Nor is the term thus ignorantly misapplied solely in disparagement, but occasionally in compliment; as though it implied superiority to frivolity and the mere pleasures of the moment. And this perverted use is the only one in which the word is popularly known, and the one from which the new generation are acquiring their sole notion of its meaning. Those who introduced the word, but who had for many years discontinued it as a distinctive appellation, may well feel themselves called to resume it, if by doing so they can hope to contribute anything towards rescuing it from this utter degradation.[1]

The creed which accepts as the foundation of morals, Util-

---

[1]The author of this essay has reason for believing himself to be the first person who brought the word utilitarian into use. He did not invent it, but adopted it from a passing expression in Mr. Galt's *Annals of the Parish*. After using it as a designation for several years, he and others abandoned it from a growing dislike to anything resembling a badge or watchword of sectarian distinction. But as a name for one single opinion, not a set of opinions—to denote the recognition of utility as a standard, not any particular way of applying it—the term supplies a want in the language, and offers, in many cases, a convenient mode of avoiding tiresome circumlocution.

ity, or the Greatest Happiness Principle, holds that actions are right in proportion as they tend to promote happiness, wrong as they tend to produce the reverse of happiness. By happiness is intended pleasure, and the absence of pain; by unhappiness, pain, and the privation of pleasure. To give a clear view of the moral standard set up by the theory, much more requires to be said; in particular, what things it includes in the ideas of pain and pleasure; and to what extent this is left an open question. But these supplementary explanations do not affect the theory of life on which this theory of morality is grounded—namely, that pleasure, and freedom from pain, are the only things desirable as ends; and that all desirable things (which are as numerous in the utilitarian as in any other scheme) are desirable either for the pleasure inherent in themselves, or as means to the promotion of pleasure and the prevention of pain.

Now, such a theory of life excites in many minds, and among them in some of the most estimable in feeling and purpose, inveterate dislike. To suppose that life has (as they express it) no higher end than pleasure—no better and nobler object of desire and pursuit—they designate as utterly mean and grovelling; as a doctrine worthy only of swine, to whom the followers of Epicurus were, at a very early period, contemptuously likened; and modern holders of the doctrine are occasionally made the subject of equally polite comparisons by its German, French, and English assailants.

When thus attacked, the Epicureans have always answered, that it is not they, but their accusers, who represent human nature in a degrading light; since the accusation supposes human beings to be capable of no pleasures except those of which swine are capable. If this supposition were true, the charge could not be gainsaid, but would then be no longer an imputation; for if the sources of pleasure were precisely the same to human beings and to swine, the rule of life which is good enough for the one would be good enough for the other. The comparison of the Epicurean life to that of beasts is felt as degrading, precisely because a beast's pleasures do not satisfy a human being's conception of happiness. Human beings have faculties more elevated than the animal appetites, and when once made conscious of them, do not regard anything as happiness which does not include their gratification. I do not, indeed, consider the Epicureans to have been by any means faultless in drawing out their scheme of consequences from the utilitarian principle. To do this in any sufficient manner, many Stoic, as well as Christian elements require to be included. But there is no known Epicurean theory of life which does not assign to the pleasures of the intellect, of the feelings and imagination, and of the moral sentiments, a much higher value as pleasures than to those of mere sensation. It must be admitted, however, that utilitarian writers in general have placed the superiority of mental over bodily pleasures chiefly in the greater permanency, safety, uncostliness, etc., of the former—that is, in their circumstantial advantages rather than in their intrinsic nature. And on all these points utilitarians have fully proved their case; but they might have taken the other, and, as it may be called, higher ground, with entire consistency. It is quite compatible with the principle of utility to recognise the fact, that some *kinds* of pleasure are more desirable and more valuable than others. It would be absurd that while, in estimating all other things, quality is considered as well as quantity, the estimation of pleasures should be supposed to depend on quantity alone.

If I am asked, what I mean by difference of quality in pleasures, or what makes one pleasure more valuable than another, merely as a pleasure, except its being greater in amount, there is but one possible answer. Of two pleasures, if there be one to which all or almost all who have experience of both give a decided preference, irrespective of any feeling of moral obligation to prefer it, that is the more desirable pleasure. If one of the two is, by those who are competently acquainted with both, placed so far above the other that they prefer it, even though knowing it to be attended with a greater amount of discontent, and would not resign it for any quantity of the other pleasure which their nature is capable of, we are justified in ascribing to the preferred enjoyment a superiority in quality, so far outweighing quantity as to render it, in comparison, of small account.

Now it is an unquestionable fact that those who are equally acquainted with, and equally capable of appreciating and enjoying, both, do give a most marked preference to the manner of existence which employs their higher faculties. Few human creatures would consent to be changed into any of the lower animals, for a promise of the fullest allowance of a beast's pleasures; no intelligent human being would consent to be a fool, no instructed person would be an ignoramus, no person of feeling and conscience would be selfish and base, even though they should be persuaded that the fool, the dunce, or the rascal is better satisfied with his lot than they are with theirs. They would not resign what they possess more than he for the most complete satisfaction of all the desires which they have in common with him. If they ever fancy they would, it is only in cases of unhappiness so extreme, that to escape from it they would exchange their lot for almost any other, however undesirable in their own eyes. A being of higher faculties requires more to make him happy, is capable probably of more acute suffering, and certainly accessible to it at more points, than one of an inferior type; but in spite of these liabilities, he can never really wish to sink into what he feels to be a lower grade of existence. We may give what explanation we please of this unwillingness; we may attribute it to pride, a name which is given indiscriminately to some of the most and to some of the least estimable feelings of which mankind are capable: we may refer it to the love of liberty and personal independence, an appeal to which was with the Stoics one of the most effective means for the inculcation of it; to the love of power, or to the love of excitement, both of which do really enter into and contribute to it: but its most appropriate appellation is a sense of dignity, which all human beings possess in one form or another, and in some, though by no means in exact, proportion to their higher faculties, and which is so essential a part of the happiness of those in whom it is strong, that nothing which conflicts with it could be, otherwise than momentarily, an object of desire to them. Whoever supposes that this preference takes place at a sacrifice of happiness—that the superior being, in anything like equal circumstances, is not happier than the inferior—confounds the two very different ideas, of happiness, and content. It is indisputable that the being whose capacities of enjoyment are low, has the greatest chance of having them fully satisfied; and a highly endowed being will always feel that any happiness which he can look for, as the world is constituted, is imperfect. But he can learn to bear its imperfections, if they are at all bearable; and they will not make him envy the being who is indeed unconscious of the imperfections, but only because he feels not at all the good which those imperfections qualify. It is better to be a human being dissatisfied than a pig satisfied; better to be Socrates dissatisfied than a fool satisfied. And if the fool, or the pig, are of a different opinion, it is because they only know their own side of the question. The other party to the comparison knows both sides.

It may be objected, that many who are capable of the higher pleasures, occasionally, under the influence of temptation, postpone them to the lower. But this is quite compatible with a full appreciation of the intrinsic superiority of the higher. Men often, from infirmity of character, make their election for the nearer good, though they know it to be the less valuable; and this no less when the choice is between two bodily pleasures, than when it is between bodily and mental. They pursue sensual indulgences to the injury of health, though perfectly aware that health is the greater good. It may be further objected, that many who begin with youthful enthusiasm for everything noble, as they advance in years sink into indolence and selfishness. But I do not believe that those who undergo this very common change, voluntarily choose the lower description of pleasures in preference to the higher. I believe that before they devote themselves exclusively to the one, they have already become incapable of the other. Capacity for the nobler feelings is in most natures a very tender plant, easily killed, not only by hostile influences, but by mere want of sustenance; and in the majority of young persons it speedily dies away if the occupations to which their position in life has devoted them, and the society into which it has thrown them, are not favourable to keeping that higher capacity in exercise. Men lose their high aspirations as they lose their intellectual tastes, because they have not time or opportunity for indulging them; and they addict themselves to inferior pleasures, not because they deliberately prefer them, but because they are either the only ones to which they have access, or the only ones which they are any longer capable of enjoying. It may be questioned whether any one who has remained equally susceptible to both classes of pleasures, ever knowingly and calmly preferred the lower; though many, in all ages, have broken down in an ineffectual attempt to combine both.

From this verdict of the only competent judges, I apprehend there can be no appeal. On a question which is the best worth having of two pleasures, or which of two modes of existence is the most grateful to the feelings, apart from its moral attributes and from its consequences, the judgment of those who are qualified by knowledge of both, or, if they differ, that of the majority among them, must be admitted as final. And there needs be the less hesitation to accept this judgment respecting the quality of pleasures, since there is no other tribunal to be referred to even on the question of quantity. What means are there of determining which is the acutest of two pains, or the intensest of two pleasurable sensations, except the general suffrage of those who are familiar with both? Neither pains nor pleasures are homogeneous, and pain is always heterogeneous with pleasure. What is there to decide whether a particular pleasure is worth purchasing at the cost of a particular pain, except the feelings and judgment of the experienced? When, therefore, those feelings and judgment declare the pleasures derived from the higher faculties to be preferable *in kind*, apart from the question of intensity, to those of which the animal nature, disjoined from the higher faculties, is susceptible, they are entitled on this subject to the same regard.

I have dwelt on this point, as being a necessary part of a perfectly just conception of Utility or Happiness, considered as the directive rule of human conduct. But it is by no means an indispensable condition to the acceptance of the utilitarian standard; for that standard is not the agent's own greatest happiness, but the greatest amount of happiness altogether; and if it may possibly be doubted whether a noble character is always the happier for its nobleness, there can be no doubt that it makes other people happier, and that the world in general is immensely a gainer by it. Utilitarianism, therefore, could only attain its end by the general cultivation of nobleness of character, even if each individual were only benefited by the nobleness of others, and his own, so far as happiness is concerned, were a sheer deduction from the benefit. But the bare enunciation of such an absurdity as this last, renders refutation superfluous.

According to the Greatest Happiness Principle, as above explained, the ultimate end, with reference to and for the sake of which all other things are desirable (whether we are considering our own good or that of other people), is an existence exempt as far as possible from pain, and as rich as possible in enjoyments, both in point of quantity and quality; the test of quality, and the rule for measuring it against quantity, being the preference felt by those who in their opportunities of experience, to which must be added their habits of self-consciousness and self-observation, are best furnished with the means of comparison. This, being, according to the utilitarian opinion, the end of human action, is necessarily also the standard of morality; which may accordingly be defined, the rules and precepts for human conduct, by the observance of which an existence such as has been described might be, to the greatest extent possible, secured to all mankind; and not to them only, but, so far as the nature of things admits, to the whole sentient creation.

Morality Is Governed by Willing to Do Right

IMMANUEL KANT

Immanuel Kant (1724-1804) is considered one of the greatest Western philosophers. In addition to his contributions to the theory of knowledge and the philosophy of religion, Kant is the chief proponent of a major type of ethical theory. His chief works in ethics are the *Critique of Practical Reason* and the *Fundamental Principles of the Metaphysics of Morals*, from which this selection is taken. Kant does not believe that the consequences of actions determine whether those actions are right or wrong. This means that he is not a consequentialist. Kant espouses a kind of "deontology," named after the Greek word for "obligation." He argues that human reason is not capable of leading human beings to happiness because humans tend to make bad choices based upon strong inclinations. It follows that seeking happiness hardly qualifies as a goal for human morality. Rather, humans are equipped to will what is

From Immanuel Kant, *Fundamental Principles of the Metaphysics of Morals*, 6th ed., translated by T.K. Abbott. London: Longmans, Green and Co., 1907.

good and worthy, even if the consequences are unknown or personally undesirable. The human intellect can guide the will by discerning what rules or maxims particular actions presuppose and embody. If these rules can be universalized, i.e., if they can be applied to everybody, then the rules are acceptable and actions which follow from them are not only allowed, but obligatory. The performance of such actions is virtuous if the performance is motivated by the duty to perform obligatory actions rather than by some desire or inclination to perform the actions. The only inherently valuable thing in the world is a Good Will, a will which is motivated by duty.

QUESTIONS

1. How does Kant attempt to show that all things other than Good Will are somehow lacking in intrinsic, unconditional value? What do you think he means by "intrinsic, unconditional value"?
2. According to the author, how good a candidate is reason for the job of leading a person to a life of enjoyment or happiness?
3. What does Kant think reason is actually good for? Why is it really needed?
4. How is it possible for Kant to say that actions which are consistent with duty can sometimes actually lack moral worth? What examples does he use?
5. According to the author, how could a cold and indifferent man be a better philanthropist than a naturally sensitive and generous man?
6. How does Kant define "duty"? How much moral weight does duty carry?
7. What role does the author say intellect plays in the determination of the will?
8. What test does Kant apply to a maxim to decide whether the maxim should be followed or not?

■ ■ ■

Nothing can possibly be conceived in the world, or even out of it, which can be called good without qualification, except a Good Will. Intelligence, wit, judgment, and the other *talents* of the mind, however they may be named, or courage, resolution, perseverance, as qualities of temperament, are undoubtedly good and desirable in many respects; but these gifts of nature may also become extremely bad and mischievous if the will which is to make use of them, and which, therefore, constitutes what is called *character*, is not good. It is the same with the *gifts of fortune*. Power, riches, honor, even health, and the general well-being and contentment with one's condition which is called *happiness*, inspire pride, and often presumption, if there is not a good will to correct the influence of these on the mind, and with this also to rectify the whole principle of acting, and adapt it to its end. The sight of a being who is not adorned with a single feature of a pure and good will, enjoying unbroken prosperity, can never give pleasure to an impartial rational spectator. Thus a good will appears to constitute the indispensable condition even of being worthy of happiness.

There are even some qualities which are of service to this good will itself, and may facilitate its action, yet which have no intrinsic unconditional value, but always presuppose a good will, and this qualifies the esteem that we justly have for them, and does not permit us to regard them as absolutely good. Moderation in the affections and passions, self-control and calm deliberation are not only good in many respects, but even seem to constitute part of the intrinsic worth of the person; but they are far from deserving to be called good without qualification, although they have been so unconditionally praised by the ancients. For without the principles of a good will, they may become extremely bad, and the coolness of a villain not only makes him far more dangerous, but also directly makes him more abominable in our eyes than he would have been without it.

A good will is good, not because of what it performs or effects, not by its aptness for the attainment of some proposed end, but simply by virtue of the volition; that is, it is good in itself, and considered by itself is to be esteemed much higher than all that can be brought about by it in favor of any inclination, nay even of the sum total of all inclinations. Even if it should happen that, owing to special disfavor of fortune, or the niggardly provision of a stepmotherly nature, this will should wholly lack power to accomplish its purpose, if with its greatest efforts it should yet achieve nothing, and there should remain only the good will (not, to be sure, a mere wish, but the summoning of all means in our power), then, like a jewel, it would still shine by its own light, as a thing which has its whole value in itself. Its usefulness or fruitlessness can neither add to nor take away anything from this value. It would be, as it were, only the setting to enable us to handle it the more conveniently in common commerce or to attract to it the attention of those who are not yet connoisseurs, but not to recommend it to true connoisseurs, or to determine its value.

There is, however, something so strange in this idea of the absolute value of the mere will, in which no account is taken of its utility, that notwithstanding the thorough assent of even common reason to the idea, yet a suspicion must arise that it may perhaps really be the product of mere high-flown fancy, and that we may have misunderstood the purpose of nature in assigning reason as the governor of our will. Therefore, we will examine this idea from this point of view.

In the physical constitution of an organized being, that is, a being adapted suitably to the purposes of life, we assume it as a fundamental principle that no organ for any purpose will be found but what is also the fittest and best adapted for that purpose. Now in a being which has reason and a will, if the proper object of nature were its *conservation*, its *welfare*, in a word, its *happiness*, then nature would have hit upon a very bad arrangement in selecting the reason of the creature to carry out this purpose. For all actions which the creature has to perform with a view to this purpose, and the whole rule of its conduct, would be far more surely prescribed to it by instinct, and that end would have been attained thereby much more certainly than it ever can be by reason. Should reason have been communicated to this favored creature over and above, it must only have served it to contemplate the happy constitution of its nature, to admire it, to congratulate itself thereon, and to feel thankful for it to the beneficent cause, but not that it should subject its desires to that weak and delusive guidance, and meddle bunglingly with the purpose of nature. In a word, nature would have taken care that reason should not break forth into *practical exercise*, nor have the presumption, with its weak insight, to think out for itself the plan of happiness, and of the means of attaining it. Nature would not only have taken on herself the choice of the ends, but also of the means, and with wise foresight would have entrusted both to instinct.

And, in fact, we find that the more a cultivated reason applies itself with deliberate purpose to the enjoyment of life and happiness, so much the more does the man fail of true satisfaction. And from this circumstance there arises in many, if they are candid enough to confess it, a certain degree of *misology*, that is, hatred of reason, especially in the case of those who are most experienced in the use of it, because after calculating all the advantages they derive, I do not say from the invention of all the arts of common luxury, but even from the sciences (which seem to them to be after all only a luxury of the understanding), they find that they have, in fact, only brought more trouble on their shoulders, rather than gained in happiness; and they end by envying, rather than despising, the more common stamp of men who keep closer to the guidance of mere instinct, and do not allow their reason much influence on their conduct. And thus we must admit that the judgment of those who would very much lower the lofty eulogies of the advantages which reason gives us in regard to the happiness and satisfaction of life, or who would even reduce them below zero, is by no means morose or ungrateful to the goodness with which the world is governed, but that there lies at the root of these judgments the idea that our existence has a different and far nobler end, for which, and not for happiness, reason is properly intended, and which must, therefore, be regarded as the supreme condition to which the private ends of man must, for the most part, be postponed.

For as reason is not competent to guide the will with certainty in regard to its objects and the satisfaction of all our wants (which it to some extent even multiplies), this being an end to which an implanted instinct would have led with much greater certainty; and since, nevertheless, reason is imparted to us as a practical faculty, i.e., as one which is to have influence on the *will*, therefore, admitting that nature generally in the distribution of her capacities has adapted the means to the end, its true destination must be to produce a *will*, not merely good as a *means* to something else, but *good in itself*, for which reason was absolutely necessary. This will, then, though not indeed the sole and complete good, must be the supreme good and the condition of every other, even of the desire of happiness. Under these circumstances, there is nothing inconsistent with the wisdom of nature in the fact that the cultivation of the reason, which is requisite for the first and unconditional purpose, does in many ways interfere, at least in this life, with the attainment of the second, which is always conditional, namely, happiness. Nay, it may even reduce it to nothing, without nature thereby failing of her purpose. For reason recognizes the establishment of a good will as its highest practical destination, and in attaining this purpose is capable only of a satisfaction of its own proper kind, namely, that from the attainment of an end, which end again is determined by reason only, notwithstanding that this may involve many a disappointment to the ends of inclination.

We have then to develop the notion of a will which deserves to be highly esteemed for itself, and is good without a view to anything further, a notion which exists already in the sound natural understanding, requiring rather to be cleared up than to be taught, and which in estimating the value of our actions always takes the first place, and constitutes the condition of all the rest. In order to do this we will take the notion of duty, which includes that of a good will, although implying certain subjective restrictions and hindrances. These, however, far from concealing it, or rendering it unrecognizable, rather bring it out by contrast, and make it shine forth so much the brighter.

I omit here all actions which are already recognized as inconsistent with duty, although they may be useful for this or that purpose, for with these the question whether they are done *from duty* cannot arise at all, since they even conflict with it. I also set aside those actions which really conform to duty, but to which men have *no* direct *inclination*, performing them because they are impelled thereto by some other inclination. For in this case we can readily distinguish whether the action which agrees with duty is done *from duty*, or from a selfish view. It is much harder to make this distinction when the action accords with duty, and the subject has besides a *direct* inclination to it. For example, it is always a matter of duty that a dealer should not overcharge an inexperienced purchaser, and wherever there is much commerce the prudent tradesman does not overcharge, but keeps a fixed price for everyone, so that a child buys of him as well as any other. Men are thus *honestly* served; but this is not enough to make us believe that the tradesman has so acted from duty and from principles of honesty: his own advantage required it: it is out of the question in this case to suppose that he might besides have a direct inclination in favor of the buyers, so that, as it were, from love he should give no advantage to one over another. Accordingly the action was done neither from duty nor from direct inclination, but merely with a selfish view.

On the other hand, it is a duty to maintain one's life; and, in addition, everyone has also a direct inclination to do so. But on this account the often anxious care which most men take for it has no intrinsic worth, and their maxim has no moral import. They preserve their life *as duty requires*, no doubt, but not *because duty requires*. On the other hand, if adversity and hopeless sorrow have completely taken away the relish for life, if the unfortunate one, strong in mind, indignant at his fate rather than desponding or dejected, wishes for death, and yet preserves his life without loving it—not from inclination or fear, but from duty—then this maxim has a moral worth.

To be beneficent when we can is a duty; and besides this, there are many minds so sympathetically constituted that, without any other motive of vanity or self-interest, they find a pleasure in spreading joy around them and can take delight in the satisfaction of others so far as it is their own work. But I maintain that in such a case an action of this kind, however proper, however amiable it may be, has nevertheless no true moral worth, but is on a level with other inclinations, e.g., the inclination to honor, which, if it is happily directed to that which is in fact of public utility and accordant with duty, and consequently honorable, deserves praise and encouragement, but not esteem. For the maxim lacks the moral import, namely, that such actions be done *from duty*, not from inclination. Put the case that the mind of that philanthropist were clouded by sorrow of his own, extinguishing all sympathy with the lot of others, and that while he still has the power to benefit others in distress, he is not touched by their trouble because he is absorbed with his own; and now suppose that he tears himself out of this dead insensibility, and performs the action without any inclination to it, but simply from duty, then only has his action its genuine moral worth. Further still; if nature has put little sympathy in the heart of this or that man; if he, supposed to be an upright man, is by temperament cold and indifferent to the sufferings of others, perhaps because in respect of his own he is provided with the special gift of patience and fortitude, and supposes, or even requires, that others should have the same—and such a man would certainly not be the meanest product of nature—but if nature had not specially framed him for a philanthropist, would he not still find in himself a source from [which to derive a far] higher worth than [any] that a good-natured temperament [might have]? Unquestionably. It is just in this that the moral worth of the character is brought out which is incomparably the highest of all, namely, that he is beneficent, not from inclination, but from duty.

To secure one's own happiness is a duty, at least indirectly; for discontent with one's condition, under a pressure of many anxieties and amidst unsatisfied wants, might easily become a great *temptation to transgression of duty*. But here again, without looking to duty, all men have already the strongest and most intimate inclination to happiness, because it is just in this idea that all inclinations are combined in one total. But the precept of happiness is often of such a sort that it greatly interferes with some inclinations, and yet a man cannot form any definite and certain conception of the sum of satisfaction of all of them which is called happiness. It is not then to be wondered at that a single inclination, definite both as to what it promises and as to the time within which it can be gratified, is often able to overcome such a fluctuating idea, and that a gouty patient, for instance, can choose to enjoy what he likes, and to suffer what he may, since, according to his calculation, on this occasion at least, he has [only] not sacrificed the enjoyment of the present moment to a possibly mistaken expectation of a happiness which is supposed to be found in health. But even in this case, if the general desire for happiness did not influence his will, and supposing that in his particular case health was not a necessary element in his calculation, there yet remains in this, as in all other cases, this law, namely, that he should promote his happiness not from inclination but from duty, and by this would his conduct first acquire true moral worth.

It is in this manner, undoubtedly, that we are to understand those passages of Scripture also in which we are commanded to love our neighbor, even our enemy. For love, as an affection, cannot be commanded, but beneficence for duty's sake may; even though we are not impelled to it by any inclination—nay, are even repelled by a natural and unconquerable aversion. This is *practical* love, and not *pathological*—a love which is seated in the will, and not in the propensions of sense—in principles of action and not of tender sympathy; and it is this love alone which can be commanded.

The second proposition is: That an action done from duty

derives its moral worth, *not from the purpose* which is to be attained by it, but from the maxim by which it is determined, and therefore does not depend on the realization of the object of the action, but merely on the *principle of volition* by which the action has taken place, without regard to any object of desire. It is clear from what precedes that the purposes which we may have in view in our actions, or their effects regarded as ends and springs of the will, cannot give to actions any unconditional or moral worth. In what, then, can their worth lie, if it is not to consist in the will and in reference to its expected effect? It cannot lie anywhere but in the *principle of the will* without regard to the ends which can be attained by the action. For the will stands between its *a priori* principle, which is formal, and its *a posteriori* spring, which is material, as between two roads, and as it must be determined by something, it follows that it must be determined by the formal principle of volition when an action is done from duty, in which case every material principle has been withdrawn from it.

The third proposition, which is a consequence of the two preceding, I would express thus: *Duty is the necessity of acting from respect for the law.* I may have *inclination* for an object as the effect of my proposed action, but I cannot have *respect* for it, just for this reason, that it is an effect and not an energy of will. Similarly, I cannot have respect for inclination, whether my own or another's; I can at most, if my own, approve it; if another's, sometimes even love it; i.e., look on it as favorable to my own interest. It is only what is connected with my will as a principle, by no means as an effect—what does not subserve my inclination, but overpowers it, or at least in case of choice excludes it from its calculation—in other words, simply the law of itself which can be an object of respect, and hence a command. Now an action done from duty must wholly exclude the influence of inclination, and with it every object of the will, so that nothing remains which can determine the will except the *law*, and subjectively *pure respect* for this practical law, and consequently the maxim that I should follow this law even to the thwarting of all my inclinations.

Thus the moral worth of an action does not lie in the effect expected from it, nor in any principle of action which requires to borrow its motive from this expected effect. For all these effects—agreeableness of one's condition, and even the promotion of the happiness of others—could have been also brought about by other causes, so that for this there would have been no need of the will of a rational being; whereas, it is in this alone that the supreme and unconditional good can be found. The pre-eminent good which we call moral can, therefore, consist in nothing else than the *conception of law* in itself, *which certainly is only possible in a rational being*, in so far as this conception, and not the expected effect, determines the will. This is a good which is already present in the person who acts accordingly, and we have not to wait for it to appear first in the result.

But what sort of law can that be, the conception of which must determine the will, even without paying any regard to the effect expected from it, in order that this will may be called good absolutely and without qualification? As I have deprived the will of every impulse which could arise to it from obedience to any law, there remains nothing but the universal conformity of its actions to law in general, which alone is to serve the will as a principle, i.e., I am never to act otherwise than so *that I could also will that my maxim should become a universal law*. Here now, it is the simple conformity to law in general, without assuming any particular law applicable to certain actions, that serves the will as its principle, and must so serve it, if duty is not to be a vain delusion and a chimerical notion. The common reason of men in its practical judgments perfectly coincides with this, and always has in view the principle here suggested. Let the question be, for example: May I, when in distress, make a promise with the intention not to keep it? I readily distinguish here between the two significations which the question may have: Whether it is prudent, or whether it is right, to make a false promise. The former may undoubtedly often be the case. I see clearly, indeed, that it is not enough to extricate myself from a present difficulty by means of this subterfuge, but it must be well considered whether there may not hereafter spring from this lie much greater inconvenience than that from which I now free myself, and as, with all my supposed *cunning*, the consequences cannot be so easily foreseen but that credit once lost may be much more injurious to me than any mischief which I seek to avoid at present, it should be considered whether it would not be more *prudent* to act herein according to a universal maxim, and to make it a habit to promise nothing except with the intention of keeping it. But it is soon clear to me that such a maxim will still only be based on the fear of consequences. Now it is a wholly different thing to be truthful from duty, and to be so from apprehension of injurious consequences. In the first case, the very notion of the action already implies a law for me; in the second case, I must first look about elsewhere to see what results may be combined with it which would affect myself. For to deviate from the principle of duty is beyond all doubt wicked; but to be unfaithful to my maxim of prudence may often be very advantageous to me, although to abide by it is certainly safer. The shortest way, however, and an unerring one, to discover the answer to this question whether a lying promise is consistent with duty, is to ask myself, Should I be content that my maxim (to extricate myself from difficulty by a false promise) should hold good as a universal law, for myself as well as for others? and should I be able to say to myself, "Everyone may make a deceitful promise when he finds himself in a difficulty from which he cannot otherwise extricate himself"? Then I presently become aware that while I can will the lie, I can by no means will that lying should be a universal law. For with such a law there would be no promises at all, since it would be in vain to allege my intention in regard to my future actions to those who would not believe this allegation, or if they overhastily did so would pay me back in my own coin. Hence my maxim, as soon as it should be made a universal law, would necessarily destroy itself.

I do not, therefore, need any far-reaching penetration to discern what I have to do in order that my will may be morally good. Inexperienced in the course of the world, incapable of being prepared for all its contingencies, I only ask myself: Canst thou also will that thy maxim should be a universal law? If not, then it must be rejected, and that not because of a disadvantage accruing from it to myself or even to others, but because it cannot enter as a principle into a possible universal legislation, and reason extorts from me immediate respect for such legislation. I do not indeed as yet *discern* on what this respect is based (this the philosopher may inquire), but at least I understand this, that it is an estimation of the worth which far outweighs all worth of what is recommended by inclination, and that the necessity of acting from *pure* respect for the practical law is what constitutes duty, to which every other motive must give place, because it is the condition of a will being good *in itself*, and the worth of such a will is above everything.

Morality Is Relative

Ruth Benedict

Ruth Benedict (1887-1948) was an outstanding American anthropologist and popular author whose writings, especially her book *Patterns of Culture*, significantly influenced her generation. Benedict begins her analysis by observing that certain isolated and primitive cultures consider individuals normal who have personality traits that civilized cultures would consider abnormal and vice versa. She uses this to illustrate her thesis that social systems are patterns of ideas and practices that develop in certain directions over time. Some patterns, for example, emphasize paranoia; some, trust. Individuals whose dispositions are paranoid are considered normal in paranoid cultures and deviant in trusting cultures. Benedict believes that, much like languages, these emphases develop as a result of historical and environmental influences. She believes that what is morally good in a given culture is simply a result of how the pattern for that particular culture has developed. People find it difficult to accept the valuations given by

Ruth Benedict, "Defense of Moral Relativism," *Journal of General Psychology* 10 (1934): 59-82. Reprinted with permission of the Helen Dwight Reid Educational Foundation. Published by Heldref Publications, 1319 18th St. NW, Washington, DC 20036-1802.

other cultures because they have been so heavily influenced by their own culture that they assume their values are objective. Benedict asserts that all cultural moral values are relative and that we cannot judge the values of other cultures.

QUESTIONS

1. Why, according to Benedict, are certain primitive, isolated peoples valuable for study?
2. What examples does the author use to explain the origins of normality and abnormality?
3. Who, according to Benedict, was the deviant in the Melanesian culture? What would she say to you if you told her that the culture itself was sick, not the man the Melanesians rejected?
4. Benedict suggests that one solution to the tendency that some people have towards megalomania and paranoia is to incorporate these as essential attributes of a civilization. Do you agree that this is an acceptable solution? Why or why not?
5. What point is the author making when she compares phonetics and sexual tabus?
6. According to Benedict, with what phrase is "morally good" synonymous?
7. Do you think there is any way in which the author could judge one culture better than another?

■ ■ ■

Modern social anthropology has become more and more a study of the varieties and common elements of cultural environment and the consequences of these in human behavior. For such a study of diverse social orders primitive peoples fortunately provide a laboratory not yet entirely vitiated by the spread of a standardized world-wide civilization. Dyaks and Hopis, Fijians and Yakuts are significant for psychological and sociological study because only among these simpler peoples has there been sufficient isolation to give opportunity for the development of localized social forms. In the higher cultures the standardization of custom and belief over a couple of continents has given a false sense of the inevitability of the particular forms that have gained currency, and we need to turn to a wider survey in order to check the conclusions we hastily base upon this near-universality of familiar customs. Most of the simpler cultures did not gain the wide currency of the one which, out of our experience, we identify with human nature, but this was for various historical reasons, and certainly not for any that gives us as its carriers a monopoly of social good or of social sanity. Modern civilization, from this point of view, becomes not a necessary pinnacle of human achievement but one entry in a long series of possible adjustments.

These adjustments, whether they are in mannerisms like the ways of showing anger, or joy, or grief in any society, or in major human drives like those of sex, prove to be far more variable than experience in any one culture would suggest. In certain fields, such as that of religion or of formal marriage arrangements, these wide limits of variability are well known and can be fairly described. In others it is not yet possible to give a generalized account, but that does not absolve us of the task of indicating the significance of the work that has been done and of the problems that have arisen.

One of these problems relates to the customary modern normal-abnormal categories and our conclusions regarding them. In how far are such categories culturally determined, or in how far can we with assurance regard them as absolute? In how far can we regard inability to function socially as diagnostic of abnormality, or in how far is it necessary to regard this as a function of the culture?

As a matter of fact, one of the most striking facts that emerge from a study of widely varying cultures is the ease with which our abnormals function in other cultures. It does not matter what kind of "abnormality" we choose for illustration, those which indicate extreme instability, or those which are more in the nature of character traits like sadism or delusions of grandeur or of persecution, there are well-described cultures in which these abnormals function at ease and with honor, and apparently without danger or difficulty to the society.

The most notorious of these is trance and catalepsy. Even a very mild mystic is aberrant in our culture. But most peoples have regarded even extreme psychic manifestations not only as normal and desirable, but even as characteristic of highly valued and gifted individuals. This was true even in our own cultural background in that period when Catholicism made the ecstatic experience the mark of sainthood. It is hard for us, born and brought up in a culture that makes no use of the experience, to realize how important a role it may play and how many individuals are capable of it, once it has been given an honorable place in any society. . . .

Cataleptic and trance phenomena are, of course, only one illustration of the fact that those whom we regard as abnormals may function adequately in other cultures. Many of our culturally discarded traits are selected for elaboration in different societies. Homosexuality is an excellent example, for in this case our attention is not constantly diverted, as in the consideration of trance, to the interruption of routine activity which it implies. Homosexuality poses the problem very simply. A tendency toward this trait in our culture exposes an individual to all the conflicts to which all aberrants are always exposed, and we tend to identify the consequences of this conflict with homosexuality. But these consequences are obviously local and cultural. Homosexuals in many societies are not incompetent, but they may be if the culture asks adjustments of them that would strain any man's vitality. Wherever homosexuality has been given an honorable place in any society, those to whom it is congenital have filled adequately the honorable roles society assigns to them. Plato's *Republic* is, of course, the most convincing statement of such a reading of homosexuality. It is presented as one of the major means to the good life, and it was generally so regarded in Greece at that time.

The cultural attitude toward homosexuals has not always been on such a high ethical plane, but it has been very varied. Among many American Indian tribes there exists the institution of the berdache, as the French called them. These men-women were men who at puberty or thereafter took the dress and the occupations of women. Sometimes they married other men and lived with them. Sometimes they were men with no inversion, persons of weak sexual endowment who chose this role to avoid the jeers of the women. The berdaches were never regarded as of first-rate supernatural power, as similar men-women were in Siberia, but rather as leaders in women's occupations, good healers in certain diseases, or, among certain tribes, as the genial organizers of social affairs. In any case, they were socially placed. They were not left exposed to the conflicts that visit the deviant who is excluded from participation in the recognized patterns of his society.

The most spectacular illustrations of the extent to which normality may be culturally defined are those cultures where an abnormality of our culture is the cornerstone of their social structure. It is not possible to do justice to these possibilities in a short discussion. A recent study of an island of northwest Melanesia by Fortune describes a society built upon traits which we regard as beyond the border of paranoia. In this tribe the exogamic groups look upon each other as prime manipulators of black magic, so that one marries always into an enemy group which remains for life one's deadly and unappeasable foes. They look upon a good garden crop as a confession of theft, for everyone is engaged in making magic to induce into his garden the productiveness of his neighbors'; therefore no secrecy in the island is so rigidly insisted upon as the secrecy of a man's harvesting of his yams. Their polite phrase at the acceptance of a gift is, "And if you now poison me, how shall I repay you this present?" Their preoccupation with poisoning is constant; no woman ever leaves her cooking pot for a moment untended. Even the great affinal economic exchanges that are characteristic of this Melanesian culture area are quite altered in Dobu since they are incompatible with this fear and distrust that pervades the culture. They go farther and people the whole world outside their own quarters with such malignant spirits that all-night feasts and ceremonials simply do not occur here. They have even rigorous religiously enforced customs that forbid the sharing of seed even in one family group. Anyone else's food is deadly poison to you, so that communality of stores is out of the question. For some months before harvest the whole society is on the verge of starvation, but if one falls to the temptation and eats up one's seed yams, one is an outcast and a beachcomber for life. There is no coming back. It involves, as a matter of course, divorce and the breaking of all social ties.

Now in this society where no one may work with another and no one may share with another, Fortune describes the individual who was regarded by all his fellows as crazy. He was not one of those who periodically ran amok and, beside himself and frothing at the mouth, fell with a knife upon anyone he could reach. Such behavior they did not regard as putting anyone outside the pale. They did not even put the individuals who were known to be liable to these attacks under any kind of control.

They merely fled when they saw the attack coming on and kept out of the way. "He would be all right tomorrow." But there was one man of sunny, kindly disposition who liked work and liked to be helpful. The compulsion was too strong for him to repress it in favor of the opposite tendencies of his culture. Men and women never spoke of him without laughing; he was silly and simple and definitely crazy. Nevertheless, to the ethnologist used to a culture that has, in Christianity, made his type the model of all virtue, he seemed a pleasant fellow. . . .

Among the Kwakiutl it did not matter whether a relative had died in bed of disease, or by the hand of any enemy, in either case death was an affront to be wiped out by the death of another person. The fact that one had been caused to mourn was proof that one had been put upon. A chief's sister and her daughter had gone up to Victoria, and either because they drank bad whiskey or because their boat capsized they never came back. The chief called together his warriors. "Now I ask you, tribes, who shall wail? Shall I do it or shall another?" The spokesman answered, of course, "Not you, Chief. Let some other of the tribes." Immediately they set up the war pole to announce their intention of wiping out the injury, and gathered a war party. They set out, and found seven men and two children asleep and killed them. "Then they felt good when they arrived at Sebaa in the evening."

The point which is of interest to us is that in our society those who on that occasion would feel good when they arrived at Sebaa that evening would be the definitely abnormal. There would be some, even in our society, but it is not a recognized and approved mood under the circumstances. On the Northwest Coast those are favored and fortunate to whom that mood under those circumstances is congenital, and those to whom it is repugnant are unlucky. This latter minority can register in their own culture only by doing violence to their congenial responses and acquiring others that are difficult for them. The person, for instance, who, like a Plains Indian whose wife has been taken from him, is too proud to fight, can deal with the Northwest Coast civilization only by ignoring its strongest bents. If he cannot achieve it, he is the deviant in that culture, their instance of abnormality.

This head-hunting that takes place on the Northwest Coast after a death is no matter of blood revenge or of organized vengeance. There is no effort to tie up the subsequent killing with any responsibility on the part of the victim for the death of the person who is being mourned. A chief whose son has died goes visiting wherever his fancy dictates, and he says to his host, "My prince has died today, and you go with him." Then he kills him. In this, according to their interpretation, he acts nobly because he has not been downed. He has thrust back in return. The whole procedure is meaningless without the fundamental paranoid reading of bereavement. Death, like all the other untoward accidents of existence, confounds man's pride and can only be handled in the category of insults.

Behavior honored upon the Northwest Coast is one which is recognized as abnormal in our civilization, and yet it is sufficiently close to the attitudes of our own culture to be intelligible to us and to have a definite vocabulary with which we may discuss it. The megalomaniac paranoid trend is a definite danger in our society. It is encouraged by some of our major preoccupations, and it confronts us with a choice of two possible attitudes. One is to brand it as abnormal and reprehensible, and is the attitude we have chosen in our civilization. The other is to make it an essential attribute we have chosen in our civilization. The other is to make it an essential attribute of ideal man, and this is the solution in the culture of the Northwest Coast.

These illustrations, which it has been possible to indicate only in the briefest manner, force upon us the fact that normality is culturally defined. An adult shaped to the drives and standards of either of these cultures, if he were transported into our civilization, would fall into our categories of abnormality. He would be faced with the psychic dilemmas of the socially unavailable. In his own culture, however, he is the pillar of society, the end result of socially inculcated mores, and the problem of personal instability in his case simply does not arise.

No one civilization can possibly utilize in its mores the whole potential range of human behavior. Just as there are great numbers of possible phonetic articulations, and the possibility of language depends on a selection and standardization of a few of these in order that speech communication may be possible at all, so the possibility of organized behavior of every sort, from the fashions of local dress and houses to the dicta of a people's ethics and religion, depends upon a similar selection among the possible behavior traits. In the field of recognized economic obligations or sex tabus this selection is as nonrational and subconscious a process as it is in the field of phonetics. It is a process which goes on in the group for long periods of time and is historically conditioned by innumerable accidents of isolation or of contact of peoples. In any comprehensive study of psychology, the selection that different cultures have made in the course of history within the great circumference of potential behavior is of great significance.

Every society, beginning with some slight inclination in one direction or another, carries its preference farther and farther, integrating itself more and more completely upon its chosen basis, and discarding those types of behavior that are uncongenial. Most of those organizations of personality that seem to us most uncontrovertibly abnormal have been used by different civilizations in the very foundations of their institutional life. Conversely the most valued traits of normal individuals have been looked on in differently organized cultures as aberrant. Normality, in short, within a very wide range, is culturally defined. It is primarily a term for the socially elaborated segment of human behavior in any culture; and abnormality, a term for the segment that that particular civilization does not use. The very eyes with which we see the problem are conditioned by the long traditional habits of our own society.

It is a point that has been made more often in relation to ethics than in relation to psychiatry. We do not any longer make the mistake of deriving the morality of our locality and decade directly from the inevitable constitution of human nature. We do not elevate it to the dignity of a first principle. We recognize that morality differs in every society, and is a convenient term for socially approved habits. Mankind has always preferred to say, "It is morally good," rather than "It is habitual," and the fact of this preference is matter enough for a critical science of ethics. But historically the two phrases are synonymous.

The concepts of the normal is properly a variant of the concept of the good. It is that which society has approved. A normal action is one which falls well within the limits of expected behavior for a particular society. Its variability among different peoples is essentially a function of the variability of the behavior patterns that different societies have created for themselves, and can never be wholly divorced from a consideration of culturally institutionalized types of behavior.

Each culture is a more or less elaborate working-out of the potentialities of the segment it has chosen. In so far as a civilization is well integrated and consistent within itself, it will tend to carry farther and farther, according to its nature, its initial impulse toward a particular type of action, and from the point of view of any other culture those elaborations will include more and more extreme and aberrant traits.

Each of these traits, in proportion as it reinforces the chosen behavior patterns of that culture, is for that culture normal. Those individuals to whom it is congenial either congenitally, or as the result of childhood sets, are accorded prestige in that culture, and are not visited with the social contempt or disapproval which their traits would call down upon them in a society that was differently organized. On the other hand, those individuals whose characteristics are not congenial to the selected type of human behavior in that community are the deviants, no matter how valued their personality traits may be in a contrasted civilization.

The Dobuan who is not easily susceptible to fear of treachery, who enjoys work and likes to be helpful, is their neurotic and regarded as silly. On the Northwest Coast the person who finds it difficult to read life in terms of an insult contest will be the person upon whom fall all the difficulties of the culturally unprovided for. The person who does not find it easy to humiliate a neighbor, nor to see humiliation in his own experience, who is genial and loving, may, of course, find some unstandardized way of achieving satisfactions in his society, but not in the major patterned responses that his culture requires of him. If he is born to play an important role in a family with many hereditary privileges, he can succeed only by doing violence to his whole personality. If he does not succeed, he has betrayed his culture; that is, he is abnormal.

I have spoken of individuals as having sets toward certain types of behavior, and of these sets as running sometimes counter to the types of behavior which are institutionalized in the culture to which they belong. From all that we know of contrasting cultures it seems clear that differences of temperament occur in every society. The matter has never been made the subject of investigation, but from the available material it would appear that these temperament types are very likely of universal recurrence. That is, there is an ascertainable range of human behavior that is found wherever a sufficiently large series of individuals is observed. But the proportion in which behavior types stand to one another in different societies is not universal. The vast majority of the individuals in any group are shaped to the fashion of that culture. In other words, most individuals are plastic to the moulding force of the society into which they are born. In a society that values trance, as in India, they will have supernormal experience. In a society that institutionalizes homosexuality, they will be homosexual. In a society that sets the gathering of possessions as the chief human objective, they will amass property. The deviants, whatever the type of behavior the culture has institutionalized, will remain few in number, and there seems no more difficulty in moulding that vast malleable majority to the "normality" of what we consider an aberrant trait, such as delusions of reference, than to the normality of such accepted behavior patterns as acquisitiveness. The small proportion of the number of the deviants in any culture is not a function of the sure instinct with which that society has built itself upon the fundamental sanities, but of the universal fact that, happily, the majority of mankind quite readily take any shape that is presented to them.

Moral Absolutes Must Be Learned

ARISTOTLE

Aristotle (384-322 B.C.) and his teacher, Plato, are the two ancient Greek philosophers who have most influenced Western thought. Aristotle was an encyclopedic thinker who studied nearly every branch of learning that was known in his day. His work included but was not limited to physics, metaphysics, politics, biology, and ethics. The present selection is taken from his *Nicomachean Ethics*. Aristotle was ultimately more interested in developing people who were inclined to do the right things than in formulating detailed rules for behavior. He believed that virtues are not inborn, but developed in the context of training and repetition. Eventually individuals develop habits which dispose them to make good choices. In general, making a good choice means choosing a mean or

From Aristotle, *Nicomachean Ethics*, translated by R.W. Browne. London: George Bell & Sons, 1895.

middle point between extremes which are in themselves bad choices. For example, it is not good to eat too little or too much, but to eat in moderation, which is between the two extremes. Aristotle was a careful observer of human nature and he realized that the lure of pleasure and personal styles and preferences often makes it difficult to choose the mean. He goes on to list the virtues he has identified along with associated vices. This list has influenced Western understanding of what it means to be a virtuous person for over two thousand years.

QUESTIONS

1. How does Aristotle relate virtue to habit?
2. How precise does the author think we can be when we talk about virtues? Why is this so?
3. Why does Aristotle think we must avoid both excess and deficiency (defect)?
4. According to the author, how can responses to pain and pleasure make a person either virtuous or not virtuous? Why then is education so important?
5. How does Aristotle distinguish between acts which are virtuous and people who are virtuous?
6. What relationship holds between personal choice and praise and blame, according to the author?
7. Can you give an example of a mean between two vices? Is this mean, in your opinion, a virtue?
8. According to Aristotle, in what sorts of cases are there no means?
9. How many virtues does Aristotle mention? Can you list them?
10. Do you think the virtues that applied to Aristotle's time apply today? Why or why not?
11. What does the author mean by "bringing ourselves far from the side of error, we shall arrive at the mean"?
12. Why does Aristotle say that pleasure is most to be guarded against?

■ ■ ■

How virtue is produced, and increased.

Virtue being twofold, one part intellectual and the other moral, intellectual virtue has its origin and increase for the most part from teaching; therefore it stands in need of experience and time; but moral virtue arises from habit, whence also it has got its name [*ēthiké*], which is only in a small degree altered from [*ethos*—"habit"]. Whence it is also clear, that not one of the moral virtues springs up in us by nature, for none of those things which exist by nature experience alteration from habit; for instance, the stone which by nature goes downwards could never be accustomed to go upwards, not even if one should attempt ten thousand times, by throwing it up, to give it this habit; nor could fire be accustomed to burn downwards; nor could anything else which has one natural bent get another different one from habit. The virtues, then, are produced in us neither by nature nor contrary to nature, but, we being naturally adapted to receive them, and this natural capacity is perfected by habit. Further, in every case where anything is produced in us naturally, we first get the capacities for doing these things, and afterwards perform the energies; which is evident in the case of the senses; for it was not from frequently seeing or frequently hearing that we got the senses, but, on the contrary, we had them first, and then used them, and did not get them by having used them. But we get the virtues by having first performed the energies, as is the case also in all the other arts; for those things which we must do after having learnt them we learn to do by doing them; as, for example, by building houses men become builders, and by playing on the harp, harp-players; thus, also, by doing just actions we become just, by performing temperate actions, temperate, and by performing brave actions we become brave. . . .

That excess and defect destroy virtue, but that being in the mean preserves it.

Since our present treatise is not for the purpose of mere speculation, as all others are, for the object of our investigation is not the knowing what virtue is, but to become good (since otherwise there would be no use in it), it is necessary to study the subject of actions, and how we must perform them; for these have entire influence over our habits to cause them to become of a certain character, as we have said. Now, to say that we must act according to right reason is a general maxim, and let it be assumed; but we will speak hereafter about it, and about the nature of right reason, and its relation to the other virtues. But this point must first be fully granted, that everything said on moral subjects ought to be said in outline, and not with exactness; just as we said in the beginning, that arguments must be demanded of such a nature only as the subject-matter admits; but the subjects of moral conduct and of expediency have no stability, just as also things wholesome. But if the treatment of the subject generally is of this nature, still less does it admit of exactness in particulars; for it comes under no art or set of precepts, but it is the duty of the agents themselves to look to the circumstances of the occasion, just as is the case in the arts of medicine and navigation. But although the subject before us is of this description, yet we must endeavour to do the best we can to help it.

This, then, we must first observe, that things of this kind are naturally destroyed both by defect and excess (for it is necessary in the case of things which cannot be seen to make use of illustrations which can be seen), just as we see in the case of strength and health; for too much as well as too little exercise destroys strength. In like manner drink and food, whether there be too little or too much of them, destroy health, but moderation in quantity causes, increases, and preserves it. The same thing, therefore, holds good in the case of temperance, and courage, and the other virtues; for he who flies from and is afraid of everything, and stands up against nothing, becomes a coward; and he who fears nothing at all, but goes boldly at everything, becomes rash. In like manner, he who indulges in the enjoyment of every pleasure, and refrains from none, is intemperate; but he who shuns all, as clowns do, becomes a kind of insensible man. For temperance and courage are destroyed both by the excess and the defect, but are preserved by the mean. . . .

The case with the virtues is the same; for by abstaining from pleasures we become temperate, and when we have become so, we are best able to abstain from them. The same also is the case with courage; for by being accustomed to despise objects of fear, and to bear them, we become brave, and when we have become so, we are best able to bear them.

That virtue is concerned with pleasures and pains.

But we must make the pleasure or pain which follows after acts a test of the habits; for he who abstains from the bodily pleasures, and in this very thing takes pleasure, is temperate; but he who feels pain at it is intemperate; and he who meets dangers and rejoices at it, or at least feels no pain, is brave; but he who feels pain is a coward; for moral virtue is conversant with pleasures and pains; for by reason of pleasure we do what is wicked, and through pain we abstain from honourable acts. Therefore it is necessary to be in some manner trained immediately from our childhood, as Plato says, to feel pleasure and pain at proper objects; for this is right education. Again, if the virtues are conversant with actions and passions, and pleasure and pain are consequent upon every action and passion, on this account, also, virtue must be conversant with pleasures and pains. Punishments also, which are inflicted by means of pleasure and pain, indicate the same thing; for they are kinds of remedies, and remedies naturally work by contraries. Again, as we said before, every habit of the soul has a natural relation and reference to those things by which it naturally becomes better and worse. But habits become bad by means of pleasures and pains, by pursuing or avoiding either improper ones, or at improper times, in improper ways, or improperly in any other manner, which reason determines.

Hence some have even defined the virtues to be certain states of apathy and tranquillity; but not correctly, in that they speak absolutely, and not in relation to propriety of time or manner, and so on through the other categories. Therefore virtue is supposed to be such as we have said, in relation to pleasures and pains, and apt to practise the best things; and vice is the contrary.

These subjects may also become plain to us from the following considerations. Since there are three things which lead us to choice, and three to aversion,—the honourable, the expedient, and the pleasant; and three contraries to them,—the disgraceful, the inexpedient, and the painful; on all these subjects the good man is apt to be right in his actions, and the bad man is apt to be wrong, and especially on the subject of pleasure; for this is common to all living creatures, and accompanies all things which are the objects of choice; for both the honourable and the expedient appear pleasant. Again, from our infancy it has grown up with all of us; and therefore it is difficult to rub out this affection, which is, as it were, engrained in our very existence. Again, we make pleasure and pain the rule of our actions, some of us in a greater, some in less degree. For this reason, therefore, it is necessary that our whole business must be with these subjects; for, to feel pleasure or pain, properly or improperly, makes no slight difference to our actions. Again, it is more difficult to resist pleasure than anger, as Heraclitus says, and both art and excellence are always conversant with that which is more difficult; for excellence in this case is superior. So that, for this reason also, the whole business of virtue, and political philosophy, must be with pleasures and pains; for he who makes a proper use of these will be good, and he who makes a bad use will be bad. Now on the point that virtue is conversant with pleasures and pains, and that it is increased and destroyed by means of the same things from which it originally sprung, when they are differently circumstanced; and that its energies are employed on those things out of which it originates, let enough have been said.

That men become just and temperate by performing just and temperate actions.

But a person may be in difficulty as to what we mean when we say that it is necessary for men to become just by performing just actions, and temperate by performing temperate ones; for if they do just and temperate actions, they are already just and temperate; just as, if they do grammatical and musical actions, they are grammarians and musicians. Or, is this not the case in the arts also? for it is possible to do a grammatical action accidentally, or at another's suggestion. A man, therefore, will only then be a grammarian, when he not only does a grammatical action, but also does it grammatically, that is, in accordance with the grammatical science, which he possesses in himself. . . .

Acts then are called just and temperate, when they are such

as the just or temperate man would do; but he who performs these acts is not a just and temperate man, but he who performs them in such a manner as just and temperate men do them. It is well said, therefore, that from performing just actions, a man becomes just; and from performing temperate ones, temperate; but without performing them no person would even be likely to become good. But the generality of men do not do these things, but taking refuge in words, they think that they are philosophers, and that in this manner they will become good men; and what they do is like what sick people do, who listen attentively to their physicians, and then do not attend to the things which they prescribe. Just as these, then, will never be in a good state of body under such treatment, so those will never be in a good state of mind, if this is their philosophy.

Definition of Moral Virtue

What is the "genus" of virtue. That it is a habit.

But we must next find out what the genus of virtue is. Since, then, the qualities which have their origin in the soul are three,—Passions, Capacities, and Habits,—Virtue must be some one of these. By passions, I mean, Desire, Anger, Fear, Confidence, Envy, Joy, Love, Hatred, Regret, Emulation, Pity; in a word, those feelings which are followed by pleasure or pain; by capacities, those qualities by means of which we are said to be able to be under the influence of these passions; as those by means of which we are able to feel anger, pain, or pity; by habits, those by means of which we are well or ill disposed with relation to the passions; as with relation to being made angry, if we feel anger too vehemently or too remissly, we are ill disposed; if we do it moderately, well disposed; and in like manner with relation to the others.

Neither the virtues, therefore, nor the vices are passions; because we are not called good or bad according to our passions, but according to our virtues or vices, and because we are neither praised nor blamed according to our passions (for the man who fears or is angry, is not praised; nor is the man who is simply angry, blamed; but the man who is angry in a certain way); but according to our virtues and vices, we are praised or blamed. Again, we feel anger and fear without deliberate preference; but the virtues are acts of deliberate preference, or at any rate, not without deliberate preference. But besides these things, we are said to be "moved" by our passions, but we are not said to be moved, but in some way to be "disposed," by our virtues and vices. For these reasons, also, they are not capacities; for we are neither called good nor bad, neither praised nor blamed, for our being able to feel passions simply. And again, we have our capacities by nature; but we do not become good or bad by nature; but of this we have already spoken. If, then, the virtues are neither passions nor capacities, it remains that they are habits. What, therefore, the "genus" of virtue is, has been sufficiently shown.

That virtue is a mean [middle] state, and how it is so.

But it is necessary not only to say that virtue is a habit, but also what sort of a habit it is. We must say, therefore, that every virtue both makes that of which it is the virtue to be in a good state, and makes its work good also; for instance, the virtue of the eye makes both the eye and the work of the eye good; for by the virtue of the eye we see well. In like manner, the virtue of a horse makes a horse good, and good in speed, and in carrying its rider, and in standing the attack of the enemy. If, then, this is the case in all instances, the virtue of man also must be a habit, from which man becomes good, and from which he will perform his work well. . . .

It is possible to go wrong in many ways (for evil, as the Pythagoreans conjectured, is of the nature of the infinite, but good of the finite); but we can go right in one way only; and for this reason the former is easy, and the latter difficult; it is easy to miss a mark, but difficult to hit it; and for these reasons, therefore, the excess and defect belong to vice, but the mean state to virtue; for, "we are good in one way only, but bad in all sorts of ways."

Virtue, therefore, is a "habit, accompanied with deliberate preference, in the relative mean, defined by reason, and as the prudent man would define it." It is a mean state between two vices, one in excess, the other in defect; and it is so, moreover, because of the vices one division falls short of, and the other exceeds what is right, both in passions and actions, whilst virtue discovers the mean and chooses it. Therefore, with reference to its essence, and the definition which states its substance, virtue is a mean state; but with reference to the standard of "the best" and "the excellent," it is an extreme. But it is not every action, nor every passion, which admits of the mean state; for some have their badness at once implied in their name; as, for example, malevolence, shamelessness, envy; and amongst actions, adultery, theft, homicide. For all these, and such as these, are so called from their being themselves bad, not because their excesses or defects are bad. In these, then, it is impossible ever to be right, but we must always be wrong. Nor does the right or wrong in such cases as these depend at all upon the person with whom, or the time when, or the manner in which, adultery is committed; but absolutely the doing of any one of these things is wrong. It would be equally absurd, then, to require a mean state, and an excess, and a defect, in injustice, and cowardice, and intemperance. For thus there would be a mean state of excess and defect, and an excess of excess, and a defect of defect. But just as there is no excess and defect of temperance and courage (owing to the fact that the mean is in some sense an extreme), so neither in the case of these is there a mean state, excess, or defect; but however they be done, sin is committed. For, in a word, there is neither a mean state of excess and defect, nor an excess and defect of a mean state.

An enumeration of mean [moderate] habits.

But it is necessary that this should not only be stated generally, but that it should also be applicable to the particular cases; for in discussions on subjects of moral action, universal statements are apt to be too vague, but particular ones are more consistent with truth; for actions are conversant with particulars; but it is necessary that the statements should agree with these. . . . Now, on the subject of fear and confidence, courage is the mean state. Of the persons who are in excess, he who is in the excess of fearlessness has no name; but there are many cases without names; and he who is in the excess of confidence, is called rash; but he who is in the excess of fear, but in the defect of confidence, is cowardly.

On the subject of pleasures and pains (but not all pleasures and pains, and less in the case of pains than pleasures), temperance is the mean state, and intemperance the excess. But there are, in fact, none who are in the defect on the subject of pleasures; therefore these also have no name; but let them be called insensible.

On the subject of the giving and receiving of money, liberality is the mean state, and the excess and defect, prodigality and illiberality. But in these, the excess and defect are mutually contrary to each other; for the prodigal man is in the excess in giving money, but is in the defect in receiving; but the illiberal man is in the excess in receiving, but in the defect in giving. Now, therefore, we are speaking on these points as in an outline, and summarily, because we consider this sufficient; but afterwards more accurate distinctions shall be drawn respecting them.

But on the subject of money there are other dispositions also: magnificence is a mean state; but the magnificent man differs from the liberal man; for one has to do with great things, the other with small ones; the excess is bad taste and vulgar profusion, the defect shabbiness. But these differ from the vices which are related to liberality; but their points of difference shall be stated hereafter.

On the subject of honour and dishonour, magnanimity is the mean; the excess, a vice called empty vanity; the defect, meanness of spirit.

But as we said that liberality, when compared with magnificence, differed from it in being concerned with small things, so there is a kind of feeling which, being itself about small honour, has the same relation to magnanimity, which is about great honour; for it is possible to desire honour as we ought, and more than we ought, and less than we ought. Now he who is in the excess in the desire of honour is called ambitious, and he who is in the defect unambitious, but he that is in the mean has no name; and the dispositions are likewise nameless, except that of the ambitious, which is called ambition; and from this cause the extremes claim the middle place. And we sometimes call him who is in the mean ambitious, and sometimes unambitious; and sometimes we praise the ambitious man, and sometimes the man who is unambitious. But hereafter the reason why we do this will be explained; but now let us go on speaking of the others in the way in which we have begun.

There are also on the subject of anger an excess, a defect, and a mean state; but since they may be said to be nameless, and as we call him who is in the mean meek, we will call the mean meekness; but of the extremes, let him who is in excess be called passionate, and the vice passion; him who is in defect insensible to anger, and the defect insensibility to anger. . . .

But there are also mean states both in the passions and also in cases which concern the passions; for modesty is not a virtue; and yet the modest man is praised; for in this case also there is one who is said to be in the mean, another in the extreme, of excess (as the bashful, who is ashamed at everything); the man who is deficient in shame, or does not feel it at all, is impudent, but he who is in the mean is modest. But indignation is a mean state between envy and malevolence; but these affections are concerned with the pain and pleasure which are felt at the circumstances of our neighbours; for he who is apt to feel indignation, feels pain at those who are undeservedly successful; but the envious man, going beyond him, feels pain at everyone's success; and the malevolent man falls so far short of being pained, that he even rejoices. . . .

Characteristics of the Extreme and Mean States: Practical Corollaries

How virtues and vices are opposed to one another.

But since there are three dispositions,—two vicious, one in excess and the other in defect, and one virtuous, namely, the mean state, they are all in some sense opposed to each other; for the extremes are opposed both to the mean state and to each other, and the mean state to the extremes. For as the equal when compared with the less is greater, and when compared with the greater is less; so the mean states when compared with the defects are in excess, and when compared with the excesses are in defect, both in the passions and in the actions; for the brave man in comparison with the coward appears rash; and in comparison with the rash man a coward. In like manner also the temperate man in comparison with the insensible is intemperate, and in comparison with the intemperate is insensible; and the liberal man in comparison with the illiberal is prodigal, and in comparison with the prodigal is illiberal.

Therefore those who are in the extreme thrust away from

them him who is in the mean state, each to the other, and the coward calls the brave man rash, and the rash man calls him a coward; and so on in the other cases. But though they are thus opposed to each other, there is a greater opposition between the extremes one to the other, than to the mean; for these stand further apart from each other than from the mean; just as the great is further from the small, and the small from the great, than either from the equal. Again, there appears in some extremes some resemblance to the mean, as rashness seems to resemble courage, and prodigality liberality; but there is the greatest dissimilarity between the extremes. Now things that are furthest apart from each other are defined to be opposites; so that those that are further off are more opposite. But in some cases the defect is more opposed to the mean, and in some cases the excess; as, for example, rashness, which is the excess, is not so much opposed to courage as cowardice, which is the defect; and insensibility, which is the defect, is less opposed to temperance than intemperance, which is the excess.

But this happens for two reasons; the first from the nature of the thing itself; for from one extreme being nearer and more like the mean than the other, it is not this but its opposite which we set down as most opposite; as, since rashness appears to be nearer and more like courage than cowardice, and cowardice less like than rashness, we oppose cowardice to courage rather than rashness, because those things that are further from the mean appear to be more opposite to it. This, therefore, is one reason arising from the nature of the thing itself; the other originates in ourselves; for those things to which we are more naturally disposed, appear to be more contrary to the mean; as, for instance, we are more naturally disposed to pleasures, and therefore we are more easily carried away to intemperance than to propriety of conduct. These, then, to which the inclination is more decided, we call more opposite; and for this reason, intemperance, which is the excess, is more opposite to temperance.

How we shall arrive at the mean and at excellence.

Now that moral virtue is a mean state, and how, and that it is a mean state between two vices, one on the side of excess, and the other on the side of defect; and that is so from being apt to aim at the mean in passions and actions, has been sufficiently proved. It is therefore difficult also to be good; for in each case it is difficult to find the mean; just as it is not in every man's power, but only in the power of him who knows how, to find the centre of a circle; and thus it is easy, and in every man's power, to be angry, and to give and spend money; but to determine the person to whom, and the quantity, and the time, and the motive, and the manner, is no longer in every man's power, nor is it easy; therefore excellence is rare, and praiseworthy, and honourable. It is therefore needful for him who aims at the mean, first to keep away from that extreme which is more contrary, like the advice that Calypso gave:

> "Keep the ship clear of this smoke and surge."

For of the extremes, one is more and one less erroneous.

Since, then, it is difficult to hit the mean exactly, we must, as our second trial, choose the least of these evils; and this will be best done in the manner which we have stated. But it is necessary to consider to which of the vices we ourselves are most inclined; for some of us are naturally disposed to one, and some to another; and this we shall be able to discover from the pleasure and pain which arise in us. But it is necessary to drag ourselves away towards the opposite extreme; for by bringing ourselves far from the side of error, we shall arrive at the mean; as people do with crooked sticks to make them straight. But in every case we must be most upon our guard against what is pleasant, and pleasure, for we are not unbiassed judges of it. Just, then, as the Trojan elders felt respecting Helen, must we feel respecting pleasure, and in all cases pronounce sentence as they did; for thus, by "sending it away," we shall be less likely to fall into error. By so doing, then, to speak summarily, we shall be best able to hit the mean. But perhaps this may be difficult, and especially in particular cases; for it is not easy to define the manner, and the persons, and the occasions, and the length of time for a person to be angry; for we sometimes praise those who are in the defect, and call them meek; and sometimes those who are easily angered, and call them manly. But he who transgresses the right a little is not blamed, whether it be on the side of excess or defect, but he who does it too much; for he does not escape notice. But it is not easy to define verbally how far, and to what point, a man is blameable, nor is anything else that is judged of by the common feeling and sense of mankind easy to be defined; but such questions as these belong to particular cases, and the decision of them belongs to moral perception. What we have said hitherto, therefore, proves that the mean state is in every case praiseworthy, but that we must incline sometimes towards excess, and sometimes towards deficiency; for thus we shall most easily hit the mean and that which is excellent.

Morality Only Makes Sense for the Atheist

BERTRAND RUSSELL

Bertrand Russell (1872-1970) was one of the most popular and influential philosophers of the twentieth century. In addition to his significant contributions to logic, metaphysics, and mathematics, he made contributions to the philosophy of religion. The following essay, entitled "A Free Man's Worship," presents an atheistic perspective on morality. Russell clearly does not believe in God. He considers the world a place of terrible power and suffering that a good God could not have created. The world is utterly indifferent to humanity and will ultimately destroy not only individuals, but also the human race itself, Bertrand concludes. The gods humans create are only reflections of the power we see in the world, and they, like the power, are not worthy of worship. Once this is courageously recognized, Russell argues, it is possible to build a morality and a worship that is not based on naive and unrealistic expectations about the world. This is done first by creat-

Bertrand Russell, "A Free Man's Worship," *Independent Review*, December 1903.

ing a vision of good and beauty in our minds and imaginations. We must then live, as much as the world will allow us and until it destroys us, according to that vision and not in submission to the power of the world. This includes helping our fellow humans in the midst of our shared suffering and taking comfort in the fact that the past, which cannot be changed, forms a kind of record of the good and noble deeds we have done. In this kind of life, and in no other, there is enlightenment, joy, and freedom.

QUESTIONS

1. Why does Russell compare the real world to the world of Dr. Faustus?
2. Why does the author reject the existence of God?
3. How, according to the author, is Man free despite the powerful forces of nature?
4. What, according to Russell, do savages worship? What does this kind of worship amount to?
5. What does the author say motivates Man to create God?
6. What is Man's true freedom, according to Russell? Why is even indignation wrong?
7. To what degree does the author think humans should submit to power?
8. How does Russell believe we obtain a vision of heaven? Where does this vision exist?
9. What virtues does the author say we obtain when we achieve victory over the powers of darkness?
10. How does Russell define a free Man's worship?
11. In what sense does the author think that humans can be immortal?

■ ■ ■

To Dr Faustus in his study Mephistopheles told the history of the Creation, saying:

'The endless praises of the choirs of angels had begun to grow wearisome; for, after all, did He not deserve their praise? Had He not given them endless joy? Would it not be more amusing to obtain undeserved praise, to be worshipped by beings whom He tortured? He smiled inwardly, and resolved that the great drama should be performed.

'For countless ages the hot nebula whirled aimlessly through space. At length it began to take shape, the central mass threw off planets, the planets cooled, boiling seas and burning mountains heaved and tossed, from black masses of cloud hot sheets of rain deluged the barely solid crust. And now the first germ of life grew in the depths of the ocean, and developed rapidly in the fructifying warmth into vast forest trees, huge ferns springing from the damp mould, sea monsters breeding, fighting, devouring, and passing away. And from the monsters, as the play unfolded itself, Man was born, with the power of thought, the knowledge of good and evil, and the cruel thirst for worship. And Man saw that all is passing in this mad, monstrous world, that all is struggling to snatch, at any cost, a few brief moments of life before Death's inexorable decree. And Man said: "There is a hidden purpose, could we but fathom it, and the purpose is good; for we must reverence something and in the visible world there is nothing worthy of reverence." And Man stood aside from the struggle, resolving that God intended harmony to come out of chaos by human efforts. And when he followed the instincts which God had transmitted to him from his ancestry of beasts of prey, he called it Sin, and asked God to forgive him. But he doubted whether he could be justly forgiven, until he invented a divine Plan by which God's wrath was to have been appeased. And seeing the present was bad, he made it yet worse, that thereby the future might be better. And he gave God thanks for the strength that enabled him to forgo even the joys that were possible. And God smiled; and when he saw that Man had become perfect in renunciation and worship, he sent another sun through the sky, which crashed into Man's sun; and all returned again to nebula.

'"Yes," he murmured, "it was a good play; I will have it performed again."'

Such, in outline, but even more purposeless, more void of meaning, is the world which Science presents for our belief. Amid such a world, if anywhere, our ideals henceforward must find a home. That Man is the product of causes which had no prevision of the end they were achieving; that his origin, his growth, his hopes and fears, his loves and his beliefs, are but the outcome of accidental collocations of atoms; that no fire, no heroism, no intensity of thought and feeling, can preserve an individual life beyond the grave; that all the labours of the ages, all the devotion, all the inspiration, all the noonday brightness of human genius, are destined to extinction in the vast death of the solar system, and that the whole temple of Man's achievement must inevitably be buried beneath the debris of a universe in ruins—all these things, if not quite beyond dispute, are yet so nearly certain, that no philosophy which rejects them can hope to stand. Only within the scaffolding of these truths, only on the firm foundation of unyielding despair, can the soul's habitation henceforth be safely built.

How, in such an alien and inhuman world, can so powerless a creature as Man preserve his aspirations untarnished? A strange mystery it is that Nature, omnipotent but blind, in the revolutions of her secular hurryings through the abysses of space, has brought forth at last a child, subject still to her power, but gifted with sight, with knowledge of good and evil, with the capacity of judging all the works of his unthinking Mother. In spite of Death, the mark and seal of the parental control, Man is yet free, during his brief years, to examine, to criticize, to know, and in imagination to create. To him alone, in the world with which he is acquainted, this freedom belongs; and in this lies his superiority to the resistless forces that control his outward life.

The savage, like ourselves, feels the oppression of his impotence before the powers of Nature; but having in himself nothing that he respects more than Power, he is willing to prostrate himself before his gods, without inquiring whether they are worthy of his worship. Pathetic and very terrible is the long history of cruelty and torture, of degradation and human sacrifice, endured in the hope of placating the jealous gods: surely, the trembling believer thinks, when what is most precious has been freely given, their lust for blood must be appeased, and more will not be required. The religion of Moloch—as such creeds may be generically called—is in essence the cringing submission of the slave, who dare not, even in his heart, allow the thought that his master deserves no adulation. Since the independence of ideals is not yet acknowledged, Power may be freely worshipped, and receive an unlimited respect, despite its wanton infliction of pain.

But gradually, as morality grows bolder, the claim of the ideal world begins to be felt; and worship, if it is not to cease, must be given to gods of another kind than those created by the savage. Some, though they feel the demands of the ideal, will still consciously reject them, still urging that naked Power is worthy of worship. Such is the attitude inculcated in God's answer to Job out of the whirlwind: the divine power and knowledge are paraded, but of the divine goodness there is no hint. Such also is the attitude of those, who, in our own day, base their morality upon the struggle for survival, maintaining that the survivors are necessarily the fittest. But others, not content with an answer so repugnant to the moral sense, will adopt the position which we have become accustomed to regard as specially religious, maintaining that, in some hidden manner, the world of fact is really harmonious with the world of ideals. Thus Man creates God, all-powerful and all-good, the mystic unity of what is and what should be.

But the world of fact, after all, is not good; and, in submitting our judgment to it, there is an element of slavishness from which our thoughts must be purged. For in all things it is well to exalt the dignity of Man, by freeing him as far as possible from the tyranny of non-human Power. When we have realized that Power is largely bad, that man, with his knowledge of good and evil, is but a helpless atom in a world which has no such knowledge, the choice is again presented to us: Shall we worship Force, or shall we worship Goodness? Shall our God exist and be evil, or shall he be recognized as the creation of our own conscience?

The answer to this question is very momentous, and affects profoundly our whole morality. The worship of Force, to which Carlyle and Nietzsche and the creed of Militarism have accustomed us, is the result of failure to maintain our own ideals against a hostile universe: it is itself a prostrate submission to evil, a sacrifice of our best to Moloch. If strength indeed is to be respected, let us respect rather the strength of those who refuse that false 'recognition of facts' which fails to recognize that facts are often bad. Let us admit that, in the world we know, there are many things that would be better otherwise, and that the ideals to which we do and must adhere are not realized in the realm of matter. Let us preserve our respect for truth, for beauty, for the ideal of perfection which life does not permit us to attain, though none of these things meet with the approval of the unconscious universe. If Power is bad, as it seems to be, let us reject it from our hearts. In this lies Man's true freedom: in determination to worship only the God created by our own love of the good, to respect only the heaven which inspires the insight of our best moments. In action, in desire, we must submit perpetually to the tyranny of outside forces; but in thought, in aspiration, we are free, free from our fellow-men, free from the petty planet on which our bodies impotently crawl, free even, while we live, from the tyranny of death. Let us learn, then, that energy of faith which enables us to live constantly in the vision of the good; and let us descend, in action, into the world of fact, with that vision always before us.

When first the opposition of fact and ideal grows fully visible, a spirit of fiery revolt, of fierce hatred of the gods, seems necessary to the assertion of freedom. To defy with Promethean constancy a hostile universe, to keep its evil always in view, always actively hated, to refuse no pain that the malice of Power can invent, appears to be the duty of all who will not bow before the inevitable. But indignation is still a bondage, for it compels our thoughts to be occupied with an evil world; and in the fierceness of desire from which rebellion springs there is a kind of self-assertion which it is necessary for the wise to overcome. Indignation is a submission of our thoughts, but not of our desires; the Stoic freedom in which wisdom consists is found in the submission of our desires, but not of our thoughts. From the submission of our desires springs the virtue of resignation; from the freedom of our thoughts springs the whole world of art and philosophy, and the vision of beauty by which, at last, we half reconquer the reluctant world. But the vision of beauty is possible only to unfettered contemplation, to thoughts not weighted by the load of eager wishes; and thus Freedom comes only to those who no longer ask of life that it shall yield them any of those personal goods that are subject to the mutations of Time.

Although the necessity of renunciation is evidence of the existence of evil, yet Christianity, in preaching it, has shown a wisdom exceeding that of the Promethean philosophy of rebellion. It must be admitted that, of the things we desire, some, though they prove impossible, are yet real goods; others, however, as ardently longed for, do not form part of a fully purified ideal. The belief that what must be renounced is bad, though sometimes false, is far less often false than untamed passion supposes; and the creed of religion, by providing a reason for proving that it is never false, has been the means of purifying our hopes by the discovery of many austere truths.

But there is in resignation a further good element: even real goods, when they are unattainable, ought not to be fretfully desired. To every man comes, sooner or later, the great renunciation. For the young, there is nothing unattainable; a good thing desired with the whole force of a passionate will, and yet impossible, is to them not credible. Yet, by death, by illness, by poverty, or by the voice of duty, we must learn, each one of us, that the world was not made for us, and that, however beautiful may be the things we crave, Fate may nevertheless forbid them. It is the part of courage, when misfortune comes, to bear without repining the ruin of our hopes, to turn away our thoughts from vain regrets. This degree of submission to Power is not only just and right: it is the very gate of wisdom.

But passive renunciation is not the whole of wisdom; for not by renunciation alone can we build a temple for the worship of our own ideals. Haunting foreshadowings of the temple appear in the realm of imagination, in music, in architecture, in the untroubled kingdom of reason, and in the golden sunset magic of lyrics, where beauty shines and glows, remote from the touch of sorrow, remote from the fear of change, remote from the failures and disenchantments of the world of fact. In the contemplation of these things the vision of heaven will shape itself in our hearts, giving at once a touchstone to judge the world about us, and an inspiration by which to fashion to our needs whatever is not incapable of serving as a stone in the sacred temple.

Except for those rare spirits that are born without sin, there is a cavern of darkness to be traversed before that temple can be entered. The gate of the cavern is despair, and its floor is paved with the gravestones of abandoned hopes. There Self must die; there the eagerness, the greed of untamed desire must be slain, for only so can the soul be freed from the empire of Fate. But out of the cavern the Gate of Renunciation leads again to the daylight of wisdom, by whose radiance a new insight, a new joy, a new tenderness, shine forth to gladden the pilgrim's heart.

When, without the bitterness of impotent rebellion, we have learnt both to resign ourselves to the outward rule of Fate and to recognize that the non-human world is unworthy of our worship, it becomes possible at last so to transform and refashion the unconscious universe, so to transmute it in the crucible of imagination, that a new image of shining gold replaces the old idol of clay. In all the multiform facts of the world—in the visual shapes of trees and mountains and clouds, in the events of the life of man, even in the very omnipotence of Death—the insight of creative idealism can find the reflection of a beauty which its own thoughts first made. In this way mind asserts its subtle mastery over the thoughtless forces of Nature. The more evil the material with which it deals, the more thwarting to untrained desire, the greater is its achievement in inducing the reluctant rock to yield up its hidden treasures, the prouder its victory in compelling the opposing forces to swell the pageant of its triumph. Of all the arts, Tragedy is the proudest, the most triumphant; for it builds its shining citadel in the very centre of the enemy's country, on the very summit of his highest mountain; from its impregnable watch towers, his camps and arsenals, his columns and forts, are all revealed; within its walls the free life continues, while the legions of Death and Pain and Despair, and all the servile captains of tyrant Fate, afford the burghers of that dauntless city new spectacles of beauty. Happy those sacred ramparts, thrice happy the dwellers on that all-seeing eminence. Honour to those brave warriors who, through countless ages of warfare, have preserved for us the priceless heritage of liberty, and have kept undefiled by sacrilegious invaders the home of the unsubdued.

But the beauty of Tragedy does but make visible a quality which, in more or less obvious shapes, is present always and everywhere in life. In the spectacle of Death, in the endurance of intolerable pain, and in the irrevocableness of a vanished past, there is a sacredness, an overpowering awe, a feeling of the vastness, the depth, the inexhaustible mystery of existence, in which, as by some strange marriage of pain, the sufferer is bound to the world by bonds of sorrow. In these moments of insight, we lose all eagerness of temporary desire, all struggling and striving for petty ends, all care for the little trivial things that, to a superficial view, make up the common life of day by day; we see, surrounding the narrow raft illumined by the flickering light of human comradeship, the dark ocean on whose rolling waves we toss for a brief hour; from the great night without, a chill blast breaks in upon our refuge; all the loneliness of humanity amid hostile forces is concentrated upon the individual soul, which must struggle alone, with what of courage it can command, against the whole weight of a universe that cares nothing for its hopes and fears. Victory, in this struggle with the powers of darkness, is the true baptism into the glorious company of heroes, the true initiation into the overmastering beauty of human existence. From that awful encounter of the soul with the outer world, enunciation, wisdom, and charity are born; and with their birth a new life begins. To take into the inmost shrine of the soul the irresistible forces whose puppets we seem to be—Death and change, the irrevocableness of the past, and the powerlessness of man before the blind hurry of the universe from vanity to vanity—to feel these things and know them is to conquer them.

This is the reason why the Past has such magical power. The beauty of its motionless and silent pictures is like the enchanted purity of late autumn, when the leaves, though one breath would make them fall, still glow against the sky in golden glory. The Past does not change or strive; like Duncan, after life's fitful fever it sleeps well; what was eager and grasping, what was petty and transitory, has faded away, the things that were beautiful and eternal shine out of it like stars in the night. Its beauty, to a soul not worthy of it, is unendurable; but to a soul which has conquered Fate it is the key of religion.

The life of Man, viewed outwardly, is but a small thing in comparison with the forces of Nature. The slave is doomed to worship Time and Fate and Death, because they are greater than anything he finds in himself, and because all his thoughts are of things which they devour. But, great as they are, to think of them greatly, to feel their passionless splendour, is greater still. And such thought makes us free men; we no longer bow before the inevitable in Oriental subjection, but we absorb it, and make it a part of ourselves. To abandon the struggle for private happiness, to expel all eagerness of temporary desire, to burn with passion for eternal things—this is emancipation, and this is the free man's worship. And this liberation is effected by a contemplation of Fate; for Fate itself is subdued by the mind which leaves nothing to be purged by the purifying fire of Time.

United with his fellow-men by the strongest of all ties, the tie of a common doom, the free man finds that a new vision is with him always, shedding over every daily task the light of love. The life of Man is a long march through the night, surrounded by invisible foes, tortured by weariness and pain, towards a goal that few can hope to reach, and where none may tarry long. One by one, as they march, our comrades vanish from our sight, seized by the silent orders of omnipotent Death. Very brief is the time in which we can help them, in which their happiness or misery is decided. Be it ours to shed sunshine on their path, to lighten their sorrows by the balm of sympathy, to give them the pure joy of a never-tiring affection, to strengthen failing courage, to instil faith in hours of despair. Let us not weigh in grudging scales their merits and demerits, but let us think only of their need—of the sorrows, the difficulties, perhaps the blindnesses, that make the misery of their lives; let us remember that they are fellow-sufferers in the same darkness, actors in the same tragedy with ourselves. And so, when their day is over, when their good and their evil have become eternal by the immortality of the past, be it ours to feel that, where they suffered, where they failed, no deed of ours was the cause; but wherever a spark of the divine fire kindled in their hearts, we were ready with encouragement, with sympathy, with brave words in which high courage glowed.

Brief and powerless is Man's life; on him and all his race the slow, sure doom falls pitiless and dark. Blind to good and evil, reckless of destruction, omnipotent matter rolls on its relentless way; for Man, condemned today to lose his dearest, tomorrow himself to pass through the gate of darkness, it remains only to cherish, ere yet the blow falls, the lofty thoughts that ennoble his little day; disdaining the coward terrors of the slave of Fate, to worship at the shrine that his own hands have built; undismayed by the empire of chance, to preserve a mind free from the wanton tyranny that rules his outward life; proudly defiant of the irresistible forces that tolerate, for a moment, his knowledge and his condemnation, to sustain alone, a weary but unyielding Atlas, the world that his own ideals have fashioned despite the trampling march of unconscious power.

Morality Only Makes Sense If There Is a God

George Mavrodes

George Mavrodes is a professor of philosophy at the University of Michigan. He received a B.D. at Western Baptist Theological Seminary and a Ph.D. from the University of Michigan. He has authored numerous articles in the philosophy of religion and edited *The Rationality of Belief in God*. The present viewpoint, which he entitled "Religion and the Queerness of Morality," is a response to the previous viewpoint, Bertrand Russell's "A Free Man's Worship." Mavrodes believes that morality entails real, binding obligations. This means that people can be obligated to go against their self-interest, even to the point of death. Obligations at this level of significance require strong grounding and justification to make rational sense. In the universe which Russell accepts, values, persons, and consciousness have emerged by accident from an unconscious process and are not in any sense significant in the scheme of things. They are not what Mavrodes calls "deeply grounded." There is consequently no way to justify significant obligations for self-sacrifice in such a universe. How can a person be asked to give up all that he or she has, for example, to save some other person's life if that other life is itself just a chance happening of no ultimate significance or value? What personal benefits could one derive from such an act of self-sacrifice in Russell's universe? Such an obligation would be rationally unjustified and absurd. In a universe created by a personal God, however, consciousness, values and personhood are part of the deep structure of reality. They are of ultimate significance to the Creator. Strong obligations to persons make good rational sense in such a universe.

QUESTIONS

1. According to the author, in what two ways might morality depend upon religion?
2. How does Mavrodes summarize the features of the Russellian world? What is a Russellian benefit?
3. What kind of obligations would make the actual world crazy and absurd, according to the author?
4. Why does Mavrodes think it is important to distinguish between moral feelings and moral obligations?
5. How do Baier and Brandt answer the question Why should I be moral? Why are their answers unsatisfactory, according to Mavrodes?
6. In what kind of world does Mavrodes think morality could disappear and nothing be lost?

■ ■ ■

Many arguments for the existence of God may be construed as claiming that there is some feature of the world that would somehow make no sense unless there was something else that had a stronger version of that feature or some analogue of it. So, for example, the cosmological line of argument may be thought of as centering upon the claim that the way in which the world exists (called "contingent" existence) would be incomprehensible unless there were something else—that is, God—that had a stronger grip upon existence (that is, "necessary" existence).

Now, a number of thinkers have held a view something like this with respect to morality. They have claimed that in some important way morality is dependent upon religion—dependent, that is, in such a way that if religion were to fail, morality would fail also. And they have held that the dependence was more than psychological, that is, if religion were to fail, it would somehow be *proper* (perhaps logically or perhaps in some other way) for morality to fail also. One way of expressing this theme is by Dostoevsky's "If there is no God, then everything is permitted," a sentiment that in this century has been prominently echoed by Sartre. But perhaps the most substantial philosophical thinker of the modern period to espouse this view, though in a rather idiosyncratic way, was Immanual Kant, who held that the existence of God was a necessary postulate of 'practical' (that is, moral) reason.[1]

On the other hand, it has recently been popular for moral philosophers to deny this theme and to maintain that the dependence of morality on religion is, at best, merely psychological. Were religion to fail, so they apparently hold, this would grant no sanction for the failure of morality. For morality stands on its own feet, whatever those feet may turn out to be.

Now, the suggestion that morality somehow depends on religion is rather attractive to me. It is this suggestion that I wish to explore in this paper, even though it seems unusually difficult to formulate clearly the features of this suggestion that make it attractive. . . .

First, then, the nonreligious view. I take a short and powerful statement of it from a 1903 essay by Bertrand Russell, "A Free Man's Worship."

> That man is the product of causes which had no prevision of the end they were achieving; that his origin, his growth, his hopes

[1] Perhaps, however, Kant was not entirely clear on this point, for in some places he talks as though it is only the *possibility* of God's existence that is a necessary postulate of morality. For a discussion of this point see M. Jamie Ferreira, "Kant's Postulate: The Possibility or the Existence of God?" *Kant-Studien* 17, no. 1 (1983): 75-80.

> and fears, his loves and his beliefs are but the outcome of accidental collocations of atoms; that no fire, no heroism, no intensity of thought and feeling, can preserve an individual life beyond the grave; that all the labors of the ages, all the devotion, all the inspiration, all the noonday brightness of human genius, are destined to extinction in the vast death of the solar system, and that the whole temple of man's achievement must inevitably be buried beneath the debris of a universe in ruins—all these things, if not quite beyond dispute, are yet so nearly certain that no philosophy which rejects them can hope to stand. Only within the scaffolding of these truths, only on the firm foundation of unyielding despair, can the soul's habitation henceforth be safely built.

For convenience, I will call a world that satisfies the description given here a "Russellian world." But we are primarily interested in what the status of morality would be in the actual world if that world should turn out to be Russellian. I shall therefore sometimes augment the description of a Russellian world with obvious features of the actual world.

What are the most relevant features of a Russellian world? The following strike me as especially important: (1) Such phenomena as minds, mental activities, consciousness, and so forth are the products of entities and causes that give no indication of being mental themselves. In Russell's words, the causes are "accidental collocations of atoms" with "no prevision of the end they were achieving." Though not stated explicitly by Russell, we might add the doctrine, a commonplace in modern science, that mental phenomena—and indeed life itself—are comparative latecomers in the long history of the earth. (2) Human life is bounded by physical death and each individual comes to a permanent end at his physical death. We might add to this the observation that the span of human life is comparatively short, enough so that in some cases we can, with fair confidence, predict the major consequences of certain actions insofar as they will affect a given individual throughout his whole remaining life. (3) Not only each individual but also the human race as a species is doomed to extinction "beneath the debris of a universe in ruins."

So much, then, for the main features of a Russellian world. Because the notion of benefits and goods plays an important part in the remainder of my discussion, I want to introduce one further technical expression—"Russellian benefit." A Russellian benefit is one that could accrue to a person in a Russellian world. A contented old age would be, I suppose, a Russellian benefit, as would a thrill of sexual pleasure or a good reputation. Going to heaven when one dies, though a benefit, is not a Russellian benefit. Russellian benefits are only the benefits possible in a Russellian world. But one can have Russellian benefits even if the world is not Russellian. In such a case there might, however, also be other benefits, such as going to heaven.

Could the actual world be Russellian? Well, I take it to be an important feature of the actual world that human beings exist in it and that in it their actions fall, at least sometimes, within the sphere of morality—that is, they have moral obligations to act (or to refrain from acting) in certain ways. And if they do not act in those ways, then they are properly subject to a special and peculiar sort of adverse judgment (unless it happens that there are special circumstances that serve to excuse their failure to fulfill the obligations). People who do not fulfill their obligations are not merely stupid or weak or unlucky; they are morally reprehensible. . . .

I claim that in the actual world we have some obligations that, when we fulfill them, will confer on us no net Russellian benefit—in fact, they will result in a Russellian loss. If the world is Russellian, then Russellian benefits and losses are the only benefits and losses, and also then we have moral obligations whose fulfillment will result in a net loss of good to the one who fulfills them. I suggest, however, that it would be very strange to have such obligations—strange not simply in the sense of being unexpected or surprising but in some deeper way. I do not suggest that it is strange in the sense of having a straightforward logical defect, of being self-contradictory to claim that we have such obligations. Perhaps the best thing to say is that were it a fact that we had such obligations, then the world that included such a fact would be absurd—we would be living in a crazy world. . . .

The existence of morality in a Russellian world, it may be said, is not at all absurd because its existence there can be given a perfectly straightforward explanation: morality has a survival value for a species such as ours because it makes possible continued cooperation and things of that sort. So it is no more absurd that people have moral obligations than it is absurd that they have opposable thumbs.

I think that this line of explanation will work only if one analyzes obligations into feelings, or beliefs. I think it is plausible (though I am not sure it is correct) to suppose that everyone's having feelings of moral obligation might have a survival value for a species such as Man, given of course that these feelings were attached to patterns of action that contributed to such survival. And if that is so, then it is not implausible to suppose that there may be a survival value for the species even in a moral feeling that leads to the death of the individual who has it. So far so good. But this observation, even if true, is not relevant to the queerness with which I am here concerned. For I have not suggested that the existence of moral feelings would be absurd in a Russellian world; it is rather the existence of moral *obligations* that is absurd, and I think it important to make the distinction. It is quite possible, it seems to me, for one to feel (or to believe) that he has a certain obligation without actually having it, and also vice versa. Now, beliefs and feelings will presumably have some effect upon actions, and this effect may possibly contribute to the survival of the species. But, so far as I can see, the addition of actual moral obligations to these moral beliefs and feelings will make no further contribution to action nor will the actual obligations have an effect upon action in the absence of the corresponding feelings and beliefs. So it seems that neither with nor without the appropriate feelings will moral obligations contribute to the survival of the species. Consequently, an "evolutionary" approach such as this cannot serve to explain the existence of moral obligations, unless one rejects my distinction and equates the obligations with the feelings.

And finally, I think that morality will not be queer in the way I allege, or at least it will not be as queer as I think, if it should be the case that every obligation yields a Russellian benefit to the one who fulfills it. Given the caveat expressed earlier, one can perhaps make some sense out of the notion of a Russellian good or benefit for a sentient organism in a Russellian world. And one could, I suppose, without further queerness imagine that such an organism might aim toward achieving such goods. And we could further suppose that there were certain actions—those that were "obligations"—that would, in contrast with other actions, actually yield such benefits to the organism that performed them. And finally, it might not be too implausible to claim that an organism that failed to perform such an action was defective in some way and that some adverse judgment was appropriate.

Morality, however, seems to require us to hold that certain organisms (namely, human beings) have in addition to their ordinary properties and relations another special relation to certain actions. This relation is that of being "obligated" to perform those actions. And some of those actions are pretty clearly such that they will yield only Russellian losses to the one who performs them. Nevertheless, we are supposed to hold that a person who does not perform an action to which he is thus related is defective in some serious and important way and an adverse judgment is appropriate against him. And that certainly does seem odd. . . .

The oddity we have been considering is, I suspect, the most important root of the celebrated and somewhat confused question, "Why should I be moral?" (Characteristically, I think, the person who asks that question is asking to have the queerness of that situation illuminated.) From time to time there are philosophers who make an attempt to argue—perhaps only a halfhearted attempt—that being moral really is in one's interest after all. Kurt Baier, it seems to me, proposes a reply of this sort. He says:

> Moralities are systems of principles whose acceptance by everyone as overruling the dictates of self-interest is in the interest of everyone alike though following the rules of a morality is not of course identical with following self-interest. . . .
>
> The answer to our question 'Why should we be moral?' is therefore as follows. We should be moral because being moral is following rules designed to overrule self-interest whenever it is in the interest of everyone alike that everyone should set aside his interest.

As I say, this seems to be an argument to the effect that it really is in everyone's interest to be moral. I suppose that Baier is here probably talking about Russellian interests. At least, we must interpret him in that way if his argument is to be applicable in this context, and I will proceed on that assumption. But how exactly is the argument to be made out?

It appears here to begin with a premise something like

> (A) It is in everyone's best interest (including mine, presumably) for everyone (including me) to be moral.

This premise itself appears to be supported earlier by reference to Hobbes. As I understand it, the idea is that without morality people will live in a "state of nature," and life will be nasty, brutish, and short. Well, perhaps so. At any rate, let us accept (A) for the moment. From (A) we can derive

> (B) It is in my best interest for everyone (including me) to be moral.

And from (B) perhaps one derives

> (C) It is in my best interest for me to be moral.

And (C) may be taken to answer the question, "Why should I be moral?" Furthermore, if (C) is true, then moral obligation will at least not have the sort of queerness that I have been alleging.

Unfortunately, however, the argument outlined above is invalid. The derivation of (B) from (A) *may* be all right, but the derivation of (C) from (B) is invalid. What does follow from (B) is

> (C′) It is in my best interest for me to be moral if everyone else is moral.

The argument thus serves to show that it is in a given person's interest to be moral only on the assumption that everyone else in the world is moral. It might, of course, be difficult to find someone ready to make that assumption. . . .

Hobbes may have been right in supposing that life in the state of nature would be short, etc. But some lives are short anyway. In fact, some lives are short just because the demands of morality are observed. Such a life is not bound to have been shorter in the state of nature. Nor is it bound to have been less happy, less pleasurable, and so forth. In fact, does it not seem obvious that *my* best Russellian interest will be further advanced in a situation in which everyone else acts morally but I act immorally (in selected cases) than it will be in case everyone, including me, acts morally? It certainly seems so. It can, of course, be observed that if I act immorally then so will other people, perhaps reducing my benefits. In the present state of the world that is certainly true. But in the present state of the world it is also true, as I observed earlier, that many other people will act immorally *anyway*, regardless of what I do.

A more realistic approach is taken by Richard Brandt. He asks, "Is it *reasonable* for me to do my duty if it conflicts seriously with my personal welfare?" After distinguishing several possible senses of this question, he chooses a single one to discuss further, presumably a sense that he thinks important. As reformulated, the question is now: "Given that doing x is my duty and that doing some conflicting act y will maximize my personal welfare, will the performance of x instead of y satisfy my reflective preferences better?" And the conclusion to which he comes is that "the correct answer may vary from one person to another. It depends on what kind of person one is, what one cares about." And within Russellian limits Brandt must surely be right in this. But he goes on to say, "It is, of course, no defense of one's failure to do one's duty, before others or society, to say that doing so is not 'reasonable' for one in this sense." And this is just to bring the queer element back in. It is to suppose that besides "the kind of person" I am and my particular, pattern of "cares" and interests there is something else, my duty, which may go against these and in any case properly overrides them. And one feels that there must be some sense of "reasonable" in which one can ask whether a world in which that is true is a reasonable world, whether such a world makes any sense. . . .

I turn now to another sort of view, stronger I think than any of these others, which accepts that queerness but goes no further. And one who holds this view will also hold, I think, that the question "Why should I be moral?" must be rejected in one way or another. A person who holds this view will say that it is simply a fact that we have the moral obligations that we do have, and that is all there is to it. If they sometimes result in a loss of good, then that too is just a fact. These may be puzzling or surprising facts, but there are lots of puzzling and surprising things about the world. In a Russellian world, morality will be, I suppose, an "emergent" phenomenon; it will be a feature of certain effects though it is not a feature of their causes. But the wetness of water is an emergent feature, too. It is not a property of either hydrogen or oxygen. And there is really nothing more to be said; somewhere we must come to an end of reasons and explanations. We have our duties. We can fulfill them and be moral, or we can ignore them and be immoral. If all that is crazy and absurd—well, so be it. Who are we to say that the world is not crazy and absurd? . . .

This brings to an end the major part of my discussion. If I have been successful at all you will have shared with me to some extent in the sense of the queerness of morality, its absurdity in a Russellian world. If you also share the conviction that it cannot in the end be absurd in that way, then perhaps you will also be attracted to some religious view of the world. Perhaps you also will say that morality must have some deeper grip upon the world than a Russellian view allows. And, consequently, things like mind and purpose must also be deeper in the real world than they would be in a Russellian world. They must be more original, more controlling. The accidental collocation of atoms cannot be either primeval or final, nor can the grave be an end. But of course that would be only a beginning, a sketch waiting to be filled in.

We cannot here do much to fill it in further. But I should like to close with a final, and rather tentative suggestion, as to a direction in which one might move in thinking about the place of morality in the world. It is suggested to me by certain elements in my own religion, Christianity.

I come more and more to think that morality, while a fact, is a twisted and distorted fact. Or perhaps better, that it is a barely recognizable version of another fact, a version adapted to a twisted and distorted world. It is something like, I suppose, the way in which the pine that grows at timberline, wind blasted and twisted low against the rock, is a version of the tall and symmetrical tree that grows lower on the slopes. I think it may be that the related notions of sacrifice and gift represent (or come close to representing) the fact, that is, the pattern of life, whose distorted version we know here as morality. Imagine a situation, an "economy" if you will, in which no one ever buys or trades for or seizes any good thing. But whatever good he enjoys it is either one which he himself has created or else one which he receives as a free and unconditional gift. And as soon as he has tasted it and seen that it is good he stands ready to give it away in his turn as soon as the opportunity arises. In such a place, if one were to speak either of his rights or his duties, his remark might be met with puzzled laughter as his hearers struggled to recall an ancient world in which those terms referred to something important.

We have, of course, even now some occasions that tend in this direction. Within some families perhaps, or even in a regiment in desperate battle, people may for a time pass largely beyond morality and live lives of gift and sacrifice. On those occasions nothing would be lost if the moral concepts and the moral language were to disappear. But it is probably not possible that such situations and occasions should be more than rare exceptions in the daily life of the present world. Christianity, however, which tells us that the present world is "fallen" and hence leads us to expect a distortion in its important features, also tells us that one day the redemption of the world will be complete and that then all things shall be made new. And it seems to me to suggest an "economy" more akin to that of gift and sacrifice than to that of rights and duties. If something like that should be true, then perhaps morality, like the Marxist state, is destined to whither away (unless perchance it should happen to survive in hell).

Christianity, then, I think is related to the queerness of morality in one way and perhaps in two. In the first instance, it provides a view of the world in which morality is not an absurdity. It gives morality a deeper place in the world than does a Russellian view and thus permits it to "make sense." But in the second instance, it perhaps suggests that morality is not the deepest thing, that it is provisional and transitory, that it is due to serve its use and then to pass away in favor of something richer and deeper. Perhaps we can say that it begins by inverting the quotation with which I began and by telling us that, since God exists, not everything is permitted; but it may also go on to tell us that, since God exists, in the end there shall be no occasion for any prohibition.

Morality Is Innate

W.T. STACE

W.T. Stace (1886-1967) was educated at Trinity College, Dublin, and served in the British Civil Service in Ceylon. He came to teach at Princeton University in 1932 and later wrote a series of influential books including *Time and Eternity* and *The Concept of Morals*, from which the present selection is taken. Stace argues that moral standards are objective in the strong sense that they are the same cross-culturally. He does not mean that particular moral rules, which are conditioned by different cultural factual understandings, are identical. He argues that only very general moral laws or values are the same. He identifies altruism as the fundamental and most general moral law. Stace claims to have discovered this law in various stages of development in different cultures, from primitive intuitions to sophisticated intellectual formulations. He argues that the more altruistic a culture is the more morally advanced it is. He accuses cultural relativists of simplistic and faulty reasoning when they fail to recognize different developmental stages of altruism and confuse these stages with fundamentally different values. Stace thinks this is like classifying a human child and a human adult as different species. Stace is comfortable using the data presented by the relativists to argue for objective standards and he asserts that there can be no such thing as moral progress in a culture if there is not some objective standard to use to judge the culture at each stage.

QUESTIONS

1. Why does Stace begin by distinguishing between particularmaxims and general moral laws?
2. According to the author, why will there always be differences of opinion about particular moral details between cultures even if a general moral law is held in common?
3. Is Stace optimistic that most people will recognize an abstract formulation of a moral truth?
4. In what state does the author expect to find the principle of altruism among primitive peoples?
5. According to Stace, how does altruism first appear?
6. How does Stace argue that burning witches could be altruistic?
7. According to the author, how is altruism connected to human social relations?
8. Why is moral progress impossible for the relativist, according to the author?
9. How does Stace distinguish between higher and lower moralities?

■ ■ ■

Let us begin by carefully explaining what we do *not* mean, in order that what we *do* mean may appear in its true light. We really do assert that all men at all times and in all lands do subscribe and have subscribed to one and the same morality. But there are many different senses in which this might be maintained. And some of these senses of the proposition really are ridiculous and contrary to all evidence. Let us eliminate these false and absurd senses of the doctrine. And let us then see whether we may not be left with something which can reasonably be believed.

First of all, then, I do *not* mean that all the peoples and races of the world take the same views as we do of murder, stealing, suicide, sex intercourse, truthfulness, courage, honesty. We should look, amid differing moral systems, not for a consensus of opinions upon the *particular* duties of life, or the *particular* maxims of morality, but for some recognition of the *general* law of morals. This general law is the principle of altruism. This is the *essence* of morals. And all that is asserted is that all moralities have this for their essence. There are certain to be many different views as to what particular kinds of action are altruistic. . . .

Hence, even in the same country, in the same age, and given the same sets of circumstances, there will always be differences of opinion as to particular duties and maxims of morality. All we can reasonably expect to find, therefore, amid the various moralities of the world, is a certain uniformity of *inner spirit*, not a one to one correspondence of particular details. Failure to understand this is one cause of the widespread acceptance of the doctrine of ethical relativity. We shall look to see whether we can discern amid different moral codes the inner spirit of altruism as their essence.

Secondly, I do not mean that all human beings have always accepted the morality of altruism *in the form or in the words* in which it is expressed here. "Act always so as to increase human happiness as much as possible. And at the same time act on the principle that all persons, including yourself, are intrinsically of equal value." It would indeed be ridiculous to maintain that everyone has always accepted *this formulation* of morality. So far as I know, no one except myself has ever expressed the essence of morals precisely in this way. And now that it has been so expressed, ninety per cent of humanity will be incapable of even understanding what the words mean. And of those who do understand it, probably far more than ninety per cent will flatly refuse to accept it. . . .

When it is said that the principle of altruism is found everywhere, this does *not* mean that it is found everywhere complete and fully developed. Among primitive peoples, I have no doubt, it is found only in rudimentary, foetus-like, or stunted forms. Logically, no doubt, a person must either have an idea or not have it. Or at any rate this will be true if by an idea one means an explicit belief, a proposition held before the intellect with its determinate parts of subject, copula, and predicate. Either it is asserted or it is not asserted. It may, of course, be merely entertained. But in any case it exists in the mind either full-blown or not at all. But ideas, for the most part, are not propositions. They appear in the human mind, first of all, as vague feelings. It is only after a long evolution that they slowly begin to take on, in the mind's womb, the form of explicit judgments with the differentiated parts of subject, predicate, and copula. Often enough they do not finally take on this form till they are expressed in words to other people. They lurk in dark places of the mind, obscure, unverbalized, formless. Even the owner of them scarcely knows that they are there until, for some reason or other, the searchlight is turned upon them. Ideas are organisms. They proliferate and grow. They develop from rudimentary beginnings. And as a human foetus may be unrecognizable as human, so may an idea in its origins be unrecognizable as identical with what it is to become when it is fully developed.

Now what is alleged regarding the principle of altruism is this. If you take an advanced code of morals, such as that of Christianity, or that of Confucius, you will probably find the principle stated somewhere in its literature, or in the sayings of its prophets, fairly explicitly—though even here you will never find it stated in its abstract form with philosophical accuracy. It will be expressed in literary, as distinguished from philosophical or scientific, language. For it was not intended for philosophers or scientists, but for the masses of men. Thus in Christian literature it appears as the golden rule, and in many other forms too. But if you take some primitive moral code, that of a people relatively savage and uncivilized, you will not find it stated in explicit form at all. Such a people might even repudiate it as ridiculous if it were put to them in its complete and developed shape. And yet it may be there, deeply buried among their chaotic and primitive notions, forming the living principle and root out of which those notions are slowly growing. And it may be there in a form so primitive and crude that it may require considerable penetration and insight to recognize it at all. And as it frequently happens that the more learning a man possesses, the less insight he has, it is not to be wondered at that there are men whose minds are choked with masses of anthropological facts, which are yet barren and useless because they cannot penetrate to the spirit which informs those facts. . . .

The ethical relativist is fond of pointing to different levels of moral development and declaring that they exhibit different and mutually inconsistent sets of moral codes. In one age and place, he tells us, it is considered quite right for the inhabitants of one village, or the members of a wandering tribe, to murder, pillage, and destroy the property of people living a few miles away. In another age and place, the same identical acts are considered immoral. Obviously you have here two quite different and mutually contradictory moral codes. And you are supposed from this to conclude to the truth of the doctrine of ethical relativity.

Could anything be more shallow? Surely this is due to looking unintelligently at the dead surfaces of things and having no insight into their living pulsating interiors. If we treat the facts as dessicated museum specimens, we may well arrive at such conclusions. We attach our labels to the dead specimens, and we find that they differ from one another. They are therefore different sets of moral ideas, they have nothing in common, they contradict one another, and consequently they contradict the whole idea of a universal morality. But this is to forget that morals are human and therefore grow. If the biologist were to take the corpses of a human foetus, a child, and a grown man, dry them, and pin them down in glass cases, as we pin down dead butterflies, he might perhaps conclude that he had before him three entirely different species of animals. Their characters might well appear mutually inconsistent. Biologists do not make these silly mistakes because, being themselves living and growing beings, they interpret the facts with the conceptions of life and growth in their minds. But the ethical relativist is apparently determined to interpret living facts as if they were dead ones. He cannot see that the continuous extensions of the application of the sentiment of altruism, its extension from the family to the tribe, from the tribe to the nation, from the nation to humanity, are an example, not of a heterogeneous collection of different and mutually inconsistent ideas, but of a single idea in different stages of its growth. . . .

Another frequent source of confusion is the failure to distinguish between means and ends. The moral man aims always and everywhere at one single end, the happiness of others. But in different countries and different ages opinions differ as to the best means of achieving this end. And straightway these differences of means are seized upon as importing different moral standards, although it is plain that it is the end which is the standard, not the means. For example, our forefathers burned witches alive, while we regard such action with horror. This is not, as is commonly supposed, evidence of mutually incompatible moral standards. It is evidence of the existence of different opinions as to how one and the same standard should be applied, and as to the means which should be adopted to achieve the standard. For our forefathers did not burn witches for amusement. Or if any of them were so motivated, they would not have met with general approval. They burned them because they genuinely believed that this was one essential means towards the saving of souls—whether the souls of the witches themselves or of those innocents whom they might delude if allowed to live. That is to say, their action was altruistic. They were therefore guided by exactly the same moral standard as are modern persons who do not burn witches, but who instead endow hospitals or send missionaries to non-Christian lands.

To sum up what has so far been said. There actually is a single universal morality which all humanity has recognized in the past and recognizes today. But this bold statement does not *mean* that men's moral ideas about particular duties or crimes are everywhere the same. It is compatible with the widest differences in such matters. It does not mean that the single moral law is everywhere understood as being the abstract principle which we formulated. It is compatible with an almost universal refusal to admit that that principle is the true law of morals at all. Finally, it does not mean that the principle of altruism, in any shape or form, appears in all moral codes in an easily recognizable or fully developed form. What it does mean is that the principle of altruism is the abstract statement of that which, whether as vague feeling or as conceptual idea, is everywhere the moving spirit and the inner life of whatever morality exists. Here it is no more than a scarcely visible seed. There it is a full grown tree. Here it is dim and misty. There it shines out with the purity of a star. Here it is overlaid and encrusted with barbarities. There it is found nearly pure. Wherever there is morality at all, there, in that place, there is altruism in greater or less degree. Where there is no altruism—and there may be, for all I know, tribes of men so low that they exhibit no altruism at all, though I doubt it—there, in that place, there is no morality.

Take any set of so-called moral ideas. First pare away from it the irrational taboos and prejudices, the mere physical dislikes, the local and inessential customs and traditions, with which—in the minds of its adherents (and in the minds of ethical relativists)—it is invariably mixed up. Pare away next those customs which, though not irrational nor of merely physical origin, are based on sanitary, medical, or other non-ethical considerations. Try to get at the *essence* of the morality in question, and you will find that this essence consists in the idea of altruism, that is, the idea of being fair, kind, just, considerate (so far as these terms are understood), to one's neighbour (whoever, at the particular stage of development, is understood to be one's neighbour), of treating him as one would oneself like to be treated, the idea of having regard for the needs and desires of other people—in a word, the idea of unselfishness. The statement that all men recognize the same morality means only that the idea of the obligation to behave thus is found, in some shape or form, in greater degree or less, in every human society; that this is the pith and marrow of whatever morality any particular human society does actually recognize. Does it require learned disquisitions in anthropology, expeditions to the Antipodes, the ostentatious display of "evidence" gathered from the ends of the earth, to prove that this is true? Surely not. For how could it possibly be false? It is impossible to believe that human beings exist, the core of whose essential relations to one another does not consist in at least an elementary consideration for one another's needs, desires, and feelings—that is to say, in some form and degree of altruistic action. For such consideration is the necessary prerequisite of any sort of social intercourse. And social intercourse of some kind is universal in all humanity, because it is as necessary to the human animal as is bread. Human beings simply could not meet, live together, exchange amenities of any kind, without such consideration. It is therefore not conceivable that there should exist social groups who are without the notion of altruism, or among whom the notion is not the foundation of their relations to one another. Morality is nothing but the necessary relations to one another of human beings. It is simply the set of principles which governs those relations. And it is a necessity of human nature that these principles should always be of the nature of altruism, that is, that they should be based upon mutual consideration. And it therefore follows that the essential idea of morality must be the same everywhere. There is no need to penetrate the jungles of Africa, the steppes of Siberia, in search of evidence of this. One must believe it, unless one thinks, with Hobbes, that there are, or may have been, men fundamentally anti-social, living in a war of all against all, even against their own children. And I am not aware that any anthropologist supports Hobbes's abstractions in this respect. . . .

I pointed out that ethical relativity renders meaningless many moral judgments which form an essential part of the beliefs of all cultured persons, and which we are all persuaded, in practice, do have both meaning and truth. Among these were all judgments which compare one moral code with another for the purpose of deciding which is the "higher," which the "lower"—judgments such as that Christian ethics are higher than the ethics of Australian bushmen. Also all judgments which assert that there has been, or ever could be, any "progress" in moral ideas were, we saw, meaningless if ethical relativity is true. For according to that doctrine there can be no common moral standard by which different moral systems can be judged. Hence the ethical relativist can give no better account of such judgments than to say that they express nothing but our egoism and self-conceit. "Higher" can mean nothing except "more like me and my ideas." Thus the ethical relativist made complete nonsense of our moral beliefs.

It is already partly possible to give intelligible meaning to such judgments in the light of the considerations adduced. They cannot indeed be finally and fully justified until we have discovered the empirical meaning of the word "ought." But already we can go a long way towards understanding them. This is because we have discovered a common standard by reference to which all local and ephemeral standards and ideas can be judged. This common standard is the principle of altruism.

A lower morality is one in which the altruistic principle, though it is present, is undeveloped. A higher morality is one in which it is more perfectly developed. The difference is a difference in the degree of unselfishness demanded by the moralities in question. If Christianity contains the highest ethical doctrine yet given to the world, this is because in it the principle of unselfishness shines out pure and clear, and because the principle is extended to all human beings; whereas in lower moralities the idea of altruism is dim, is obscured by other elements, is encrusted with barbarisms and even cruelties, is narrowly and meanly interpreted, and is extended only to a man's immediate friends, family, fellow tribesmen, or fellow nationals. Progress in moral ideas means, in our view, not egregious self-conceit, but the steady development and unfolding of more and more altruistic rules of conduct.

This is surely a more sensible view than that which denies to the idea of higher and lower moralities any legitimate meaning at all. It is no wonder that plain sensible men are suspicious of philosophy and reject its claims to intellectual leadership when they find that philosophers become so dazzled and bewildered by their own brilliant but empty dialectic that they lose all touch with the actual world, lose touch with man's moral intuitions, cannot keep their feet upon the earth, but drift off into a cloudland, of clever falsehoods. For this is what they do when they allow themselves, in the interests of a hair-brained theory, to deny meaning to plain statements of fact of which everyone, except themselves, knows the meaning. Then it is that we see exhibited before our eyes the spectacle of cleverness without wisdom, of learning without sense.

How Are Governments Constituted?

Chapter Preface

Death and taxes are said to be inevitable, and taxes presuppose some form of government. Why does government seem so inevitable and what is its purpose? What makes a government just and legitimate? Who should pick leaders and how much power should these leaders have over people's lives? What is the basis for law? Political philosophers are concerned with these kinds of questions. One way to explain the near universal existence of government is to consider the alternative. English philosopher Thomas Hobbes, an atheist, paints a pessimistic picture of what human beings are like without government in a brutish "state of nature." There is no justice or God-ordained set of civil laws, only individuals competing with one another for limited resources that are necessary for survival. No security or cultural progress is possible until each person turns over his right to self-governance to an absolute sovereign power that can institute laws, create justice, and protect individuals and their property from one another. Fellow English philosopher John Locke, a theist, is less pessimistic about the state of nature and believes that many God-given rights exist even without government. He agrees, however, with Hobbes that government is necessary to protect people and property. Since he takes a less extreme view of the state of nature than Hobbes does, Locke does not think it is necessary to give as much power to government as Hobbes does, and Locke argues that men dissolve bad governments.

Another issue surrounding governments is what rights should a government protect—and, perhaps more importantly, whom should the government protect? Locke believes government should protect private property. Private property comes into existence when people "mix" their labor, which they own, with things in the environment like land or materials, thus "improving" these things by making them more valuable and useful to people. Money, which makes it possible to store wealth in a nonperishable form, provides the necessary wealth for the development of science and industry. Locke's teachings were used to justify the American Revolution. German philosopher Karl Marx attacks private property. He argues that, once industrial and scientific progress reaches a certain point, private ownership of the means of industrial production becomes concentrated in the hands of the bourgeois class, who oppress the workers, the proletariat class, and make their lives impossible. Marx believes that, as part of an inevitable historical process, the proletariat will rise against the minority bourgeoisie and abolish private property in favor of a socialist state where the means of production will be owned by all and used for the common good. He argues that a higher kind of morality and justice would then emerge.

Harvard philosopher John Rawls does not agree with Marx that justice ultimately requires the abolition of private property, but he believes that a just state must consider the interests of the least well-off and not merely the most successful members of society. He argues that a just society is one that a rational person would choose given the qualification that he or she would not know in advance what social and economic position they would have in that society. Since the rational person might end up somewhere near the bottom of the society, such a person would want to insure that the political and economic structures of society would make life reasonably good for people at the bottom.

Libertarian philosopher John Hospers has a much different approach to justice. He is not interested in setting up mechanisms that will particularly benefit the least well-off. Rather, he begins with a strong affirmation of individual rights to life and property and wants to prevent government, which he considers highly dangerous, from taking control of people's lives. When government forces people to work to pay unnecessary taxes, says Hospers, it makes slaves of them. Hospers argues that the government only exists to provide protection for persons, property, and contracts. Government may not decide what people can and cannot do, as long as their actions do not harm others. Government does not have the right to enforce benevolence or impose a governmental educational agenda on people.

Governments Exist to Provide Security

THOMAS HOBBES

English philosopher Thomas Hobbes (1588-1679) made significant contributions to metaphysics, psychology, and political philosophy. He was impressed by the laws of physical science and the precise logic of geometry. In his masterpiece, *Leviathan*, he attempts to explain the authority governments have to rule and the duty citizens have to obey governments. In the present viewpoint, extracted from *Leviathan*, Hobbes presents his reasoning without any appeal to a divine mandate or plan. Rather, he begins with his understanding of human nature and carefully argues for the necessity and moral justification of both an absolute sovereign and of certain individual rights. In a state of nature, one in which there is no sovereign, human beings function only as competitive individuals at war with one another over resources they all desire. Hobbes claims that there is no security or stability, and

From *Leviathan* by Thomas Hobbes. Oxford: Clarendon Press, 1909.

human life is "solitary, poor, nasty, brutish, and short." This terrible situation can only be corrected by a power great enough to compel individual humans to obedience. Humans create such a power by covenanting together and each transferring the right that he has to govern himself to a sovereign who establishes law and order in exchange for the transfer. A just society then becomes possible where humans can devote their energy to science and commerce and productive living rather than to mere self-defense against one another.

QUESTIONS

1. What, according to Hobbes, is the origin of war? What is it like to live in a state of war?
2. How does the author distinguish between a right and a law? What are the first two laws of nature?
3. What, according to Hobbes, is impossible for a person to abandon or transfer? Why?
4. How does the author explain the origin of justice?
5. What reasons does Hobbes give for claiming that justice is rational and injustice irrational?
6. According to the author, how does a commonwealth do what the laws of nature cannot?

■ ■ ■

Of the Natural Condition of Mankind as Concerning Their Felicity and Misery

Men by nature equal. Nature hath made men so equal, in the faculties of the body, and mind; as that though there be found one man sometimes manifestly stronger in body, or of quicker mind than another; yet when all is reckoned together, the difference between man, and man, is not so considerable, as that one man can thereupon claim to himself any benefit, to which another may not pretend, as well as he. For as to the strength of body, the weakest has strength enough to kill the strongest, either by secret machination, or by confederacy with others, that are in the same danger with himself.

And as to the faculties of the mind, setting aside the arts grounded upon words, and especially that skill of proceeding upon general, and infallible rules, called science; which very few have, and but in few things; as being not a native faculty, born with us; nor attained, as prudence, while we look after somewhat else, I find yet a greater equality amongst men, than that of strength. For prudence, is but experience; which equal time, equally bestows on all men, in those things they equally apply themselves unto. That which may perhaps make such equality incredible, is but a vain conceit of one's own wisdom, which almost all men think they have in a greater degree, than the vulgar; that is, than all men but themselves, and a few others, whom by fame, or for concurring with themselves, they approve. For such is the nature of men, that howsoever they may acknowledge many others to be more witty, or more eloquent, or more learned; yet they will hardly believe there be many so wise as themselves; for they see their own wit at hand, and other men's at a distance. But this proveth rather that men are in that point equal, than unequal. For there is not ordinarily a greater sign of the equal distribution of any thing, than that every man is contented with his share.

From equality proceeds diffidence. From this equality of ability, ariseth equality of hope in the attaining of our ends. And therefore if any two men desire the same thing, which nevertheless they cannot both enjoy, they become enemies; and in the way to their end, which is principally their own conservation, and sometimes their delectation only, endeavour to destroy, or subdue one another. And from hence it comes to pass, that where an invader hath no more to fear, than another man's single power; if one plant, sow, build, or possess a convenient seat, others may probably be expected to come prepared with forces united, to dispossess, and deprive him, not only of the fruit of his labour, but also of his life, or liberty. And the invader again is in the like danger of another.

From diffidence war. And from this diffidence of one another, there is no way for any man to secure himself, so reasonable, as anticipation; that is, by force, or wiles, to master the persons of all men he can, so long, till he see no other power great enough to endanger him: and this is no more than his own conservation requireth, and is generally allowed. Also because there be some, that taking pleasure in contemplating their own power in the acts of conquest, which they pursue farther than their security requires; if others, that otherwise would be glad to be at ease within modest bounds, should not by invasion increase their power, they would not be able, long time, by standing only on their defence, to subsist. And by consequence, such augmentation of dominion over men being necessary to a man's conservation, it ought to be allowed him.

Again, men have no pleasure, but on the contrary a great deal of grief, in keeping company, where there is no power able to over-awe them all. For every man looketh that his companion should value him, at the same rate he sets upon himself: and upon all signs of contempt, or undervaluing, naturally endeavours, as far as he dares, (which amongst them that have no common power to keep them in quiet, is far enough to make them destroy each other), to extort a greater value from his contemners, by damage; and from others, by the example.

So that in the nature of man, we find three principal causes of quarrel. First, competition; secondly, diffidence; thirdly, glory.

The first, maketh men invade for gain; the second, for safety; and the third, for reputation. The first use violence, to make themselves masters of other men's persons, wives, children, and cattle; the second, to defend them; the third, for trifles, as a word, a smile, a different opinion, and any other sign of undervalue, either direct in their persons, or by reflection in their kindred, their friends, their nation, their profession, or their name.

Out of civil states, there is always war of every one against every one. Hereby it is manifest, that during the time men live without a common power to keep them all in awe, they are in that condition which is called war; and such a war, as is of every man, against every man. For WAR, consisteth not in battle only, or the act of fighting; but in a tract of time, wherein the will to contend by battle is sufficiently known: and therefore the notion of *time*, is to be considered in the nature of war; as it is in the nature of weather. For as the nature of foul weather, lieth not in a shower or two of rain; but in an inclination thereto of many days together: so the nature of war, consisteth not in actual fighting; but in the known disposition thereto, during all the time there is no assurance to the contrary. All other time is PEACE.

The incommodities of such a war. Whatsoever therefore is consequent to a time of war, where every man is enemy to every man, the same is consequent to the time, wherein men live without other security, than what their own strength, and their own invention shall furnish them withal. In such condition, there is no place for industry; because the fruit thereof is uncertain: and consequently no culture of the earth; no navigation, nor use of the commodities that may be imported by sea; no commodious building; no instruments of moving, and removing, such things as require much force; no knowledge of the face of the earth; no account of time; no arts; no letters; no society; and which is worst of all, continual fear, and danger of violent death; and the life of man, solitary, poor, nasty, brutish, and short.

It may seem strange to some man, that has not well weighed these things; that nature should thus dissociate, and render men apt to invade, and destroy one another: and he may therefore, not trusting to this inference, made from the passions, desire perhaps to have the same confirmed by experience. Let him therefore consider with himself, when taking a journey, he arms himself, and seeks to go well accompanied; when going to sleep, he locks his doors; when even in his house he locks his chests; and this when he knows there be laws, and public officers, armed, to revenge all injuries shall be done him; what opinion he has of his fellow-subjects, when he rides armed; of his fellow citizens, when he locks his doors; and of his children, and servants, when he locks his chests. Does he not there as much accuse mankind by his actions, as I do by my words? But neither of us accuse man's nature in it. The desires, and other passions of man, are in themselves no sin. No more are the actions, that proceed from those passions, till they know a law that forbids them: which till laws be made they cannot know; nor can any law be made, till they have agreed upon the person that shall make it.

It may peradventure be thought, there was never such a time, nor condition of war as this; and I believe it was never generally so, over all the world: but there are many places, where they live so now. For the savage people in many places of America, except the government of small families, the concord whereof dependeth on natural lust, have no government at all; and live at this day in that brutish manner, as I said before. Howsoever, it may be perceived what manner of life there would be, where there were no common power to fear, by the manner of life, which men that have formerly lived under a peaceful government, use to degenerate into, in a civil war.

But though there had never been any time, wherein particular men were in a condition of war one against another; yet in all times, kings, and persons of sovereign authority, because of their independency, are in continual jealousies, and in the state and posture of gladiators; having their weapons pointing, and their eyes fixed on one another; that is, their forts, garrisons, and guns upon the frontiers of their kingdoms; and continual spies upon their neighbours; which is a posture of war. But because they uphold thereby, the industry of their subjects; there does not follow from it, that misery, which accompanies the liberty of particular men.

In such a war nothing is unjust. To this war of every man, against every man, this also is consequent; that nothing can be unjust. The notions of right and wrong, justice and injustice have there no place. Where there is no common power, there is no law: where no law, no injustice. Force, and fraud, are in war the two cardinal virtues. Justice, and injustice are none of the faculties neither of the body, nor mind. If they were, they might be in a man that were alone in the world, as well as his senses, and passions. They are qualities, that relate to men in society, not in solitude. It is consequent also to the same condition, that there be no propriety, no dominion, no *mine* and *thine* distinct; but only that to be every man's, that he can get: and for so long, as he can keep it. And thus much for the ill condition, which man by mere nature is actually placed in; though with a possibility to come out of it, consisting partly in the passions, partly in his reason.

The passions that incline men to peace. The passions that incline men to peace, are fear of death; desire of such things as are necessary to commodious living; and a hope by their industry to obtain them. And reason suggesteth convenient articles of peace, upon which men may be drawn to agreement. These articles, are they, which otherwise are called the Laws of Nature. . . .

Of the First and Second Natural Laws, and of Contracts

Right of nature what. THE RIGHT OF NATURE, which writers commonly call *jus naturale*, is the liberty each man hath, to use his own power, as he will himself, for the preservation of his own nature; that is to say, of his own life; and consequently, of doing any thing, which in his own judgment, and reason, he shall conceive to be the aptest means thereunto.

Liberty what. By LIBERTY is understood, according to the proper signification of the word, the absence of external impediments: which impediments, may oft take away part of a man's power to do what he would; but cannot hinder him from using the power left him, according as his judgment, and reason shall dictate to him.

A law of nature what. Difference of right and law. A LAW OF NATURE, *lex naturalis,* is a precept or general rule, found out by reason, by which a man is forbidden to do that, which is destructive of his life, or taketh away the means of preserving the same; and to omit that, by which he thinketh it may be best preserved. For though they that speak of this subject, use to confound *jus,* and *lex, right* and *law*: yet they ought to be distinguished; because RIGHT, consisteth in liberty to do, or to forbear: whereas LAW, determineth, and bindeth to one of them: so that law, and right, differ as much, as obligation, and liberty; which in one and the same matter are inconsistent.

Naturally every man has right to every thing. The fundamental law of nature. And because the condition of man, as hath been declared, is a condition of war of every one against every one; in which case every one is governed by his own reason; and there is nothing he can make use of, that may not be a help unto him, in preserving his life against his enemies; it followeth, that in such a condition, every man has a right to every thing; even to one another's body. And therefore, as long as this natural right of every man to every thing endureth, there can be no security to any man, how strong or wise soever he be, of living out the time, which nature ordinarily alloweth men to live. And consequently it is a precept, or general rule of reason, *that every man, ought to endeavour peace, as far as he has hope of obtaining it; and when he cannot obtain it, that he may seek, and use, all helps, and advantages of war.* The first branch of which rule, containeth the first, and fundamental law of nature; which is, *to seek peace, and follow it.* The second, the sum of the right of nature; which is, *by all means we can, to defend ourselves.*

The second law of nature. From this fundamental law of nature, by which men are commanded to endeavour peace, is derived this second law; *that a man be willing, when others are so too, as far-forth, as for peace, and defence of himself he shall think it necessary, to lay down this right to all things; and be contented with so much liberty against other men, as he would allow other men against himself.* For as long as every man holdeth this right, of doing any thing he liketh; so long are all men in the condition of war. But if other men will not lay down their right, as well as he; then there is no reason for any one, to divest himself of his: for that were to expose himself to prey, which no man is bound to, rather than to dispose himself to peace. This is that law of the Gospel; *whatsoever you require that others should do to you, that do ye to them*. And that law of all men, *quod tibi fieri non vis, alteri ne feceris*.

What it is to lay down a right. To *lay down* a man's *right* to any thing, is to *divest* himself of the *liberty*, of hindering another of the benefit of his own right to the same. For he that renounceth, or passeth away his right, giveth not to any other man a right which he had not before; because there is nothing to which every man had not right by nature: but only standeth out of his way, that he may enjoy his own original right, without hindrance from him; not without hindrance from another. So that the effect which redoundeth to one man, by another man's defect of right, is but so much diminution of impediments to the use of his own right original.

Renouncing a right, what it is. Transferring right what. Obligation. Duty. Injustice. Right is laid aside, either by simply renouncing it; or by transferring it to another. By *simply* RENOUNCING; when he cares not to whom the benefit thereof redoundeth. By TRANSFERRING; when he intendeth the benefit thereof to some certain person, or persons. And when a man hath in either manner abandoned, or granted away his right; then he is said to be OBLIGED, or BOUND, not to hinder those to whom such right is granted, or abandoned, from the benefit of it: and that he *ought*, and it is his DUTY, not to make void that voluntary act of his own: and that such hindrance is INJUSTICE, and INJURY, as being *sine jure;* the right being before renounced, or transferred. So that *injury*, or *injustice*, in the controversies of the world, is somewhat like to that, which in the disputations of scholars is called *absurdity*. For as it is there called an absurdity, to contradict what one maintained in the beginning: so in the world, it is called injustice, and injury, voluntarily to undo that, which from the beginning he had voluntarily done. The way by which a man either simply renounceth, or transferreth his right, is a declaration, or signification, by some voluntary and sufficient sign, or signs, that he doth so renounce, or transfer; or hath so renounced, or transferred the same, to him that accepteth it. And these signs are either words only, or actions only; or, as it happeneth most often, both words and actions. And the same are the BONDS, by which men are bound, and obliged: bonds, that have their strength, not from their own nature, for nothing is more easily broken than a man's word, but from fear of some evil consequence upon the rupture.

Not all rights are alienable. Whensoever a man transferreth his right, or renounceth it; it is either in consideration of some right reciprocally transferred to himself; or for some other good he hopeth for thereby. For it is a voluntary act: and of the voluntary acts of every man, the object is some *good to himself*. And therefore there be some rights, which no man can be understood by any words, or other signs, to have abandoned, or transferred. As first a man cannot lay down the right of resisting them, that assault him by force, to take away his life; because he cannot be understood to aim thereby, at any good to himself. The same may be said of wounds, and chains, and imprisonment; both because there is no benefit consequent to such patience; as there is to the patience of suffering another to be wounded, or imprisoned: as also because a man cannot tell, when he seeth men proceed against him by violence, whether they intend his death or not. And lastly the motive, and end for which this renouncing, and transferring of right is introduced, is nothing else but the security of a man's person, in his life, and in the means of so preserving life, as not to be weary of it. And therefore if a man by words, or other signs, seem to despoil himself of the end, for which those signs were intended; he is not to be understood as if he meant it, or that it was his will; but that he was ignorant of how such words and actions were to be interpreted.

Contract what. The mutual transferring of right, is that which men call CONTRACT.

There is difference between transferring of right to the thing; and transferring, or tradition, that is delivery of the thing itself. For the thing may be delivered together with the translation of the right; as in buying and selling with ready-money; or exchange of goods, or lands: and it may be delivered some time after.

Covenant what. Again, one of the contractors, may deliver the thing contracted for on his part, and leave the other to perform his part at some determinate time after, and in the mean time be trusted; and then the contract on his part, is called PACT, or COVENANT: or both parts may contract now, to perform hereafter: in which cases, he that is to perform in time to come, being trusted, his performance is called *keeping of promise*, or faith; and the failing of performance, if it be voluntary, *violation of faith*. . . .

Covenants how made void. Men are freed of their covenants two ways; by performing; or by being forgiven. For performance, is the natural end of obligation; and forgiveness, the restitution of liberty; as being a retransferring of that right, in which the obligation consisted.

Covenants extorted by fear are valid. Covenants entered into by fear, in the condition of mere nature, are obligatory. For example, if I covenant to pay a ransom, or service for my life, to an enemy; I am bound by it: for it is a contract, wherein one receiveth the benefit of life; the other is to receive money, or service for it; and consequently, where no other law, as in the condition of mere nature, forbiddeth the performance, the covenant is valid. Therefore prisoners of war, if trusted with the payment of their ransom, are obliged to pay it: and if a weaker prince, make a disadvantageous peace with a stronger, for fear; he is bound to keep it; unless, as hath been said before, there ariseth some new, and just cause of fear, to renew the war. And even in commonwealths, if I be forced to redeem myself from a thief by promising him money, I am bound to pay it, till the civil law discharge me. For whatsoever I may lawfully do without obligation, the same I may lawfully covenant to do through fear: and what I lawfully covenant, I cannot lawfully break. . . .

Of Other Laws of Nature

The third law of nature, justice. From that law of nature, by which we are obliged to transfer to another, such rights, as being retained, hinder the peace of mankind, there followeth a third; which is this, *that men perform their covenants made:* without which, covenants are in vain, and but empty words; and the right of all men to all things remaining, we are still in the condition of war.

Justice and injustice what. And in this law of nature, consisteth the fountain and original of JUSTICE. For where no covenant hath preceded, there hath no right been transferred, and every man has right to every thing; and consequently, no action can be unjust. But when a covenant is made, then to break it is *unjust:* and the definition of INJUSTICE, is no other than *the not performance of covenant.* And whatsoever is not unjust, is *just.*

Justice and propriety begin with the constitution of commonwealth. But because covenants of mutual trust, where there is a fear of not performance on either part, as hath been said are invalid; though the original of justice be the making of covenants; yet injustice actually there can be none, till the cause of such fear be taken away; which while men are in the natural condition of war, cannot be done. Therefore before the names of just, and unjust can have place, there must be some coercive power, to compel men equally to the performance of their covenants, by the terror of some punishment, greater than the benefit they expect by the breach of their covenant; and to make good that propriety, which by mutual contract men acquire, in recompense of the universal right they abandon: and such power there is none before the erection of a commonwealth. And this is also to be gathered out of the ordinary definition of justice in the Schools: for they say, that *justice is the constant will of giving to every man his own.* And therefore where there is no *own,* that is no propriety, there is no injustice; and where there is no coercive power erected, that is, where there is no commonwealth, there is no propriety; all men having right to all things: therefore where there is no commonwealth, there nothing is unjust. So that the nature of justice, consisteth in keeping of valid covenants: but the validity of covenants begins not but with the constitution of a civil power, sufficient to compel men to keep them: and then it is also that propriety begins.

Justice not contrary to reason. The fool hath said in his heart, there is no such thing as justice; and sometimes also with his tongue; seriously alleging, that every man's conservation, and contentment, being committed to his own care, there could be no reason, why every man might not do what he thought conduced thereunto: and therefore also to make, or not make; keep, or not keep covenants, was not against reason, when it conduced to one's benefit. He does not therein deny, that there be covenants; and that they are sometimes broken, sometimes kept; and that such breach of them may be called injustice, and the observance of them justice: but he questioneth, whether injustice, taking away the fear of God, for the same fool hath said in his heart there is no God, may not sometimes stand with that reason, which dictateth to every man his own good; and particularly then, when it conduceth to such a benefit, as shall put a man in a condition, to neglect not only the dispraise, and revilings, but also the power of other men. The kingdom of God is gotten by violence: but what if it could be gotten by unjust violence? were it against reason so to get it, when it is impossible to receive hurt by it? and if it be not against reason, it is not against justice; or else justice is not to be approved for good. . . . This specious reasoning is nevertheless false.

For the question is not of promises mutual, where there is no security of performance on either side; as when there is no civil power erected over the parties promising; for such promises are no covenants: but either where one of the parties has performed already; or where there is a power to make him perform; there is the question whether it be against reason, that is, against the benefit of the other to perform, or not. And I say it is not against reason. For the manifestation whereof, we are to consider; first, that when a man doth a thing, which notwithstanding any thing can be foreseen, and reckoned on, tendeth to his own destruction, howsoever some accident which he could not expect, arriving may turn it to his benefit; yet such events do not make it reasonably or wisely done. Secondly, that in a condition of war, wherein every man to every man, for want of a common power to keep them all in awe, is an enemy, there is no man who can hope by his own strength, or wit, to defend himself from destruction, without the help of confederates; where every one expects the same defence by the confederation, that any one else does: and therefore he which declares he thinks it reason to deceive those that help him, can in reason expect no other means of safety, than what can be had from his own single power. He therefore that breaketh his covenant, and consequently declareth that he thinks he may with reason do so, cannot be received into any society, that unite themselves for peace and defence, but by the error of them that receive him; nor when he is received, be retained in it, without seeing the danger of their error; which errors a man cannot reasonably reckon upon as the means of his security:

and therefore if he be left, or cast out of society, he perisheth; and if he live in society, it is by the errors of other men, which he could not foresee, nor reckon upon; and consequently against the reason of his preservation; and so, as all men that contribute not to his destruction, forbear him only out of ignorance of what is good for themselves.

As for the instance of gaining the secure and perpetual felicity of heaven, by any way; it is frivolous: there being but one way imaginable; and that is not breaking, but keeping of covenant.

And for the other instance of attaining sovereignty by rebellion; it is manifest, that though the event follow, yet because it cannot reasonably be expected, but rather the contrary; and because by gaining it so, others are taught to gain the same in like manner, the attempt thereof is against reason. Justice therefore, that is to say, keeping of covenant, is a rule of reason, by which we are forbidden to do any thing destructive to our life; and consequently a law of nature. . . .

Justice of men and justice of actions what. The names of just, and unjust, when they are attributed to men, signify one thing; and when they are attributed to actions, another. When they are attributed to men, they signify conformity, or inconformity of manners, to reason. But when they are attributed to actions, they signify the conformity, or inconformity to reason, not of manners, or manner of life, but of particular actions. A just man therefore, is he that taketh all the care he can, that his actions may be all just: and an unjust man, is he that neglecteth it. And such men are more often in our language styled by the names of righteous, and unrighteous; than just, and unjust; though the meaning be the same. Therefore a righteous man, does not lose that title, by one, or a few unjust actions, that proceed from sudden passion, or mistake of things, or persons: nor does an unrighteous man, lose his character, for such actions, as he does, or forbears to do, for fear: because his will is not framed by the justice, but by the apparent benefit of what he is to do. That which gives to human actions the relish of justice, is a certain nobleness or gallantness of courage, rarely found, by which a man scorns to be beholden for the contentment of his life, to fraud, or breach of promise. This justice of the manners, is that which is meant, where justice is called a virtue; and injustice a vice.

But the justice of actions denominates men, not just, but *guiltless*: and the injustice of the same, which is also called injury, gives them but the name of *guilty*.

Justice of manners, and justice of actions. Again, the injustice of manners, is the disposition, or aptitude to do injury; and is injustice before it proceed to act; and without supposing any individual person injured. But the injustice of an action, that is to say injury, supposeth an individual person injured; namely him, to whom the covenant was made: and therefore many times the injury is received by one man, when the damage redoundeth to another. As when the master commandeth his servant to give money to a stranger; if it be not done, the injury is done to the master, whom he had before covenanted to obey; but the damage redoundeth to the stranger, to whom he had no obligation; and therefore could not injure him. And so also in commonwealths, private men may remit to one another their debts; but not robberies or other violences, whereby they are endamaged; because the detaining of debt, is an injury to themselves; but robbery and violence, are injuries to the person of the commonwealth.

Nothing done to a man by his own consent can be injury. Whatsoever is done to a man, conformable to his own will signified to the doer, is no injury to him. For if he that doeth it, hath not passed away his original right to do what he please, by some antecedent covenant, there is no breach of covenant; and therefore no injury done him. And if he have; then his will to have it done being signified, is a release of that covenant: and so again there is no injury done him.

Justice commutative and distributive. Justice of actions, is by writers divided into *commutative*, and *distributive*: and the former they say consisteth in proportion arithmetical; the latter in proportion geometrical. Commutative therefore, they place in the equality of value of the things contracted for; and distributive, in the distribution of equal benefit, to men of equal merit. As if it were injustice to sell dearer than we buy; or to give more to a man than he merits. The value of all things contracted for, is measured by the appetite of the contractors: and therefore the just value, is that which they be contented to give. And merit (besides that which is by covenant, where the performance on one part, meriteth the performance on the other part, and falls under justice commutative, not distributive) is not due to justice; but is rewarded of grace only. And therefore this distinction, in the sense wherein it useth to be expounded, is not right. To speak properly, commutative justice, is the justice, of a contractor; that is, a performance of covenant, in buying, and selling; hiring, and letting to hire; lending, and borrowing; exchanging, bartering, and other acts of contract.

And distributive justice, the justice of an arbitrator; that is to say, the act of defining what is just. Wherein, being trusted by them that make him arbitrator, if he perform his trust, he is said to distribute to every man his own: and this is indeed just distribution, and may be called, though improperly, distributive justice; but more properly equity; which also is a law of nature, as shall be shown in due place. . . .

Of the Causes, Generation, and Definition of a Commonwealth

The end of commonwealth, particular security. The final cause, end, or design of men, who naturally love liberty, and dominion over others, in the introduction of that restraint upon themselves, in which we see them live in commonwealths, is the foresight of their own preservation, and of a more contented life thereby; that is to say, of getting themselves out from that miserable condition of war, which is necessarily consequent, as hath been shown, to the natural passions of men, when there is no visible power to keep them in awe, and tie them by fear of punishment to the performance of their covenants, and observation of those laws of nature.

Which is not to be had from the law of nature. For the laws of nature, as *justice, equity, modesty, mercy,* and, in sum, *doing to others, as we would be done to,* of themselves, without the terror of some power, to cause them to be observed, are contrary to our natural passions, that carry us to partiality, pride, revenge, and the like. And covenants, without the sword, are but words, and of no strength to secure a man at all. Therefore notwithstanding the laws of nature (which every one hath then kept, when he has the will to keep them, when he can do it safely) if there be no power erected, or not great enough for our security; every man will, and may lawfully rely on his own strength and art, for caution against all other men. And in all places, where men have lived by small families, to rob and spoil one another, has been a trade, and so far from being reputed against the law of nature, that the greater spoils they gained, the greater was their honour; and men observed no other laws therein, but the laws of honour; that is, to abstain from cruelty, leaving to men their lives, and instruments of husbandry. And as small families did then; so now do cities and kingdoms which are but greater families, for their own security, enlarge their dominions, upon all pretences of danger, and fear of invasion, or assistance that may be given to invaders, and endeavour as much as they can, to subdue, or weaken their neighbours, by open force, and secret arts, for want of other caution, justly; and are remembered for it in after ages with honour. . . .

The generation of a commonwealth. The definition of a commonwealth. The only way to erect such a common power, as may be able to defend them from the invasion of foreigners, and the injuries of one another, and thereby to secure them in such sort, as that by their own industry, and by the fruits of the earth, they may nourish themselves and live contentedly; is, to confer all their power and strength upon one man, or upon one assembly of men, that may reduce all their wills, by plurality of voices, unto one will: which is as much as to say, to appoint one man, or assembly of men, to bear their person; and every one to own, and acknowledge himself to be author of whatsoever he that so beareth their person, shall act, or cause to be acted, in those things which concern the common peace and safety; and therein to submit their wills, every one to his will, and their judgments, to his judgment. This is more than consent, or concord; it is a real unity of them all, in one and the same person, made by covenant of every man with every man, in such manner, as if every man should say to every man, *I authorize and give up my right of governing myself, to this man, or to this assembly of men, on this condition, that though give up thy right to him, and authorize all his actions in like manner*. This done, the multitude so united in one person, is called a COMMONWEALTH, in Latin CIVITAS. This is the generation of that great LEVIATHAN, or rather, to speak more reverently, of that *mortal god*, to which we owe under the *immortal God*, our peace and defence. For by this authority, given him by every particular man in the commonwealth, he hath the use of so much power and strength conferred on him, that by terror thereof, he is enabled to form the wills of them all, to peace at home, and mutual aid against their enemies abroad. And in him consisteth the essence of the commonwealth; which, to define it, is *one person, of whose acts a great multitude, by mutual covenants one with another, have made themselves every one the author, to the end he may use the strength and means of them all, as he shall think expedient, for their peace and common defence.*

Sovereign, and subject, what. And he that carrieth this person is called SOVEREIGN, and said to have *sovereign power*; and every one besides, his SUBJECT.

The attaining to this sovereign power, is by two ways. One by natural force; as when a man maketh his children, to submit themselves, and their children to his government, as being able to destroy them if they refuse; or by war subdueth his enemies to his will, giving them their lives on that condition. The other, is when men agree amongst themselves, to submit to some man, or assembly of men, voluntarily, on confidence to be protected by him against all others. This latter, may be called a political commonwealth, or commonwealth by *institution;* and the former, a commonwealth by *acquisition*.

Governments Exist to Preserve Property

JOHN LOCKE

John Locke (1632-1704) was a major English empiricist philosopher who made major contributions to epistemology and political philosophy. His writings include *Essay Concerning Human Understanding* and *Second Treatise on Government,* from which this viewpoint is taken. Many of Locke's ideas are contained in the U. S. Declaration of Independence. Locke argues that men are created by God subject to a law of nature which gives them certain rights even in the state of nature, before any political institutions exist. In addition to natural ownership over their own bodies, men can process or improve things which make up their common environment. They can harvest plants for food or plant a field, for example. When men add their labor to things these things become more valuable and are then the private property or possessions of those who have "mixed" their labor with them. Men have rights to use and enjoy their prop-

From *Two Treatises on Government* by John Locke. London: Everyman's Library, 1924.

erty subject to the limitation that they may not take more than they can actually utilize. They have the right to exchange their possessions for whatever they choose. When they agreed by mutual consent that certain things like pieces of metal or jewels can be exchanged for useful but perishable things like food, money and a new way of accumulating wealth was born. Men choose to leave the state of nature and form a government with laws and judges and power to enforce laws in order to protect their lives and property in a better way than is possible in the state of nature. They do this by consenting to transfer their natural rights to the government in exchange for these advantages. The government is obligated not to extend its power beyond what is necessary to provide these advantages. If it does, the people can dissolve it and form another.

QUESTIONS

1. According to Locke, what is the law of nature? How much power does it give individuals over other individuals?
2. Where, according to the author, can we actually find people in the state of nature?
3. How does private property arise, according to Locke? What limits apply on what can be claimed as private?
4. According to the author, how does money originate and what effect does it have on the extent of a man's possessions?
5. How, according to Locke, does a person become a member of a society?
6. According to the author, what do people give up and gain when they become a part of a political society? Is it a worthwhile trade?

■ ■ ■

Of the State of Nature

To understand Political Power right, and derive it from its Original, we must consider what State all Men are naturally in, and that is, a *State of perfect Freedom* to order their Actions, and dispose of their Possessions, and Persons as they think fit, within the bounds of the Law of Nature, without asking leave, or depending upon the Will of any other Man.

A *State* also *of Equality*, wherein all the Power and Jurisdiction is reciprocal, no one having more than another: there being nothing more evident, than that Creatures of the same species and rank promiscuously born to all the same advantages of Nature, and the use of the same faculties, should also be equal one amongst another without Subordination or Subjection, unless the Lord and Master of them all, should by any manifest Declaration of his Will set one above another, and confer on him by an evident and clear appointment an undoubted Right to Dominion and Sovereignty. . . .

But though this be a *State of Liberty*, yet it is *not a State of Licence*, though Man in that State have an uncontroleable Liberty, to dispose of his Person or Possessions, yet he has not Liberty to destroy himself, or so much as any Creature in his Possession, but where some nobler use, than its bare Preservation calls for it. The *State of Nature* has a Law of Nature to govern it, which obliges every one: And Reason, which is that Law, teaches all Mankind, who will but consult it, that being all equal and independent, no one ought to harm another in his Life, Health, Liberty, or Possessions. For Men being all the Workmanship of one Omnipotent, and infinitely wise Maker; All the Servants of one Sovereign Master, sent into the World by his order and about his business, they are his Property, whose Workmanship they are, made to last during his, not one anothers Pleasure. And being furnished with like Faculties, sharing all in one Community of Nature, there cannot be supposed any such *Subordination* among us, that may Authorize us to destroy one another, as if we were made for one anothers uses, as the inferior ranks of Creatures are for ours. Every one as he is *bound to preserve himself*, and not to quit his Station wilfully; so by the like reason when his own Preservation comes not in competition, ought he, as much as he can, *to preserve the rest of Mankind*, and may not unless it be to do Justice on an Offender, take away, or impair the life, or what tends to the Preservation of the Life, the Liberty, Health, Limb or Goods of another.

And that all Men may be restrained from invading others Rights, and from doing hurt to one another, and the Law of Nature be observed, which willeth the Peace and *Preservation of all Mankind*, the *Execution* of the Law of Nature is in that State, put into every Mans hands, whereby every one has a right to punish the transgressors of that Law to such a Degree, as may hinder its Violation. For the *Law of Nature* would, as all other Laws that concern Men in this World, be in vain, if there were no body that in the State of Nature, had a *Power to Execute* that Law, and thereby preserve the innocent and restrain offenders, and if any one in the State of Nature may punish another, for any evil he has done, every one may do so. For in that *State of perfect Equality*, where naturally there is no superiority or jurisdiction of one, over another, what any may do in Prosecution of that Law, every one must needs have a Right to do.

And thus in the State of Nature, *one Man comes by a Power over another*; but yet no Absolute or Arbitrary Power, to use a Criminal when he has got him in his hands, according to the passionate heats, or boundless extravagancy of his own Will, but only to retribute to him, so far as calm reason and conscience dictates, what is proportionate to his Transgression, which is so much as may serve for *Reparation* and *Restraint*. For these two are the only reasons, why one Man may lawfully do harm to another, which is that we call *punishment*. In transgressing the Law of Nature, the Offender declares himself to live by another Rule, than that of *reason* and common Equity, which is that measure God has set to the actions of Men, for their mutual security: and so he becomes dangerous to Mankind, the tye, which is to secure them from injury and violence, being slighted and broken by him. Which being a trespass against the whole Species, and the Peace and Safety of it, provided for by the Law of Nature, every man upon this score, by the Right he hath to preserve Mankind in general, may restrain, or where it is necessary, destroy things noxious to them, and so may bring such evil on any one, who hath transgressed that Law, as may make him repent the doing of it, and thereby deter him, and by his Example others, from doing the like mischief. And in this case, and upon this ground, *every Man hath a Right to punish the Offender, and be Executioner of the Law of Nature. . . .*

Besides the Crime which consists in violating the Law, and varying from the right Rule of Reason, whereby a Man so far becomes degenerate, and declares himself to quit the Principles of Human Nature, and to be a noxious Creature, there is commonly *injury* done to some Person or other, and some other Man receives damage by his Transgression, in which Case he who hath received any damage, has besides the right of punishment common to him with other Men, a particular Right to seek *Reparation* from him that has done it. And any other Person who finds it just, may also joyn with him that is injur'd, and assist him in recovering from the Offender, so much as may make satisfaction for the harm he has suffer'd. . . .

May a Man in the State of Nature *punish the lesser breaches* of that Law. It will perhaps be demanded, with death? I answer, Each Transgression may be *punished* to that *degree*, and with so much *Severity* as will suffice to make it an ill bargain to the Offender, give him cause to repent, and terrifie others from doing the like. . . .

To this strange Doctrine, *viz.* That *in the State of Nature, every one has the Executive Power* of the Law of Nature, I doubt not but it will be objected, That it is unreasonable for Men to be Judges in their own Cases, that Self-love will make Men partial to themselves and their Friends. And on the other side, that Ill Nature, Passion and Revenge will carry them too far in punishing others. And hence nothing but Confusion and Disorder will follow, and that therefore God hath certainly appointed Government to restrain the partiality and violence of Men. I easily grant, that *Civil Government* is the proper Remedy for the Inconveniences of the State of Nature, which must certainly be Great, where Men may be Judges in their own Case, since 'tis easily to be imagined, that he who was so unjust as to do his Brother an Injury, will scarce be so just as to condemn himself for it: But I shall desire those who make this Objection, to remember that *Absolute Monarchs* are but Men, and if Government is to be the Remedy of those Evils, which necessarily follow from Mens being Judges in their own Cases, and the State of Nature is therefore not to be endured, I desire to know what kind of Government that is, and how much better it is than the State of Nature, where one Man commanding a multitude, has the Liberty to be Judge in his own Case, and may do to all his Subjects whatever he pleases, without the least liberty to any one to question or controle those who Execute his Pleasure? And in whatsoever he doth, whether led by Reason, Mistake or Passion, must be submitted to? Much better it is in the State of Nature wherein Men are not bound to submit to the unjust will of another: And if he that judges, judges amiss in his own, or any other Case, he is answerable for it to the rest of Mankind. . . .

Of Property

Whether we consider natural *Reason*, which tells us, that Men, being once born, have a right to their Preservation, and consequently to Meat and Drink, and such other things, as Nature affords for their Subsistence: Or *Revelation*, which gives us an account of those Grants God made of the World to *Adam*, and to *Noah*, and his Sons, 'tis very clear, that God, as King *David* says, *Psal.* CXV. xvj. *has given the Earth to the Children of Men*, given it to Mankind in common. But this being supposed, it seems to some a very great difficulty, how any one should ever come to have a *Property* in any thing: I will not content my self to answer, That if it be difficult to make out *Property*, upon a supposition, that God gave the World to *Adam* and his Posterity in common; it is impossible that any Man, but one universal Monarch, should have any *Property*, upon a supposition, that God gave the World to *Adam*, and his Heirs in Succession, exclusive of all the rest of his Posterity. But I shall endeavour to shew, how Men might come to have a *property* in several parts of that which God gave to Mankind in common, and that without any express Compact of all the Commoners.

God, who hath given the World to Men in common, hath also given them reason to make use of it to the best advantage of Life, and convenience. The Earth, and all that is therein, is given to Men for the Support and Comfort of their being. And though all the Fruits it naturally produces, and Beasts it feeds, belong to Mankind in common, as they are produced by the spontaneous hand of Nature; and no body has originally a private dominion, exclusive of the rest of Mankind, in any of them, as they are thus in their natural state: yet being given for the use of Men, there must of necessity be a means *to appropriate* them some way or other before they can be of any use, or at all beneficial to any particular Man. The Fruit, or Venison, which nourishes the wild *Indian*, who knows no Inclosure, and is still a Tenant in common, must be his, and so his, *i.e.* a part of him, that another can no longer have any right to it, before it can do him any good for the support of his Life.

Though the Earth, and all inferior Creatures be common to all Men, yet every Man has a *Property* in his own *Person*. This no Body has any Right to but himself. The *Labour* of his Body, and the *Work* of his Hands, we may say, are properly his. Whatsoever then he removes out of the State that Nature hath provided, and left it in, he hath mixed his *Labour* with, and joyned to it something that is his own, and thereby makes it his *Property*. It being by him removed from the common state Nature placed it in, it hath by this *labour* something annexed to it, that excludes the common right of other Men. For this *Labour* being the unquestionable Property of the Labourer, no man but he can have a right to what that is once joyned to, at least where there is enough, and as good left in common for others.

He that is nourished by the Acorns he pickt up under an Oak, or the Apples he gathered from the Trees in the Wood, has certainly appropriated them to himself. No Body can deny but the nourishment is his. I ask then, When did they begin to be his? When he digested? Or when he eat? Or when he boiled? Or when he brought them home? Or when he pickt them up? And 'tis plain, if the first gathering made them not his, nothing else could. That *labour* put a distinction between them and common. That added something to them more than Nature, the common Mother of all, had done; and so they became his private right. . . .

It will perhaps be objected to this, That if gathering the Acorns, or other Fruits of the Earth, *etc.* makes a right to them, then any one may *ingross* as much as he will. To which I Answer, Not so. The same Law of Nature, that does by this means give us Property, does also *bound* that *Property* too. *God has given us all things richly*, I Tim. vi. 17. is the Voice of Reason confirmed by Inspiration. But how far has he given it us? *To enjoy*. As much as any one can make use of to any advantage of life before it spoils; so much he may by his labour fix a Property in. Whatever is beyond this, is more than his share, and belongs to others. Nothing was made by God for Man to spoil or destroy. And thus considering the plenty of natural Provisions there was a long time in the World, and the few spenders, and to how small a part of that provision the industry of one Man could extend it self, and ingross it to the prejudice of others; especially keeping within the *bounds*, set by reason of what might serve for his *use*; there could be then little room for Quarrels or Contentions about Property so establish'd.

But the *chief matter of Property* being now not the Fruits of the Earth, and the Beasts that subsist on it, but the *Earth it self*; as that which takes in and carries with it all the rest: I think it is plain, that *Property* in that too is acquired as the former. *As much Land* as a Man Tills, Plants, Improves, Cultivates, and can use the Product of, so much is his *Property*. He by his Labour does, as it were, inclose it from the Common. Nor will it invalidate his right to say, Every body else has an equal Title to it; and therefore he cannot appropriate, he cannot inclose, without the Consent of all his Fellow-Commoners, all Mankind. God, when he gave the World in common to all Mankind, commanded Man also to labour, and the penury of his Condition required it of him. God and his Reason commanded him to subdue the Earth, *i.e.* improve it for the benefit of Life, and therein lay out something upon it that was his own, his labour. He that in Obedience to this Command of God, subdued, tilled and sowed any part of it, thereby annexed to it something that was his *Property*, which another had no Title to, nor could without injury take from him. . . .

Nor is it so strange, as perhaps before consideration it may appear, that the *Property of labour* should be able to overballance the Community of Land. For 'tis *Labour* indeed that *puts the difference of value* on every thing; and let any one consider, what the difference is between an Acre of Land planted with Tobacco, or Sugar, sown with Wheat or Barley; and an Acre of the same Land lying in common, without any Husbandry upon it, and he will find, that the improvement of *labor makes* the far greater part of *the value*. I think it will be but a very modest Computation to say, that of the *Products* of the Earth useful to the Life of Man $^{9}/_{10}$ are the *effects of labour*: nay, if we will rightly estimate things as they come to our use, and cast up the several Expences about them, what in them is purely owing to *Nature*, and what to *labour*, we shall find, that in most of them $^{99}/_{100}$ are wholly to be put on the account of *labour*.

There cannot be a clearer demonstration of any thing, than several Nations of the *Americans* are of this, who are rich in Land, and poor in all the Comforts of Life; whom Nature having furnished as liberally as any other people, with the materials of Plenty, *i.e.* a fruitful Soil, apt to produce in abundance, what might serve for food, rayment and delight; yet for want of improving it by labour, have not one hundredth part of the Conveniencies we enjoy: And a King of a large and fruitful Territory there feeds, lodges, and is clad worse than a day Labourer in *England*. . . .

Of the Beginning of Political Societies

Men being, as has been said, by Nature, all free, equal and independent, no one can be put out of this Estate, and subjected to the Political Power of another, without his own *Consent*. The only way whereby any one devests himself of his Natural Liberty, and *puts on the bonds of Civil Society* is by agreeing with other Men to joyn and unite into a Community, for their comfortable, safe, and peaceable living one amongst another, in a secure Enjoyment of their Properties, and a greater Security against any that are not of it. This any number of Men may do, because it injures not the Freedom of the rest; they are left as they were in the Liberty of the State of Nature. When any number of Men have so *consented to make one Community* or Government, they are thereby presently incorporated, and make *one Body Politick*, wherein the *Majority* have a Right to act and conclude the rest. . . .

For if *the consent of the majority* shall not in reason, be received, as *the act of the whole*, and conclude every individual; nothing but the consent of every individual can make any thing to be the act of the whole: But such a consent is next impossible ever to be had, if we consider the Infirmities of Health, and Avocations of Business, which in a number, though much less than that of a Common-wealth, will necessarily keep many away from the publick Assembly. To which if we add the variety of Opinions, and contrariety of Interests, which unavoidably happen in all Collections of Men, the coming into Society upon such terms, would be only like *Cato*'s coming into the Theatre, only to go out again. Such a Constitution as this would make the might *Leviathan* of a shorter duration, than the feeblest Creatures; and not let it outlast the day it was born in: which cannot be suppos'd, till we can think, that Rational Creatures should desire and constitute Societies only to be dissolved. For where the *majority* cannot conclude the rest, there they cannot act as one Body, and consequently will be immediately dissolved again. . . .

Every Man being, as has been shewed, *naturally free*, and nothing being able to put him into subjection to any Earthly Power, but only his own Consent; it is to be considered, what shall be understood to be *a sufficient Declaration of* a Mans *Consent, to make him subject* to the Laws of any Government. There is a common distinction of an express and a tacit consent, which will concern our present Case. No body doubts but an *express Consent*, of any Man, entring into any Society, makes him a perfect Member of that Society, a Subject of that Government. The difficulty is, what ought to be look'd upon as a *tacit Consent*, and how far it binds, *i.e.* how far any one shall be looked on to have consented, and thereby submitted to any Government, where he has made no Expressions of it at all. And to this I say, that every Man, that hath any Possession, or Enjoyment, of any part of the Dominions of any Government, doth thereby give his *tacit Consent*, and is as far forth obliged to Obedience to the Laws of that Government, during such Enjoyment, as any one under it; whether this his Possession be of Land, to him and his Heirs for ever, or a Lodging only for a Week; or whether it be barely travelling freely on the Highway; and in Effect, it reaches as far as the very being of any one within the Territories of that Government. . . .

But submitting to the Laws of any Country, living quietly, and enjoying Priviledges and Protection under them, *makes not a Man a Member of that Society*: This is only a local Protection and Homage due to, and from all those, who, not being in a state of War, come within the Territories belonging to any Government, to all parts whereof the force of its Law extends. But this no more *makes a Man a Member of that Society*, a perpetual Subject of that Commonwealth, than it would make a Man a Subject to another in whose Family he found it convenient to abide for some time; though, whilst he continued in it, he were obliged to comply with the Laws, and submit to the Government he found there. And thus we see, that *Foreigners*, by living all their Lives under another Government, and enjoying the Priviledges and Protection of it, though they are bound, even in Conscience, to submit to its Administration, as far forth as any Denison; yet do not thereby come to be *Subjects or Members of that Commonwealth.* Nothing can make any Man so, but his actually entering into it by positive Engagement, and express Promise and Compact. This is that, which I think, concerning the beginning of Political Societies, and that *Consent which makes any one a Member* of any Commonwealth.

Of the Ends of Political Society and Government

If man in the State of Nature be so free, as has been said; If he be absolute Lord of his own Person and Possessions, equal to the greatest, and subject to no Body, why will he part with his Freedom? Why will he give up this Empire, and subject himself to the Dominion and Controul of any other Power? To which 'tis obvious to Answer, that though in the state of Nature he hath such a right, yet the Enjoyment of it is very uncertain, and constantly exposed to the Invasion of others. For all being Kings as much as he, every Man his Equal, and the greater part no strict Observers of Equity and Justice, the enjoyment of the property he has in this state is very unsafe, very unsecure. This makes him willing to quit this Condition, which however free, is full of fears and continual dangers: And 'tis not without reason, that he seeks out, and is willing to joyn in Society with others who are already united, or have a mind to unite for the mutual *Preservation* of their Lives, Liberties and Estates, which I call by the general Name, *Property*.

The great and *chief end* therefore, of Mens uniting into Commonwealths, and putting themselves under Government, *is the Preservation of their Property*. To which in the state of Nature there are many things wanting.

First, There wants an *establish'd*, settled, known *Law*, received and allowed by common consent to be the Standard of Right and Wrong, and the common measure to decide all Controversies between them. For though the Law of Nature be plain and intelligible to all rational Creatures; yet Men being biassed by their Interest, as well as ignorant for want of study of it, are not apt to allow of it as a Law binding to them in the application of it to their particular Cases.

Secondly, In the State of Nature there wants *a known and indifferent Judge*, with Authority to determine all differences according to the established Law. For every one in that state being both Judge and Executioner of the Law of Nature, Men being partial to themselves, Passion and Revenge is very apt to carry them too far, and with too much heat, in their own Cases; as well as negligence, and unconcernedness, to make them too remiss, in other Mens.

Thirdly, In the state of Nature there often wants *Power* to back and support the Sentence when right, and to *give* it due *Execution*. They who by any Injustice offended, will seldom fail, where they are able, by force to make good their Injustice: such resistance many times makes the punishment dangerous, and frequently destructive, to those who attempt it. . . .

For in the State of Nature, to omit the liberty he has of innocent Delights, a Man has two Powers.

The first is to do whatsoever he thinks fit for the preservation of himself and others within the permission of the *Law of Nature*: by which Law common to them all, he and all the rest of *Mankind are one Community*, make up one Society distinct from all other Creatures. And were it not for the corruption, and vitiousness of degenerate Men, there would be no need of any other; no necessity that Men should separate from this great and natural Community, and by positive agreements combine into smaller and divided associations.

The other power a Man has in the State of Nature, is the *power to punish the Crimes* committed against that Law. Both these he gives up, when he joyns in a private, if I may so call it, or particular Political Society, and incorporates into any Commonwealth, separate from the rest of Mankind.

The first *Power, viz. of doing whatsoever he thought fit for the Preservation of himself*, and the rest of Mankind, *he gives up* to be regulated by Laws made by the Society, so far forth as the preservation of himself, and the rest of that Society shall require; which Laws of the Society in many things confine the liberty he had by the Law of Nature.

Secondly, the *Power of punishing* he wholly *gives up*, and engages his natural force, (which he might before imploy in the Execution of the Law of Nature, by his own single Authority, as he thought fit) to assist the Executive Power of the Society, as the Law thereof shall require. For being now in a new State, wherein he is to enjoy many Conveniencies, from the labour, assistance, and society of others in the same Community, as well as protection from its whole strength; he is to part also with as much of his natural liberty in providing for himself, as the good, prosperity, and safety of the Society shall require: which is not only necessary, but just; since the other Members of the Society do the like. . . .

The Reason why Men enter into Society, is the preservation of their Property; and the end why they chuse and authorize a Legislative, is, that there may be Laws made, and Rules set as Guards and Fences to the Properties of all the Members of the Society, to limit the Power, and moderate the Dominion of every Part and Member of the Society. For since it can never be supposed to be the Will of the Society, that the Legislative should have a Power to destroy that, which every one designs to secure, by entering into Society, and for which the People submitted themselves to the Legislators of their own making; whenever the *Legislators endeavour to take away, and destroy the Property of the People*, or to reduce them to Slavery under Arbitrary Power, they put themselves into a state of War with the People, who are thereupon absolved from any farther Obedience, and are left to the common Refuge, which God hath provided for all Men, against Force and Violence. Whensoever therefore the *Legislative* shall transgress this fundamental Rule of Society; and either by Ambition, Fear, Folly or Corruption, *endeavour to grasp* themselves, *or put into the hands of any other an Absolute Power* over the Lives, Liberties, and Estates of the People; By this breach of Trust they *forfeit the Power*, the People had put into their hands, for quite contrary ends, and it devolves to the People, who have a Right to resume their original Liberty, and, by the Establishment of a new Legislative (such as they shall think fit) provide for their own Safety and Security, which is the end for which they are in Society. . . .

To conclude, The *Power that every individual gave the Society*, when he entered into it, can never revert to the Individuals again, as long as the Society lasts, but will always remain in the Community; because without this, there can be no Community, no Common-wealth, which is contrary to the original Agreement: So also when the Society hath placed the Legislative in any Assembly of Men, to continue in them and their Successors, with Direction and Authority for providing such Successors, *the Legislative can never revert to the People* whilst that Government lasts: Because having provided a Legislative with Power to continue for ever, they have given up their Political Power to the Legislative, and cannot resume it. But if they have set Limits to the Duration of their Legislative, and made this Supreme Power in any Person, or Assembly, only temporary: Or else when by the Miscarriages of those in Authority, it is forfeited; upon the Forfeiture of their Rulers, or at the Determination of the Time set, *it reverts to the Society*, and the People have a Right to act as Supreme, and continue the Legislative in themselves, or erect a new Form, or under the old form place it in new hands, as they think good.

Proletariat Governments Will Abolish Private Property

Karl Marx

Karl Marx (1818-1883) was born in Germany but spent most of his life in exile because of his radical political activities. He and his friend and associate Friedrick Engels developed the theoretical justification for contemporary communism. The following viewpoint is extracted from the *Manifesto of the Communist Party*, which Marx coauthored with Engels, and from Marx's *Critique of the Gotha Program*. Marx begins by arguing that history is a process driven by conflicts between different socioeconomic classes. Each conflict has been temporarily resolved by a set of economic arrangements which contained within themselves the seeds of their own destruction and further class conflict. The latest structure to emerge is capitalism, which pits the bourgeoisie, who own the means of production like factories

From *The Manifesto of the Communist Party* by Karl Marx and Frederick Engels and Marx's *Critique of the Gotha Program*, in *The Marx-Engels Reader*, 2nd ed., published by W.W. Norton and Company, 1978.

and land, against the proletarians, who have only labor to contribute. The present conflict will be resolved when the means of production cease to be the private property of the bourgeoisie and become common property, to be used for the good of all. This resolution will be brought about by a series of revolutions. The final result will be a world whose concepts of justice, labor, and family are shaped by the new economic reality, just as certain traditional conceptions of justice and family are shaped by capitalist economic relationships. Class conflicts will finally end and a higher kind of society will emerge under the banner: "From each according to his ability, to each according to his needs!"

QUESTIONS

1. According to Marx, what is the basic mechanism of social history? What steps does he list?
2. How, according to the author, did bourgeois society distribute population?
3. What, according to Marx, is the origin of the proletariat? What are their lives like?
4. What kind of property does the author say must be done away with? What objections to this elimination does he respond to?
5. How, according to Marx, do people arrive at their ideas of freedom, family, and other social forms? How do communists understand these forms and the "eternal" truths which justify them?
6. According to the author, what will ultimately replace class structure? How will justice then be understood?

■ ■ ■

Bourgeois and Proletarians

The history of all hitherto existing society is the history of class struggles.

Freeman and slave, patrician and plebeian, lord and serf, guild-master and journeyman, in a word, oppressor and oppressed, stood in constant opposition to one another, carried on an uninterrupted, now hidden, now open fight, a fight that each time ended, either in a revolutionary re-constitution of society at large, or in the common ruin of the contending classes. . . .

Modern industry has established the world-market, for which the discovery of America paved the way. This market has given an immense development to commerce, to navigation, to communication by land. This development has, in its turn, reacted on the extension of industry; and in proportion as industry, commerce, navigation, railways extended, in the same proportion the bourgeoisie developed, increased its capital, and pushed into the background every class handed down from the Middle Ages.

We see, therefore, how the modern bourgeoisie is itself the product of a long course of development, of a series of revolutions in the modes of production and of exchange. . . .

The productive forces at the disposal of society no longer tend to further the development of the conditions of bourgeois property; on the contrary, they have become too powerful for these conditions, by which they are fettered, and so soon as they overcome these fetters, they bring disorder into the whole of bourgeois society, endanger the existence of bourgeois property. The conditions of bourgeois society are too narrow to comprise the wealth created by them. And how does the bourgeoisie get over these crises? On the one hand by enforced destruction of a mass of productive forces; on the other, by the conquest of new markets, and by the more thorough exploitation of the old ones. That is to say, by paving the way for more extensive and more destructive crises, and by diminishing the means whereby crises are prevented.

The weapons with which the bourgeoisie felled feudalism to the ground are now turned against the bourgeoisie itself.

But not only has the bourgeoisie forged the weapons that bring death to itself; it has also called into existence the men who are to wield those weapons—the modern working class—the proletarians.

In proportion as the bourgeoisie, *i.e.*, capital, is developed, in the same proportion is the proletariat, the modern working class, developed—a class of labourers, who live only so long as they find work, and who find work only so long as their labour increases capital. These labourers, who must sell themselves piece-meal, are a commodity, like every other article of commerce, and are consequently exposed to all the vicissitudes of competition, to all the fluctuations of the market.

Owing to the extensive use of machinery and to division of labour, the work of the proletarians has lost all individual character, and consequently, all charm for the workman. He becomes an appendage of the machine, and it is only the most simple, most monotonous, and most easily acquired knack, that is required of him. Hence, the cost of production of a workman is restricted, almost entirely, to the means of subsistence that he requires for his maintenance, and for the propagation of his race. But the price of a commodity, and therefore also of labour, is equal to its cost of production. In proportion, therefore, as the repulsiveness of the work increases, the wage decreases. Nay more, in proportion as the use of machinery and division of labour increases, in the same proportion the burden of toil also increases, whether by prolongation of the working hours, by increase of the work exacted in a given time or by increased speed of the machinery, etc. . . .

But with the development of industry the proletariat not only increases in number; it becomes concentrated in greater masses, its strength grows, and it feels that strength more. The various interests and conditions of life within the ranks of the proletariat are more and more equalised, in proportion as machinery obliterates all distinctions of labour, and nearly everywhere reduces wages to the same low level. The growing competition among the bourgeois, and the resulting commercial crises, make the wages of the workers ever more fluctuating. The unceasing improvement of machinery, ever more rapidly developing, makes their livelihood more and more precarious; the collisions between individual workmen and individual bourgeois take more and more the character of collisions between two classes. Thereupon the workers begin to form combinations (Trades Unions) against the bourgeois; they club together in order to keep up the rate of wages; they found permanent associations in order to make provision beforehand for these occasional revolts. Here and there the contest breaks out into riots. . . .

In the conditions of the proletariat, those of old society at large are already virtually swamped. The proletarian is without property; his relation to his wife and children has no longer anything in common with the bourgeois family-relations; modern industrial labour, modern subjection to capital, the same in England as in France, in America as in Germany, has stripped him of every trace of national character. Law, morality, religion, are to him so many bourgeois prejudices, behind which lurk in ambush just as many bourgeois interests.

All the preceding classes that got the upper hand, sought to fortify their already acquired status by subjecting society at large to their conditions of appropriation. The proletarians cannot become masters of the productive forces of society, except by abolishing their own previous mode of appropriation, and thereby also every other previous mode of appropriation. They have nothing of their own to secure and to fortify; their mission is to destroy all previous securities for, and insurances of, individual property.

All previous historical movements were movements of minorities, or in the interests of minorities. The proletarian movement is the self-conscious, independent movement of the immense majority, in the interests of the immense majority. The proletariat, the lowest stratum of our present society, cannot stir, cannot raise itself up, without the whole superincumbent strata of official society being sprung into the air.

Though not in substance, yet in form, the struggle of the proletariat with the bourgeoisie is at first a national struggle. The proletariat of each country must, of course, first of all settle matters with its own bourgeoisie.

In depicting the most general phases of the development of the proletariat, we traced the more or less veiled civil war, raging within existing society, up to the point where that war breaks out into open revolution, and where the violent overthrow of the bourgeoisie lays the foundation for the sway of the proletariat. . . .

All property relations in the past have continually been subject to historical change consequent upon the change in historical conditions.

The French Revolution, for example, abolished feudal property in favour of bourgeois property.

The distinguishing feature of Communism is not the abolition of property generally, but the abolition of bourgeois property. But modern bourgeois private property is the final and most complete expression of the system of producing and appropriating products, that is based on class antagonisms, on the exploitation of the many by the few.

In this sense, the theory of the Communists may be summed up in the single sentence: Abolition of private property.

We Communists have been reproached with the desire of abolishing the right of personally acquiring property as the fruit of a man's own labour, which property is alleged to be the groundwork of all personal freedom, activity and independence.

Hard-won, self-acquired, self-earned property! Do you mean the property of the petty artisan and of the small peasant, a form of property that preceded the bourgeois form? There is no need to abolish that; the development of industry has to a great extent already destroyed it, and is still destroying it daily.

Or do you mean modern bourgeois private property?

But does wage-labour create any property for the labourer? Not a bit. It creates capital, *i.e.*, that kind of property which exploits wage-labour, and which cannot increase except upon condition of begetting a new supply of wage-labour for fresh exploitation. Property, in its present form, is based on the antagonism of capital and wage-labour. Let us examine both sides of this antagonism.

To be a capitalist, is to have not only a purely personal, but a social *status* in production. Capital is a collective product, and only by the united action of many members, nay, in the last resort, only by the united action of all members of society, can it be set in motion.

Capital is, therefore, not a personal, it is a social power.

When, therefore, capital is converted into common property, into the property of all members of society, personal property is not thereby transformed into social property. It is only the social character of the property that is changed. It loses its class-character.

Let us now take wage-labour.

The average price of wage-labour is the minimum wage, *i.e.*, that quantum of the means of subsistence, which is absolutely requisite to keep the labourer in bare existence as a labourer. What, therefore, the wage-labourer appropriates by means of his labour, merely suffices to prolong and reproduce a bare existence. We by no means intend to abolish this personal appropriation of the products of labour, an appropriation that is made for the maintenance and reproduction of human life, and that leaves no surplus wherewith to command the labour of others. All that we want to do away with, is the miserable character of this appropriation, under which the labourer lives merely to increase capital, and is allowed to live only in so far as the interest of the ruling class requires it.

In bourgeois society, living labour is but a means to increase accumulated labour. In Communist society, accumulated labour is but a means to widen, to enrich, to promote the existence of the labourer.

In bourgeois society, therefore, the past dominates the present; in Communist society, the present dominates the past. In bourgeois society capital is independent and has individuality, while the living person is dependent and has no individuality.

And the abolition of this state of things is called by the bourgeois, abolition of individuality and freedom! And rightly so. The abolition of bourgeois individuality, bourgeois independence, and bourgeois freedom is undoubtedly aimed at.

By freedom is meant, under the present bourgeois conditions of production, free trade, free selling and buying.

But if selling and buying disappears, free selling and buying disappears also. This talk about free selling and buying, and all the other "brave words" of our bourgeoisie about freedom in general, have a meaning, if any, only in contrast with restricted selling and buying, with the fettered traders of the Middle Ages, but have no meaning when opposed to the Communistic abolition of buying and selling, of the bourgeois conditions of production, and of the bourgeoisie itself.

You are horrified at our intending to do away with private property. But in your existing society, private property is already done away with for nine-tenths of the population; its existence for the few is solely due to its non-existence in the hands of those nine-tenths. You reproach us, therefore, with intending to do away with a form of property, the necessary condition for whose existence is the non-existence of any property for the immense majority of society.

In one word, you reproach us with intending to do away with your property. Precisely so; that is just what we intend.

From the moment when labour can no longer be converted into capital, money, or rent, into a social power capable of being monopolised, *i.e.*, from the moment when individual property can no longer be transformed into bourgeois property, into capital, from that moment, you say, individuality vanishes.

You must, therefore, confess that by "individual" you mean no other person than the bourgeois, than the middle-class owner of property. This person must, indeed, be swept out of the way, and made impossible.

Communism deprives no man of the power to appropriate the products of society; all that it does is to deprive him of the power to subjugate the labour of others by means of such appropriation.

It has been objected that upon the abolition of private property all work will cease, and universal laziness will overtake us.

According to this, bourgeois society ought long ago to have gone to the dogs through sheer idleness; for those of its members who work, acquire nothing, and those who acquire anything, do not work. The whole of this objection is but another expression of the tautology: that there can no longer be any wage-labour when there is no longer any capital.

All objections urged against the Communistic mode of producing and appropriating material products, have, in the same way, been urged against the Communistic modes of producing and appropriating intellectual products. Just as, to the bourgeois, the disappearance of class property is the disappearance of production itself, so the disappearance of class culture is to him identical with the disappearance of all culture.

That culture, the loss of which he laments, is, for the enormous majority, a mere training to act as a machine.

But don't wrangle with us so long as you apply, to our intended abolition of bourgeois property, the standard of your bourgeois notions of freedom, culture, law, &c. Your very ideas are but the outgrowth of the conditions of your bourgeois production and bourgeois property, just as your jurisprudence is but the will of your class made into a law for all, a will, whose essential character and direction are determined by the economical conditions of existence of your class.

The selfish misconception that induces you to transform

into eternal laws of nature and of reason, the social forms springing from your present mode of production and form of property—historical relations that rise and disappear in the progress of production—this misconception you share with every ruling class that has preceded you. What you see clearly in the case of ancient property, what you admit in the case of feudal property, you are of course forbidden to admit in the case of your own bourgeois form of property.

Abolition of the family! Even the most radical flare up at this infamous proposal of the Communists.

On what foundation is the present family, the bourgeois family, based? On capital, on private gain. In its completely developed form this family exists only among the bourgeoisie. But this state of things finds its complement in the practical absence of the family among the proletarians, and in public prostitution.

The bourgeois family will vanish as a matter of course when its complement vanishes, and both will vanish with the vanishing of capital.

Do you charge us with wanting to stop the exploitation of children by their parents? To this crime we plead guilty.

But, you will say, we destroy the most hallowed of relations, when we replace home education by social.

And your education! Is not that also social, and determined by the social conditions under which you educate, by the intervention, direct or indirect, of society, by means of schools, &c.? The Communists have not invented the intervention of society in education; they do but seek to alter the character of that intervention, and to rescue education from the influence of the ruling class.

The bourgeois clap-trap about the family and education, about the hallowed co-relation of parent and child, becomes all the more disgusting, the more, by the action of Modern Industry, all family ties among the proletarians are torn asunder, and their children transformed into simple articles of commerce and instruments of labour.

But you Communists would introduce community of women, screams the whole bourgeoisie in chorus.

The bourgeois sees in his wife a mere instrument of production. He hears that the instruments of production are to be exploited in common, and, naturally, can come to no other conclusion than that the lot of being common to all will likewise fall to the women.

He has not even a suspicion that the real point aimed at is to do away with the status of women as mere instruments of production.

For the rest, nothing is more ridiculous than the virtuous indignation of our bourgeois at the community of women, which, they pretend, is to be openly and officially established by the Communists. The Communists have no need to introduce community of women; it has existed almost from time immemorial.

Our bourgeois, not content with having the wives and daughters of their proletarians at their disposal, not to speak of common prostitutes, take the greatest pleasure in seducing each other's wives.

Bourgeois marriage is in reality a system of wives in common and thus, at the most, what the Communists might possibly be reproached with, is that they desire to introduce, in substitution for a hypocritically concealed, an openly legalised community of women. For the rest, it is self-evident that the abolition of the present system of production must bring with it the abolition of the community of women springing from that system, *i.e.*, of prostitution both public and private.

The Communists are further reproached with desiring to abolish countries and nationality.

The working men have no country. We cannot take from them what they have not got. Since the proletariat must first of all acquire political supremacy, must rise to be the leading class of the nation, must constitute itself *the* nation, it is, so far, itself national, though not in the bourgeois sense of the word.

National differences and antagonisms between peoples are daily more and more vanishing, owing to the development of the bourgeoisie, to freedom of commerce, to the world-market, to uniformity in the mode of production and in the conditions of life corresponding thereto.

The supremacy of the proletariat will cause them to vanish still faster. United action, of the leading civilised countries at least, is one of the first conditions for the emancipation of the proletariat.

In proportion as the exploitation of one individual by another is put an end to, the exploitation of one nation by another will also be put an end to. In proportion as the antagonism between classes within the nation vanishes, the hostility of one nation to another will come to an end.

The charges against Communism made from a religious, a philosophical, and, generally, from an ideological standpoint, are not deserving of serious examination.

Does it require deep intuition to comprehend that man's ideas, views and conceptions, in one word, man's consciousness, changes with every change in the conditions of his material existence, in his social relations and in his social life?

What else does the history of ideas prove, than that intellectual production changes its character in proportion as material production is changed? The ruling ideas of each age have ever been the ideas of its ruling class.

When people speak of ideas that revolutionise society, they do but express the fact, that within the old society, the elements of a new one have been created, and that the dissolution of the old ideas keeps even pace with the dissolution of the old conditions of existence.

When the ancient world was in its last throes, the ancient religions were overcome by Christianity. When Christian ideas succumbed in the 18th century to rationalist ideas, feudal society fought its death battle with the then revolutionary bourgeoisie. The ideas of religious liberty and freedom of conscience merely gave expression to the sway of free competition within the domain of knowledge.

"Undoubtedly," it will be said, "religious, moral, philosophical and juridical ideas have been modified in the course of historical development. But religion, morality, philosophy, political science, and law, constantly survived this change."

"There are, besides, eternal truths, such as Freedom, Justice, etc., that are common to all states of society. But Communism abolishes eternal truths, it abolishes all religion, and all morality, instead of constituting them on a new basis; it therefore acts in contradiction to all past historical experience."

What does this accusation reduce itself to? The history of all past society has consisted in the development of class antagonisms, antagonisms that assumed different forms at different epochs.

But whatever form they may have taken, one fact is common to all past ages, *viz.*, the exploitation of one part of society by the other. No wonder, then, that the social consciousness of past ages, despite all the multiplicity and variety it displays, moves within certain common forms, or general ideas, which cannot completely vanish except with the total disappearance of class antagonisms.

The Communist revolution is the most radical rupture with traditional property relations; no wonder that its development involves the most radical rupture with traditional ideas.

But let us have done with the bourgeois objections to Communism.

We have seen above, that the first step in the revolution by the working class, is to raise the proletariat to the position of ruling class, to win the battle of democracy.

The proletariat will use its political supremacy to wrest, by degrees, all capital from the bourgeoisie, to centralise all instruments of production in the hands of the State, *i.e.*, of the proletariat organised as the ruling class; and to increase the total of productive forces as rapidly as possible.

Of course, in the beginning, this cannot be effected except by means of despotic inroads on the rights of property, and on the conditions of bourgeois production; by means of measures, therefore, which appear economically insufficient and untenable, but which, in the course of the movement, outstrip themselves, necessitate further inroads upon the old social order, and are unavoidable as a means of entirely revolutionising the mode of production.

These measures will of course be different in different countries.

Nevertheless in the most advanced countries, the following will be pretty generally applicable.

1. Abolition of property in land and application of all rents of land to public purposes.
2. A heavy progressive or graduated income tax.
3. Abolition of all right of inheritance.
4. Confiscation of the property of all emigrants and rebels.
5. Centralisation of credit in the hands of the State, by means of a national bank with State capital and an exclusive monopoly.
6. Centralisation of the means of communication and transport in the hands of the State.

7. Extension of factories and instruments of production owned by the State; the bringing into cultivation of waste-lands, and the improvement of the soil generally in accordance with a common plan.
8. Equal liability of all to labour. Establishment of industrial armies, especially for agriculture.
9. Combination of agriculture with manufacturing industries; gradual abolition of the distinction between town and country, by a more equable distribution of the population over the country.
10. Free education for all children in public schools. Abolition of children's factory labour in its present form. Combination of education with industrial production &c., &c.

When, in the course of development, class distinctions have disappeared, and all production has been concentrated in the hands of a vast association of the whole nation, the public power will lose its political character. Political power, properly so called, is merely the organised power of one class for oppressing another. If the proletariat during its contest with the bourgeoisie is compelled, by the force of circumstances, to organise itself as a class, if, by means of a revolution, it makes itself the ruling class, and, as such, sweeps away by force the old conditions of production, then it will, along with these conditions, have swept away the conditions for the existence of class antagonisms and of classes generally, and will thereby have abolished its own supremacy as a class.

In place of the old bourgeois society, with its classes and class antagonisms, we shall have an association, in which the free development of each is the condition for the free development of all.

Critique of the Gotha Program

Within the co-operative society based on common ownership of the means of production, the producers do not exchange their products; just as little does the labour employed on the products appear here *as the value* of these products, as a material quality possessed by them, since now, in contrast to capitalist society, individual labour no longer exists in an indirect fashion but directly as a component part of the total labour. The phrase "proceeds of labour," objectionable also today on account of its ambiguity, thus loses all meaning.

What we have to deal with here is a communist society, not as it has *developed* on its own foundations, but, on the contrary, just as it *emerges* from capitalist society; which is thus in every respect, economically, morally and intellectually, still stamped with the birth marks of the old society from whose womb it emerges. Accordingly, the individual producer receives back from society—after the deductions have been made—exactly what he gives to it. What he has given to it is his individual quantum of labour. For example, the social working day consists of the sum of the individual hours of work; the individual labour time of the individual producer is the part of the social working day contributed by him, his share in it. He receives a certificate from society that he has furnished such and such an amount of labour (after deducting his labour for the common funds), and with this certificate he draws from the social stock of means of consumption as much as costs the same amount of labour. The same amount of labour which he has given to society in one form he receives back in another.

Here obviously the same principle prevails as that which regulates the exchange of commodities, as far as this is exchange of equal values. Content and form are changed, because under the altered circumstances no one can give anything except his labour, and because, on the other hand, nothing can pass to the ownership of individuals except individual means of consumption. But, as far as the distribution of the latter among the individual producers is concerned, the same principle prevails as in the exchange of commodity equivalents: a given amount of labour in one form is exchanged for an equal amount of labour in another form.

Hence, *equal right* here is still in principle—*bourgeois right*, although principle and practice are no longer at loggerheads, while the exchange of equivalents in commodity exchange only exists *on the average* and not in the individual case.

In spite of this advance, this *equal right* is still constantly stigmatised by a bourgeois limitation. The right of the producers is *proportional* to the labour they supply; the equality consists in the fact that measurement is made with an *equal standard*, labour.

But one man is superior to another physically or mentally

and so supplies more labour in the same time, or can labour for a longer time; and labour, to serve as a measure, must be defined by its duration or intensity, otherwise it ceases to be a standard of measurement. This *equal* right is an unequal right for unequal labour. It recognises no class differences, because everyone is only a worker like everyone else; but it tacitly recognises unequal individual endowment and thus productive capacity as natural privileges. *It is, therefore, a right of inequality, in its content, like every right*. Right by its very nature can consist only in the application of an equal standard; but unequal individuals (and they would not be different individuals if they were not unequal) are measurable only by an equal standard in so far as they are brought under an equal point of view, are taken from one *definite* side only, for instance, in the present case, are regarded *only as workers* and nothing more is seen in them, everything else being ignored. Further, one worker is married, another not; one has more children than another, and so on and so forth. Thus, with an equal performance of labour, and hence an equal share in the social consumption fund, one will in fact receive more than another, one will be richer than another, and so on. To avoid all these defects, right instead of being equal would have to be unequal.

But these defects are inevitable in the first phase of communist society as it is when it has just emerged after prolonged birth pangs from capitalist society. Right can never be higher than the economic structure of society and its cultural development conditioned thereby.

In a higher phase of communist society, after the enslaving subordination of the individual to the division of labour, and therewith also the antithesis between mental and physical labour, has vanished; after labour has become not only a means of life but life's prime want; after the productive forces have also increased with the all-round development of the individual, and all the springs of co-operative wealth flow more abundantly—only then can the narrow horizon of bourgeois right be crossed in its entirety and society inscribe on its banner: From each according to his ability, to each according to his needs!

A Just Government Must Benefit the Least Well-Off

John Rawls

Harvard professor John Rawls (1921-) is an outstanding moral and political theorist. His *A Theory of Justice,* the source of the following viewpoint, is a twentieth-century classic. Rawls argues that a just society must conform to certain principles people would rationally choose, given the following situation. Let us say that we are born into a society with certain rights and resources, but we do not know what position we will occupy in this society. We might even be one of the least well-off persons. What sort of society would we want to be born into given typical human aspirations and our ignorance of our particular situation? Rawls thinks that we would choose a society which would give us as much liberty as possible consistent with equal liberty for others since we may well be one of those "others." He also thinks that we would want no greater social or economic inequalities than those which are necessary to allow the society to work to the advantage of everyone. A society which allows some people to own a given amount more than others, for example, might ultimately provide a better life for everyone than one which allowed no differences or too great a difference. Rawls thinks that justice and injustice are products of social institutions and cannot be blamed on the natural differences in talents or luck. Social institutions are not simple facts we must accept, but things we can change to bring them into conformity with just principles.

QUESTIONS

1. What kinds of justice does Rawls identify? What kind does he want to address in his viewpoint?
2. What does the author mean by the "original position"?
3. What two principles of justice does Rawls believe people would choose given the chance to choose their original positions? Why is a "veil of ignorance" important?
4. What, according to the author, is the only justification for political and economic inequality?
5. How does Rawls distinguish between perfect and pure procedural justice? What kinds of institutions are necessary to supplement pure procedural justice? Why?
6. Does the author believe that natural ability and/or good character make a person deserve more good things?

■ ■ ■

My aim is to present a conception of justice which generalizes and carries to a higher level of abstraction the familiar theory of the social contract as found, say, in Locke, Rousseau, and Kant. In order to do this we are not to think of the original contract as one to enter a particular society or to set up a particular form of government. Rather, the guiding idea is that the principles of justice for the basic structure of society are the object of the original agreement. They are the principles that free and rational persons concerned to further their own interests would accept in an initial position of equality as defining the fundamental terms of their association. These principles are to regulate all further agreements; they specify the kinds of social cooperation that can be entered into and the forms of government that can be established. This way of regarding the principles of justice I shall call justice as fairness.

Thus we are to imagine that those who engage in social cooperation choose together, in one joint act, the principles which are to assign basic rights and duties and to determine the division of social benefits. Men are to decide in advance how they are to regulate their claims against one another and what is to be the foundation charter of their society. Just as each person must decide by rational reflection what constitutes his good, that is, the system of ends which it is rational for him to pursue, so a group of persons must decide once and for all what is to count among them as just and unjust. The choice which rational men would make in this hypothetical situation of equal liberty, assuming for the present that this choice problem has a solution, determines the principles of justice.

In justice as fairness the original position of equality corresponds to the state of nature in the traditional theory of the social contract. This original position is not, of course, thought of as an actual historical state of affairs, much less as a primitive condition of culture. It is understood as a purely hypothetical situation characterized so as to lead to a certain conception of justice. Among the essential features of this situation is that no one knows his place in society, his class position or social status, nor does any one know his fortune in the distribution of natural assets and abilities, his intelligence, strength, and the like. I shall even assume that the parties do not know their conceptions of the good or their special psychological propensities. The principles of justice are chosen behind a veil of ignorance. This ensures that no one is advantaged or disadvantaged in the choice of principles by the outcome of natural chance or the contingency of social circumstances. Since all are similarly situated and no one is able to design principles to favor his particular condition, the principles of justice are the result of a fair agreement or bargain. For given the circumstances of the original position, the symmetry of everyone's relations to each other, this initial situation is fair between individuals as moral persons, that is, as rational beings with their own ends and capable, I shall assume, of a sense of justice. The original position is, one might say, the appropriate initial status quo, and thus the fundamental agreements reached in it are fair. This explains the propriety of the name "justice as fairness": it conveys the idea that the principles of justice are agreed to in an initial situation that is fair. The name does not mean that the concepts of justice and fairness are the same, any more than the phrase "poetry as metaphor" means that the concepts of poetry and metaphor are the same.

Justice as fairness begins, as I have said, with one of the most general of all choices which persons might make together, namely, with the choice of the first principles of a conception of justice which is to regulate all subsequent criticism and reform of institutions. Then, having chosen a conception of justice, we can suppose that they are to choose a constitution and a legislature to enact laws, and so on, all in accordance with the principles of justice initially agreed upon. Our social situation is just if it is such that by this sequence of hypothetical agreements we would have contracted into the general system of rules which defines it. Moreover, assuming that the original position does determine a set of principles (that is, that a particular conception of justice would be chosen), it will then be true that whenever social institutions satisfy these principles those engaged in them can say to one another that they are cooperating on terms to which they would agree if they were free and equal persons whose relations with respect to one another were fair. They could all view their arrangements as meeting the stipulations which they would acknowledge in an initial situation that embodies widely accepted and reasonable constraints on the choice of principles. The general recognition of this fact would provide the basis for a public acceptance of the corresponding principles of justice. No society can, of course, be a scheme of cooperation which men enter voluntarily in a literal sense; each person finds himself placed at birth in some particular position in some particular society, and the nature of this position materially affects his life prospects. Yet a society satisfying the principles of justice as fairness comes as close as a society can to being a voluntary scheme, for it meets the principles which free and equal persons would assent to under circumstances that are fair. In this sense its members are autonomous and the obligations they recognize self-imposed.

One feature of justice as fairness is to think of the parties in the initial situation as rational and mutually disinterested. This does not mean that the parties are egoists, that is, individuals with only certain kinds of interests, say in wealth, prestige, and domination. But they are conceived as not taking an interest in one another's interests. They are to presume that even their spiritual aims may be opposed, in the way that the aims of those of different religions may be opposed. Moreover, the concept of rationality must be interpreted as far as possible in the narrow sense, standard in economic theory, of taking the most effective means to given ends. I shall modify this concept to some extent, as explained later, but one must try to avoid introducing into it any controversial ethical elements. The initial situation must be characterized by stipulations that are widely accepted.

In working out the conception of justice as fairness one main task clearly is to determine which principles of justice would be chosen in the original position. To do this we must describe this situation in some detail and formulate with care the problem of choice which it presents. . . . It may be observed, however, that once the principles of justice are thought of as arising from an original agreement in a situation of equality, it is an open question whether the principle of utility would be acknowledged. Offhand it hardly seems likely that persons who view themselves as equals, entitled to press their claims upon one another, would agree to a principle which may require lesser life prospects for some simply for the sake of a greater sum of advantages enjoyed by others. Since each desires to protect his interests, his capacity to advance his conception of the good, no one has a reason to acquiesce in an enduring loss for himself in order to bring about a greater net balance of satisfaction. In the absence of strong and lasting benevolent impulses, a rational man would not accept a basic structure merely because it maximized the algebraic sum of advantages irrespective of its permanent effects on his own basic rights and interests. Thus it seems that the principle of utility is incompatible with the conception of social cooperation among equals for mutual advantage. It appears to be inconsistent with the idea of reciprocity implicit in the notion of a well-ordered society. Or, at any rate, so I shall argue.

I shall maintain instead that the persons in the initial situation would choose two rather different principles: the first requires equality in the assignment of basic rights and duties, while the second holds that social and economic inequalities, for example inequalities of wealth and authority, are just only if they result in compensating benefits for everyone, and in particular for the least advantaged members of society. These principles rule out justifying institutions on the grounds that the hardships of some are offset by a greater good in the aggregate. It may be expedient but it is not just that some should have less in order that others may prosper. But there is no injustice in the greater benefits earned by a few provided that the situation of persons not so fortunate is thereby improved. The intuitive idea is that since everyone's well-being depends upon a scheme of cooperation without which no one could have a satisfactory life, the division of advantages should be such as to draw forth the willing cooperation of everyone taking part in it, including those less well situated. Yet this can be expected only if reasonable terms are proposed. The two principles mentioned seem to be a fair agreement on the basis of which those better endowed, or more fortunate in their social position, neither of which we can be said to deserve, could expect the willing cooperation of others when some workable scheme is a necessary condition of the welfare of all. Once we decide to look for a conception of justice that nullifies the accidents of natural endowment and the contingencies of social circumstance as counters in quest for political and economic advantage, we are led to these principles. They express the result of leaving aside those aspects of the social world that seem arbitrary from a moral point of view.

The problem of the choice of principles, however, is extremely difficult. I do not expect the answer I shall suggest to be convincing to everyone. It is, therefore, worth noting from the outset that justice as fairness, like other contract views, consists of two parts: (1) an interpretation of the initial situation and of the problem of choice posed there, and (2) a set of principles which, it is argued, would be agreed to. One may accept the first part of the theory (or some variant thereof), but not the other, and conversely. The concept of the initial contractual situation may seem reasonable although the particular principles proposed are rejected. To be sure, I want to maintain that the most appropriate conception of this situation does lead to principles of justice contrary to utilitarianism and perfectionism, and therefore that the contract doctrine provides an alternative to these views. Still, one may dispute this contention even though one grants that the contractarian method is a useful way of studying ethical theories and of setting forth their underlying assumptions.

Justice as fairness is an example of what I have called a contract theory. Now there may be an objection to the term "contract" and related expressions, but I think it will serve reasonably well. Many words have misleading connotations which at first are likely to confuse. The terms "utility" and "utilitarianism" are surely no exception. They too have unfortunate suggestions which hostile critics have been willing to exploit; yet they are clear enough for those prepared to study utilitarian doctrine. The same should be true of the term "contract" applied to moral theories. As I have mentioned, to understand it one has to keep in mind that it implies a certain level of abstraction. In particular, the content of the relevant agreement is not to enter a given society or to adopt a given form of government, but to accept certain moral principles. Moreover, the undertakings referred to are purely hypothetical: a contract view holds that certain principles would be accepted in a well-defined initial situation.

The merit of the contract terminology is that it conveys the idea that principles of justice may be conceived as principles that would be chosen by rational persons, and that in this way conceptions of justice may be explained and justified. The theory of justice is a part, perhaps the most significant part, of the theory of rational choice. Furthermore, principles of justice deal with conflicting claims upon the advantages won by social cooperation; they apply to the relations among several persons or groups. The word "contract" suggests this plurality as well as the condition that the appropriate division of advantages must be in accordance with principles acceptable to all parties. The condition of publicity for principles of justice is also connoted by the contract phraseology. Thus, if these principles are the outcome of an agreement, citizens have a knowledge of the principles that others follow. It is characteristic of contract theories to stress the public nature of political principles. Finally there is the long tradition of the contract doctrine. Expressing the tie with this line of thought helps to define ideas and accords with natural piety. There are then several advantages in the use of the term "contract." With due precautions taken, it should not be misleading. . . .

Two Principles of Justice

I shall now state in a provisional form the two principles of justice that I believe would be chosen in the original position. In this section I wish to make only the most general comments, and therefore the first formulation of these principles is tentative. As we go on I shall run through several formulations and approximate step by step the final statement to be given much later. I believe that doing this allows the exposition to proceed in a natural way.

The first statement of the two principles reads as follows.

> First: each person is to have an equal right to the most extensive basic liberty compatible with a similar liberty for others.
>
> Second: social and economic inequalities are to be arranged so that they are both (a) reasonably expected to be to everyone's advantage, and (b) attached to positions and offices open to all. . . .

By way of general comment, these principles primarily apply, as I have said, to the basic structure of society. They are to govern the assignment of rights and duties and to regulate the distribution of social and economic advantages. As their formulation suggests, these principles presuppose that the social structure can be divided into two more or less distinct parts, the first principle applying to the one, the second to the other. They distinguish between those aspects of the social system that define and secure the equal liberties of citizenship and those that specify and establish social and economic inequalities. The basic liberties of citizens are, roughly speaking, political liberty (the right to vote and to be eligible for public office) together with freedom of speech and assembly; liberty of conscience and freedom of thought; freedom of the person along with the right to hold (personal) property; and freedom from arbitrary arrest and seizure as defined by the concept of the rule of law. These liberties are all required to be equal by the first principle, since citizens of a just society are to have the same basic rights.

The second principle applies, in the first approximation, to the distribution of income and wealth and to the design of organizations that make use of differences in authority and responsibility, or chains of command. While the distribution of wealth and income need not be equal, it must be to everyone's advantage, and at the same time, positions of authority and offices of command must be accessible to all. One applies the second principle by holding positions open, and then, subject to this constraint, arranges social and economic inequalities so that everyone benefits.

These principles are to be arranged in a serial order with the first principle prior to the second. This ordering means that a departure from the institutions of equal liberty required by the first principle cannot be justified by, or compensated for, by greater social and economic advantages. The distribution of wealth and income, and the hierarchies of authority, must be consistent with both the liberties of equal citizenship and equality of opportunity.

It is clear that these principles are rather specific in their content, and their acceptance rests on certain assumptions that I must eventually try to explain and justify. A theory of justice depends upon a theory of society in ways that will become evident as we proceed. For the present, it should be observed that the two principles (and this holds for all formulations) are a special case of a more general conception of justice that can be expressed as follows.

> All social values—liberty and opportunity, income and wealth, and the bases of self-respect—are to be distributed equally unless an unequal distribution of any, or all, of these values is to everyone's advantage.

Injustice, then, is simply inequalities that are not to the benefit of all. Of course, this conception is extremely vague and requires interpretation.

As a first step, suppose that the basic structure of society distributes certain primary goods, that is, things that every rational man is presumed to want. These goods normally have a use whatever a person's rational plan of life. For simplicity, assume that the chief primary goods at the disposition of society are right and liberties, powers and opportunities, income and wealth. . . . These are the social primary goods. Other primary goods such as health and vigor, intelligence and imagination, are natural goods; although their possession is influenced by the basic structure, they are not so directly under its control. Imagine, then, a hypothetical initial arrangement in which all the social primary goods are equally distributed: everyone has similar rights and duties, and income and wealth are evenly shared. This state of affairs provides a benchmark for judging improvements. If certain inequalities of wealth and organizational powers would make everyone better off than in this hypothetical starting situation, then they accord with the general conception.

Now it is possible, at least theoretically, that by giving up some of their fundamental liberties men are sufficiently compensated by the resulting social and economic gains. The general conception of justice imposes no restrictions on what sort of inequalities are permissible; it only requires that everyone's position be improved. We need not suppose anything so drastic as consenting to a condition of slavery. Imagine instead that men forego certain political rights when the economic returns are significant and their capacity to influence the course of policy by the exercise of these rights would be marginal in any case. It is this kind of exchange which the two principles as stated rule out; being arranged in serial order they do not permit exchanges between basic liberties and economic and social gains. The serial ordering of principles expresses an underlying preference among primary social goods. When this preference is rational so likewise is the choice of these principles in this order. . . .

The fact that the two principles apply to institutions has certain consequences. Several points illustrate this. First of all, the rights and liberties referred to by these principles are those which are defined by the public rules of the basic structure. Whether men are free is determined by the rights and duties established by the major institutions of society. Liberty is a certain pattern of social forms. The first principle simply requires that certain sorts of rules, those defining basic liberties, apply to everyone equally and that they allow the most extensive liberty compatible with a like liberty for all. The only reason for circumscribing the rights defining liberty and making men's freedom less extensive than it might otherwise be is that these equal rights as institutionally defined would interfere with one another.

Another thing to bear in mind is that when principles mention persons, or require that everyone gain from an inequality, the reference is to representative persons holding the various social positions, or offices, or whatever, established by the basic structure. Thus in applying the second principle I assume that it is possible to assign an expectation of well-being to representative individuals holding these positions. This expectation indicates their life prospects as viewed from their social station. In general, the expectations of representative persons depend upon the distribution of rights and duties throughout the basic structure. When this changes, expectations change. I assume, then, that expectations are connected: by raising the prospects of the representative man in one position we presumably increase or decrease the prospects of representative men in other positions. Since it applies to institutional forms, the second principle (or rather the first part of it) refers to the expectations of representative individuals. As I shall discuss below, neither principle applies to distributions of particular goods to particular individuals who may be identified by their proper names. The situation where someone is considering how to allocate certain commodities to needy persons who are known to him is not within the scope of the principles. They are meant to regulate basic institutional arrangements. We must not assume that there is much similarity from the standpoint of justice between an administrative allotment of goods to specific persons and the appropriate design of society. Our common sense intuition for the former may be a poor guide to the latter.

Now the second principle insists that each person benefit from permissible inequalities in the basic structure. This means that it must be reasonable for each relevant representative man defined by this structure, when he views it as a going concern, to prefer his prospects with the inequality to his prospects without it. One is not allowed to justify differences in income or organizational powers on the ground that the disadvantages of those in one position are outweighed by the greater advantages of those in another. Much less can infringements of liberty be counterbalanced in this way. Applied to the basic structure, the principle of utility would have us maximize the sum of expectations of representative men (weighted by the number of persons they represent, on the classical view); and this would permit us to compensate for the losses of some by the gains of others. Instead, the two principles require that everyone benefit from economic and social inequalities. . . .

Democratic Equality and the Difference Principle

To illustrate the difference principle, consider the distribution of income among social classes. Let us suppose that the various income groups correlate with representative individuals by reference to whose expectations we can judge the distribution. Now those starting out as members of the entrepreneurial class in property-owning democracy, say, have a better prospect than those who begin in the class of unskilled laborers. It seems likely that this will be true even when the social injustices which now exist are removed. What, then, can possibly justify this kind of initial inequality in life prospects? According to the difference principle, it is justifiable only if the difference in expectation is to the advantage of the representative man who is worse off, in this case the representative unskilled worker. The inequality in expectation is permissible only if lowering it would make the working class even more worse off. Supposedly, given the rider in the second principle concerning open positions, and the principle of liberty generally, the greater expectations allowed to entrepreneurs encourages them to do things which raise the long-term prospects of the laboring class. Their better prospects act as incentives so that the economic process is more efficient, innovation proceeds at a faster pace, and so on. Eventually the resulting material benefits spread throughout the system and to the least advantaged. I shall not consider how far these things are true. The point is that something of this kind must be argued if these inequalities are to be just by the difference principle.

Fair Equality of Opportunity and Pure Procedural Justice

Now I have said that the basic structure is the primary subject of justice. This means, as we have seen, that the first distributive problem is the assignment of fundamental rights and duties and the regulation of social and economic inequalities and of the legitimate expectations founded on these. Of course, any ethical theory recognizes the importance of the basic structure as a subject of justice, but not all theories regard its importance in the same way. In justice as fairness society is interpreted as a cooperative venture for mutual advantage. The basic structure is a public system of rules defining a scheme of activities that leads men to act together so as to produce a greater sum of benefits and assigns to each certain recognized claims to a share in the proceeds. What a person does depends upon what the public rules say he will be entitled to, and what a person is entitled to depends on what he does. The distribution which results is arrived at by honoring the claims determined by what persons undertake to do in the light of these legitimate expectations.

These considerations suggest the idea of treating the question of distributive shares as a matter of pure procedural justice. The intuitive idea is to design the social system so that the outcome is just whatever it happens to be, at least so long as it is within a certain range. The notion of pure procedural justice is best understood by a comparison with perfect and imperfect procedural justice. To illustrate the former, consider the simplest case of fair division. A number of men are to divide a cake: assuming that the fair division is an equal one, which procedure, if any, will give this outcome? Technicalities aside, the obvious solution is to have one man divide the cake and get the last piece, the others being allowed their pick before him. He will divide the cake equally, since in this way he assures for himself the largest share possible. This example illustrates the two characteristic features of perfect procedural justice. First, there is an independent criterion for what is a fair division, a criterion defined separately from and prior to the procedure which is to be followed. And second, it is possible to devise a procedure that is sure to give the desired outcome. Of course, certain assumptions are made here, such as that the man selected can divide the cake equally, wants as large a piece as he can get, and so on. But we can ignore these details. The essential thing is that there is an independent standard for deciding which outcome is just and a procedure guaranteed to lead to it. Pretty clearly, perfect procedural justice is rare, if not impossible, in cases of much practical interest.

Imperfect procedural justice is exemplified by a criminal trial. The desired outcome is that the defendant should be declared guilty if and only if he has committed the offense with which he is charged. The trial procedure is framed to search for and to establish the truth in this regard. But it seems impossible to design the legal rules so that they always lead to the correct result. The theory of trials examines which procedures and rules of evidence, and the like, are best calculated to advance this purpose consistent with the other ends of the law. Different arrangements for hearing cases may reasonably be expected in different circumstances to yield the right results, not always but at least most of the time. A trial, then, is an instance of imperfect procedural justice. Even though the law is carefully followed, and the proceedings fairly and properly conducted, it may reach the wrong outcome. An innocent man may be found guilty, a guilty man may be set free. In such cases we speak of a miscarriage of justice: the injustice springs from no human fault but from a fortuitous combination of circumstances which defeats the purpose of the legal rules. The characteristic mark of imperfect procedural justice is that while there is an independent criterion for the correct outcome, there is no feasible procedure which is sure to lead to it.

By contrast, pure procedural justice obtains when there is no independent criterion for the right result: instead there is a correct or fair procedure such that the outcome is likewise correct or fair, whatever it is, provided that the procedure has been properly followed. This situation is illustrated by gambling. If a number of persons engage in a series of fair bets, the distribution of cash after the last bet is fair, or at least not unfair, whatever this distribution is. I assume here that fair bets are those having a zero expectation of gain, that the bets are made voluntarily, that no one cheats, and so on. The betting procedure is fair and freely entered into under conditions that are fair. Thus the background circumstances define a fair procedure. Now any distribution of cash summing to the initial stock held by all individuals could result from a series of fair bets. In this sense all of these particular distributions are equally fair. A distinctive feature of pure procedural justice is that the procedure for determining the just result must actually be carried out; for in these cases there is no independent criterion by reference to which a definite outcome can be known to be just. Clearly we cannot say that a particular state of affairs is just because it could have been reached by following a fair procedure. This would permit far too much and would lead to absurdly unjust consequences. It would allow one to say that almost any distribution of goods is just, or fair, since it could have come about as a result of fair gambles. What makes the final outcome of betting fair, or not unfair, is that it is the one which has arisen after a series of fair gambles. A fair procedure translates its fairness to the outcome only when it is actually carried out.

In order, therefore, to apply the notion of pure procedural justice to distributive shares it is necessary to set up and to administer impartially a just system of institutions. Only against the background of a just basic structure, including a just political constitution and a just arrangement of economic and social institutions, can one say that the requisite just procedure exists. I shall describe in some detail a basic structure that has the necessary features. Its various institutions are explained and connected with the two principles of justice. The intuitive idea is familiar. Suppose that law and government act effectively to keep markets competitive, resources fully employed, property and wealth (especially if private ownership of the means of production is allowed) widely distributed by the appropriate forms of taxation, or whatever, and to guarantee a reasonable social minimum. Assume also that there is fair equality of opportunity underwritten by education for all; and that the other equal liberties are secured. Then it would appear that the resulting distribution of income and the pattern of expectations will tend to satisfy the difference principle. In this complex of institutions, which we think of as establishing social justice in the modern state, the advantages of the better situated improve the condition of the least favored. Or when they do not, they can be adjusted to do so, for example, by setting the social minimum at the appropriate level. As these institutions presently exist they are riddled with grave injustices. But there presumably are ways of running them compatible with their basic design and intention so that the difference principle is satisfied consistent with the demands of liberty and fair equality of opportunity. It is this fact which underlies our assurance that these arrangements can be made just.

The Tendency to Equality

We see then that the difference principle represents, in effect, an agreement to regard the distribution of natural talents as a common asset and to share in the benefits of this distribution whatever it turns out to be. Those who have been favored by nature, whoever they are, may gain from their good fortune only on terms that improve the situation of those who have lost out. The naturally advantaged are not to gain merely because they are more gifted, but only to cover the costs of training and education and for using their endowments in ways that help the less fortunate as well. No one deserves his greater natural capacity nor merits a more favorable starting place in society. But it does not follow that one should eliminate these distinctions. There is another way to deal with them. The basic structure can be arranged so that these contingencies work for the good of the least fortunate. Thus we are led to the difference principle if we wish to set up the social system so that no one gains or loses from his arbitrary place in the distribution of natural assets or his initial position in society without giving or receiving compensating advantages in return.

In view of these remarks we may reject the contention that the injustice of institutions is always imperfect because the distribution of natural talents and the contingencies of social circumstance are unjust, and this injustice must inevitably carry over to human arrangements. Occasionally this reflection is offered as an excuse for ignoring injustice, as if the refusal to acquiesce in injustice is on a par with being unable to accept death. The natural distribution is neither just nor unjust; nor is it unjust that men are born into society at some particular position. These are simply natural facts. What is just and unjust is the way that institutions deal with these facts. Aristocratic and caste societies are unjust because they make these contingencies the ascriptive basis for belonging to more or less enclosed and privileged social classes. The basic structure of these societies incorporates the arbitrariness found in nature. But there is no necessity for men to resign themselves to these contingencies. The social system is not an unchangeable order beyond human control but a pattern of human action. In justice as fairness men agree to share one another's fate. In designing institutions they undertake to avail themselves of the accidents of nature and social circumstance only when doing so is for the common benefit. The two principles are a fair way of meeting the arbitrariness of fortune; and while no doubt imperfect in other ways, the institutions which satisfy these principles are just.

A further point is that the difference principle expresses a conception of reciprocity. It is a principle of mutual benefit. We have seen that, at least when chain connection holds, each representative man can accept the basic structure as designed to advance his interests. The social order can be justified to everyone, and in particular to those who are least favored; and in this sense it is egalitarian. But it seems necessary to consider in an intuitive way how the condition of mutual benefit is satisfied. Consider any two representative men A and B, and let B be the one who is less favored. Actually, since we are most interested in the comparison with the least favored man, let us assume that B is this individual. Now B can accept A's being better off since A's advantages have been gained in ways that improve B's prospects. If A were not allowed his better position, B would be even worse off than he is. The difficulty is to show that A has no grounds for complaint. Perhaps he is required to have less than he might since his having more would result in some loss to B. Now what can be said to the more favored man? To begin with, it is clear that the well-being of each depends on a scheme of social cooperation without which no one could have a satisfactory life. Secondly, we can ask for the willing cooperation of everyone only if the terms of the scheme are reasonable. The difference principle, then, seems to be a fair basis on which those better endowed, or more fortunate in their social circumstances, could expect others to collaborate with them when some workable arrangement is a necessary condition of the good of all.

There is a natural inclination to object that those better situated deserve their greater advantages whether or not they are to the benefit of others. At this point it is necessary to be clear about the notion of desert. It is perfectly true that given a just system of cooperation as a scheme of public rules and the expectations set up by it, those who, with the prospect of improving their condition, have done what the system announces that it will reward are entitled to their advantages. In this sense the more fortunate have a claim to their better situation; their claims are legitimate expectations established by social institutions, and the community is obligated to meet them. But this sense of desert presupposes the existence of the cooperative scheme; it is irrelevant to the question whether in the first place the scheme is to be designed in accordance with the difference principle or some other criterion.

Perhaps some will think that the person with greater natural endowments deserves those assets and the superior character that made their development possible. Because he is more worthy in this sense, he deserves the greater advantages that he could achieve with them. This view, however, is surely incorrect. It seems to be one of the fixed points of our considered judgments that no one deserves his place in the distribution of native endowments, any more than one deserves one's initial starting place in society. The assertion that a man deserves the superior character that enables him to make the effort to cultivate his abilities is equally problematic; for his character depends in large part upon fortunate family and social circumstances for which he can claim no credit. The notion of desert seems not to apply to these cases. Thus the more advantaged representative man cannot say that he deserves and therefore has a right to a scheme of cooperation in which he is permitted to acquire benefits in ways that do not contribute to the welfare of others. There is no basis for his making this claim. From the standpoint of common sense, then, the difference principle appears to be acceptable both to the more advantaged and to the less advantaged individual. Of course, none of this is strictly speaking an argument for the principle, since in a contract theory arguments are made from the point of the original position. But these intuitive considerations help to clarify the nature of the principle and the sense in which it is egalitarian.

A Just Government Is Absolutely Minimal

JOHN HOSPERS

John Hospers (1918-) is a former professor of philosophy at the University of Southern California and past editor of *Pacific Philosophical Quarterly*. He is known for his work in political theory, ethics, and theory of knowledge. His works include *Human Conduct: Problems of Ethics* and *Libertarianism: A Political Philosophy for Tomorrow*. He was the Libertarian Party candidate for president of the United States in 1972. Hospers bases his arguments on the assumption that human beings have fundamental rights including control of their own persons and their own property. Social and political institutions, as well as the actions of other individuals, are legitimate only insofar as they respect these basic rights. The consequences of respecting rights are primarily restrictive. Institutions and other individuals may not physically harm people, steal their resources, make slaves of them, force them to do things for

Excerpted from "What Is Libertarianism?" by John Hospers, in *The Libertarian Alternative*, edited by Tibor Machan. Chicago: Nelson-Hall, 1974. Reprinted with permission.

their own good, or force them to help others in need. Governments, which are extremely powerful and dangerous, exist only to protect people from others who would violate their personal or property rights. Any other exercise of power by governments, such as taxes for welfare or laws restricting behavior that does not hurt other people, is a form of robbery and slavery rather than just governing.

QUESTIONS

1. What sorts of actions does Hospers classify as slavery?
2. According to the author, what rights do people have?
3. What is wrong, according to Hospers, with the doctrine that everybody owns everything?
4. What institution, according to the author, is the most dangerous one known to man? Why is this so?
5. What three types of laws does Hospers consider? Which ones does he consider legitimate?
6. What does the author mean by "moral cannibalism"? What examples does he give?

■ ■ ■

What Is Libertarianism?

The political philosophy that is called libertarianism (from the Latin *libertas*, liberty) is the doctrine that every person is the owner of his own life, and that no one is the owner of anyone else's life: and that consequently every human being has the right to act in accordance with his own choices, unless those actions infringe on the equal liberty of other human beings to act in accordance with their choices.

There are several other ways of stating the same libertarian thesis:

1. *No one is anyone else's master, and no one is anyone else's slave.* Since I am the one to decide how my life is to be conducted just as you decide about yours, I have no right (even if I had the power) to make you my slave and be your master, nor have you the right to become the master by enslaving me. Slavery is *forced* servitude, and since no one owns the life of anyone else, no one has the right to enslave another. Political theories past and present have traditionally been concerned with who should be the master (usually the king, the dictator, or government bureaucracy) and who should be the slaves, and what the extent of the slavery should be. Libertarianism holds that no one has the right to use force to enslave the life of another, or any portion or aspect of that life.

2. *Other men's lives are not yours to dispose of.* I enjoy seeing operas; but operas are expensive to produce. Opera-lovers often say, "The state (or the city, etc.) should subsidize opera, so that we can all see it. Also it would be for people's betterment, cultural benefit, etc." But what they are advocating is nothing more or less than legalized plunder. They can't pay for the productions themselves, and yet they want to see opera, which involves a large number of people and their labor; so what they are saying in effect is, "Get the money through legalized force. Take a little bit more out of every worker's paycheck every week to pay for the operas we want to see." But I have no right to take by force from the workers' pockets to pay for what I want.

Perhaps it would be better if he *did* go to see opera—then I should try to convince him to go voluntarily. But to take the money from him forcibly, because in my opinion it would be good for *him*, is still seizure of his earnings, which is plunder.

Besides, if I have the right to force him to help pay for my pet projects, hasn't he equally the right to force me to help pay for his? Perhaps he in turn wants the government to subsidize rock-and-roll, or his new car, or a house in the country? If I have the right to milk him, why hasn't he the right to milk me? If I can be a moral cannibal, why can't he too?

We should beware of the inventors of utopias. They would remake the world according to their vision—with the lives and fruits of the labor of *other* human beings. Is it someone's utopian vision that others should build pyramids to beautify the landscape? Very well, then other men should provide the labor; and if he is in a position of political power, and he can't get men to do it voluntarily, then he must *compel* them to "cooperate"—i.e., he must enslave them. . . .

3. *No human being should be a nonvoluntary mortgage on the life of another.* I cannot claim your life, your work, or the products of your effort as mine. The fruit of one man's labor should not be fair game for every freeloader who comes along and demands it as his own. The orchard that has been carefully grown, nurtured, and harvested by its owner should not be ripe for the plucking for any bypasser who has a yen for the ripe fruit. The wealth that some men have produced should not be fair game for looting by government, to be used for whatever purposes its representatives determine, no matter what their motives in so doing may be. The theft of your money by a robber is not justified by the fact that he used it to help his injured mother.

Libertarianism and Rights

It will already be evident that libertarian doctrine is embedded in a view of the rights of man. Each human being has the right to live his life as he chooses, compatibly with the equal rights of all other human beings to live their lives as they choose.

All man's rights are implicit in the above statement. Each man has the right to life: any attempt by others to take it away from him, or even to injure him, violates this right, through the use of coercion against him. Each man has the right to liberty: to conduct his life in accordance with the alternatives open to him without coercive action by others. And every man has the right to property: to work to sustain his life (and the lives of whichever others he chooses to sustain, such as his family) and to retain the fruits of his labor.

People often defend the rights of life and liberty but denigrate property rights, and yet the right to property is as basic as the other two: indeed, without property rights no other rights are possible. Depriving you of property is depriving you of the means by which you live. . . .

I have no right to decide how *you* should spend your time or your money. I can make that decision for myself, but not for you, my neighbor. I may deplore your choice of life-style, and I may talk with you about it provided you are willing to listen to me. But I have no right to use force to change it. Nor have I the right to decide how you should spend the money you have earned. I may appeal to you to give it to the Red Cross, and you may prefer to go to prizefights. But that is your decision, and however much I may chafe about it I do not have the right to interfere forcibly with it, for example by robbing you in order to use the money in accordance with *my* choices. (If I have the right to rob you, have you also the right to rob me?)

When I claim a right, I carve out a niche, as it were, in my life, saying in effect, "This activity I must be able to perform without interference from others. For you and everyone else, this is off limits." And so I put up a "no trespassing" sign, which marks off the area of my right. Each individual's right is his "no trespassing" sign in relation to me and others. I may not encroach on his domain any more than he upon mine, without my consent. Every right entails a duty, true—but the duty is only that of *forbearance*—that is, of *refraining* from violating the other person's right. If you have a right to life, I have no right to take your life; if you have a right to the products of your labor (property), I have no right to take it from you without your consent. The nonviolation of these rights will not guarantee you protection against natural catastrophes such as floods and earthquakes, but it will protect you against the aggressive activities *of other men*. And rights, after all, have to do with one's relations to other human beings, not with one's relations to physical nature.

Nor were these rights created by government; governments—some governments, obviously not all—*recognize* and *protect* the rights that individuals already have. Governments regularly forbid homicide and theft; and, at a more advanced stage, protect individuals against such things as libel and breach of contract. . . .

The *right to property* is the most misunderstood and unappreciated of human rights, and it is one most constantly violated by governments. "Property" of course does not mean only real estate; it includes anything you can call your own—your clothing, your car, your jewelry, your books and papers. . . .

"But why have *individual* property rights? Why not have lands and houses owned by everybody together?" Yes, this involves no violation of individual rights, as long as everybody consents to this arrangement and no one is forced to join it. The parties to it may enjoy the communal living enough (at least for a time) to overcome certain inevitable problems: that some will work and some not, that some will achieve more in an hour than others can do in a day, and still they will all get the same income. The few who do the most will in the end consider themselves "workhorses" who do the work of two or three or twelve, while the others will be "freeloaders" on the efforts of these few. But as long as they can get out of the arrangement if they no longer like it, no violation of rights is involved. They got in voluntarily, and they can get out voluntarily; no one has used force.

"But why not say that everybody owns everything? That we *all* own everything there is?"

To some this may have a pleasant ring—but let us try to analyze what it means. If everybody owns everything, then everyone has an equal right to go everywhere, do what he pleases, take what he likes, destroy if he wishes, grow crops or burn them, trample them under, and so on. Consider what it would be like in practice. Suppose you have saved money to buy a house for yourself and your family. Now suppose that the principle, "everybody owns everything," becomes adopted. Well then, why shouldn't every itinerant hippie just come in and take over, sleeping in your beds and eating in your kitchen and not bothering to replace the food supply or clean up the mess? After all, it belongs to all of us, doesn't it? So we have just as much right to it as you, the buyer, have. What happens if we *all* want to sleep in the bedroom and there's not room for all of us? Is it the strongest who wins?

What would be the result? Since no one would be responsible for anything, the property would soon be destroyed, the food used up, the facilities nonfunctional. Beginning as a house that *one* family could use, it would end up as a house that *no one* could use. And if the principle continued to be adopted, no one would build houses any more—or anything else. What for? They would only be occupied and used by others, without remuneration. . . .

How can any of man's rights be violated? Ultimately, only by the use of force. I can make suggestions to you, I can reason with you, entreat you (if you are willing to listen), but I cannot *force* you without violating your rights; only by forcing you do I cut the cord between your free decisions and your actions. Voluntary relations between individuals involve no deprivation of rights, but murder, assault, and rape do, because in doing these things I make you the unwilling victim of my actions. A man's beating his wife involves no violation of rights if she *wanted* to be beaten. *Force is behavior that requires the unwilling involvement of other persons.*

According to libertarianism, the role of government should be limited to the retaliatory use of force against those who have initiated its use. It should not enter into any other areas, such as religion, social organization, and economics.

Government is the most dangerous institution known to man. Throughout history it has violated the rights of men more than any individual or group of individuals could do: it has killed people, enslaved them, sent them to forced labor and concentration camps, and regularly robbed and pillaged them of the fruits of their expended labor. Unlike individual criminals, government has the power to arrest and try; unlike individual criminals, it can surround and encompass a person totally, dominating every aspect of one's life, so that one has no recourse from it but to leave the country (and in totalitarian nations even that is prohibited). Government throughout history has a much sorrier record than any individual, even that of a ruthless mass murderer. The signs we see on bumper stickers are chillingly accurate: "Beware: the Government Is Armed and Dangerous."

The only proper role of government, according to libertarians, is that of the protector of the citizen against aggression by other individuals. The government, of course, should never initiate aggression; its proper role is as the embodiment of the *retaliatory* use of force against anyone who initiates its use.

If each individual had constantly to defend himself against possible aggressors, he would have to spend a considerable portion of his life in target practice, karate exercises, and other means of self-defenses, and even so he would probably be helpless against groups of individuals who might try to kill, maim, or rob him. He would have little time for cultivating those qualities which are essential to civilized life, nor would improvements in science, medicine, and the arts be likely to occur. The function of government is to take this responsibility off his shoulders: the government undertakes to defend him against aggressors and to punish them if they attack him. When the government is effective in doing this, it enables the citizen to go about his business unmolested and without constant fear for his life. To do this, of course, government must have physical power—the police, to protect the citizen from aggression within its borders, and the armed forces, to protect him from aggressors outside. Beyond that, the government should not intrude upon his life, either to run his business, or adjust his daily activities, or prescribe his personal moral code. . . .

The Function of Government

What then should be the function of government? In a word, the *protection of human rights.*

1. *The right to life*: libertarians support all such legislation as will protect human beings against the use of force by others, for example, laws against killing, attempting killing, maiming, beating, and all kinds of physical violence.
2. *The right to liberty*: there should be no laws compromising in any way freedom of speech, of the press, and peaceable assembly. There should be no censorship of ideas, books, films, or of anything else by government.
3. *The right to property*: libertarians support legislation that protects the property rights of individuals against confiscation, nationalization, eminent domain, robbery, trespass, fraud and misrepresentation, patent and copyright, libel and slander. . . .

Laws may be classified into three types: (1) laws protecting individuals against themselves, such as laws against fornication and other sexual behavior, alcohol, and drugs; (2) laws protecting individuals against aggressions by other individuals, such as laws against murder, robbery, and fraud; (3) laws requiring people to help one another; for example, all laws which rob Peter to pay Paul, such as welfare.

Libertarians reject the first class of laws totally. Behavior which harms no one else is strictly the individual's own affair. Thus, there should be no laws against becoming intoxicated, since whether or not to become intoxicated is the individual's own decision: but there should be laws against driving while intoxicated, since the drunken driver is a threat to every other motorist on the highway (drunken driving falls into type 2). Similarly, there should be no laws against drugs (except the prohibition of sale of drugs to minors) as long as the taking of these drugs poses no threat to anyone else. Drug addiction is a psychological problem to which no present solution exists. Most of the social harm caused by addicts, other than to themselves, is the result of the thefts which they perform in order to continue their habit—and then the *legal* crime is the theft, not the addiction. The actual cost of heroin is about ten cents a shot; if it were legalized, the enormous traffic in illegal sale and purchase of it would stop, as well as the accompanying proselytization to get new addicts (to make more money for the pusher) and the thefts performed by addicts who often require eighty dollars a day just to keep up the habit. Addiction would not stop, but the crimes would: it is estimated that 75 percent of the burglaries in New York City today are performed by addicts, and all these crimes could be wiped out at one stroke through the legalization of drugs. (Only when the taking of drugs could be shown to constitute a threat to *others*, should it be prohibited by law. It is only laws protecting people against *themselves* that libertarians oppose.)

Laws should be limited to the second class only: aggression by individuals against other individuals. These are laws whose function is to protect human beings against encroachment by others; and this, as we have seen, is (according to libertarianism) the sole function of government.

Libertarians also reject the third class of laws totally: no one should be forced by law to help others, not even to tell them the time of day if requested, and certainly not to give them a portion of one's weekly paycheck. Governments, in the guise of humanitarianism, have given to some by taking from others (charging a "handling fee" in the process, which, because of the government's waste and inefficiency, sometimes is several hundred percent). And in so doing they have decreased incentive, violated the rights of individuals and lowered the standard of living of almost everyone.

All such laws constitute what libertarians call *moral cannibalism*. A cannibal in the physical sense is a person who lives off the flesh of other human beings. A *moral* cannibal is one who believes he has a right to live off the "spirit" of other human beings—who believes that he has a moral claim on the productive capacity, time, and effort expended by others.

It has become fashionable to claim virtually everything that one needs or desires as one's *right*. Thus, many people claim that they have a right to a job, the right to free medical care, to free food and clothing, to a decent home, and so on. Now if one asks, apart from any specific context, whether it would be desirable if everyone had these things, one might well say yes. But there is a gimmick attached to each of them: *At whose expense?* Jobs, medical care, education, and so on, don't grow on trees. These are goods and services *produced only by men*. Who then is to provide them, and under what conditions? . . .

All those who demand this or that as a "free service" are consciously or unconsciously evading the fact that there is in reality no such thing as free services. All man-made goods and services are the result of human expenditure of time and effort. There is no such thing as "something for nothing" in this world. If you demand something free, you are demanding that other men give their time and effort to you without compensation. If they voluntarily choose to do this, there is no problem; but if you demand that they be *forced* to do it, you are interfering with their right not to do it if they so choose. "Swimming in this pool ought to be free!" says the indignant passerby. What he means is that others should build a pool, others should provide the material, and still others should run it and keep it in functioning order, so that *he* can use it without fee. But what right has he to the expenditure of *their* time and effort? To expect something "for free" is to expect it *to be paid for by others* whether they choose to or not.

Many questions, particularly about economic matters, will be generated by the libertarian account of human rights and the role of government. Should government have no role in assisting the needy, in providing social security, in legislating minimum wages, in fixing prices and putting a ceiling on rents, in curbing monopolies, in erecting tariffs, in guaranteeing jobs, in managing the money supply? To these and all similar questions the libertarian answers with an unequivocal no.

"But then you'd let people go hungry!" comes the rejoinder. This, the libertarian insists, is precisely what would not happen; with the restrictions removed, the economy would flourish as never before. With the controls taken off business, existing enterprises would expand and new ones would spring into existence satisfying more and more consumer needs; millions more people would be gainfully employed instead of subsisting on welfare, and all kinds of research and production, released from the stranglehold of government, would proliferate, fulfilling man's needs and desires as never before. It has always been so whenever government has permitted men to be free traders on a free market. But *why* this is so, and how the free market is the best solution to all problems relating to the material aspect of man's life, is another and far longer story.

Glossary

Absolute, the That which is unconditioned and uncaused by anything else.

actuality/possibility For Aristotle, actuality is the realization of some form or pattern. Potentiality is the power to change form.

analytic/synthetic A statement is analytically true if it is true by virtue of the meanings of the terms which make up the statement or if its denial constitutes a contradiction. A statement is synthetically true if it is not analytically true.

a posteriori truth A proposition whose truth requires some observation or experience to verify.

a priori truth A proposition whose truth we know without reference to experience.

argument A series of propositions one of which, the conclusion, is claimed to be supported by the others.

argument from evil An argument from the reality of evil which claims to prove either that God does not exist or is not all-powerful, all-knowing, or all-good.

behaviorism The methodological principle in psychology which confines inquiry to psychological phenomena that can be behaviorally defined; the philosophical theory that when we talk about a person's mental states we are merely referring to the fact that the person has dispositions to behave in certain ways.

bourgeoisie In Marxism the bourgeoisie are the capitalists who control the means of production and the lives of the proletariat, the workers.

capitalism An economic system in which the means of production are owned by private individuals and corporations.

categorical imperative Immanuel Kant's formulation of those laws which hold categorically (unconditionally). One form states that one ought to act in such a way that one could desire that the action become a universal law.

causal explanation An explanation of the cause or causes of an event.

clear and distinct idea An idea is clear if it is present and patently evident to an attentive mind, and distinct if it is precise and different.

cogito, ergo sum "I think, therefore I am." The single indubitable truth on which Descartes's epistemology is based.

communism The political-economic philosophy developed by Marx and Engels which holds to economic determinism—that the means of production of a society determines all else, including class struggle between the bourgeoisie and the proletariat. Communism seeks to abolish private property.

consequentialism A kind of ethical theory which asserts that the rightness or wrongness of actions is determined by the consequences or effects of the actions. Utilitarianism is a form of consequentialism while Kant's theory is not.

contingent A proposition is contingent if its denial is logically possible; a being is contingent, as opposed to absolute, if it is not logically necessary.

cosmological argument An argument for the existence of God which asserts that neither the universe nor its parts are self-caused and so must have been created by God.

cultural relativism The descriptive doctrine that each culture has its own set of standards and values which may differ from the standards of other cultures.

deontological theory Ethical system in which certain features of the moral act itself have intrinsic value. Kant's system is deontological. Contrast to consequentialism.

design argument A proof for the existence of God based on the idea that the universe and its parts appear to manifest purpose and therefore require a Designer.

determinism The doctrine that claims that every event in the universe is strictly determined by the prior total state of the universe. Applied to a person's actions, he or she could not have done other than what they did.

dualism The doctrine that claims that there are two kinds of reality or substance, usually meaning physical and nonphysical (or spiritual or mental) substances, in contrast to monism.

efficient cause One of Aristotle's four kinds of causes, the agent or "doer" of an action that initiates change.

empiricism The philosophy (epistemological) that all knowledge originates in sensory experience.

epistemology The theory of the scope, structure, and justification of knowledge.

Esse ist percipi Latin for "to be is to be perceived." The basis for the philosophy of George Berkeley.

essence The set of properties making a thing uniquely the kind of thing which it is.

ethical relativism The normative doctrine that there are no absolute and universal moral laws, but that moral standards which constrain a person are merely those held by that person's culture.

ethics The study of good and evil, right and wrong.

idealism The doctrine that reality is ultimately mental (thought, consciousness) and so-called material things are manifestations of mind or consciousness.

innate ideas Concepts or ideas possessed by the mind prior to and independent of any experience.

instrumental good A good whose value and goodness derives from its contribution to some further good, as a means to an end. Also called "extrinsic good."

intentionality The characteristic of consciousness that makes it consciousness of something, that makes it point to something beyond itself.

interactionist dualism The theory that the physical body and the nonphysical mind interact with one another.

intrinsic good A value or good which is valuable in itself irrespective of whether it leads to some other value. Contrast to extrinsic or instrumental value.

Leviathan The state created by social contract. Named after the dragon in the Book of Job, this state is a "mortal God, to which we owe our peace and defense."

liberalism The political philosophy which maintains that each person should have maximum political freedom consistent with the freedom of others.

libertarianism The doctrine that we have free will. The political philosophy that government must respect individual freedoms and only act to enforce contracts, prevent fraud, and protect individuals from physical harm by others.

Marxism The socialist political philosophy of Karl Marx and Friedrich Engels that opposes capitalism in favor of the common ownership of property.

materialism The theory that only physical things exist and that "mental" things are manifestations of an underlying material reality.

metaphysics The branch of philosophy that studies the nature and fundamental attributes of being.

monism The philosophy that ultimately only one kind of substance or kind of being exists. Idealism and materialism are both monistic. Monism is opposed to dualism.

naturalism The doctrine that the physical universe is all there is and that all features of the universe can be explained by physical laws.

necessary being A being that cannot not exist, whose nonexistence is impossible and contradictory.

normative/descriptive claims A normative claim says whether something should be the case or whether it is good or evil, as "It is terrible that so many people are absent." A descriptive claim merely says what is the case, as "Many people are absent today."

omniscient All-powerful; all-knowing.

ontological argument The argument that existence of God necessarily follows from the definition or concept of God.

original position John Rawls's hypothetical condition in which rational and unbiased individuals select principles of social justice.

physicalism Materialism.

process A unit of being or reality that is in a happening or dynamic state of becoming, as opposed to a static, unchanging substance. Processes are often related to or identified with events.

proposition That which is expressed by a true or false declarative sentence. It is possible to express the same proposition, for example, that it is raining, using declarative sentences in different languages.

skepticism The doctrine that true knowledge is impossible to obtain or recognize.

substance The ultimate subject of predication; that which exists independently from other things; that which endures through change.

teleological theory See consequentialism.

theodicy The justification of the ways of God to man, especially concerning the existence and magnitude of evil.

universal Whatever is designated by a general word like "book" which applies to more than one thing.

utilitarianism The moral theory that the total balance of pleasure or satisfaction over pain which results from an action determines that action's rightness or moral goodness.

veil of ignorance John Rawls's metaphor for the hypothetical condition necessary for rational beings to select principles of justice. That condition states that they do not know what position they will occupy in the society they order by their selections.

For Further Discussion

Chapter 1

1. René Descartes and Henri Bergson both use introspection to discover reality. How does Bergson's method take advantage of the philosophical discussion and clarification that followed Descartes' earlier work?
2. John Locke and Thomas Nagel both refer to possible non-human experiences to illustrate important points. Are they making the same or different points?
3. How do you think Descartes might respond to W.V. Quine and John Ullian's strong claims for the hypothetical-deductive method?
4. Locke claims that all knowledge comes through the senses. Do you know anything that cannot be accounted for by Locke's theory? What?
5. Descartes uses skeptical doubt as a way of finding truth. How far can skepticism be pushed? Is it reasonable to make a strong claim that all knowledge is impossible? Why or why not?

Chapter 2

1. Both David Hume and Bertrand Russell refer to language as they come to opposite conclusions about universals. Why do you think they consider language important when they are arguing about metaphysics? Pick a few paragraphs from a variety of books you read and decide what assumptions about reality come packaged with the language itself, quite apart from what the authors are using the language to say. For example, what kinds of things are there in the world that correspond to nouns? How about verbs? How about prepositions? Does this help you make better sense of Hume and Russell?
2. James Feibleman tries to explain everything in terms of matter. As he argues, he refers to the methods of science. Why, in your opinion, are the methods of science useful? Do you think it is legitimate to appeal to science for arguments abut what is ultimately real?
3. Both materialists and idealists try to explain everything using only their own preferred kind of "stuff." After they have given detailed explanations from each of their perspectives, does it matter any more whether we call the "ultimately real

stuff" by the name "consciousness" as opposed to "matter" or vice versa since both theories are supposed to explain everything? Could we just call this ultimate stuff "zimbe" or make up some other name rather than continue to call it "consciousness" or "experience" or "matter," or do we lose some real insight by doing this? What do you think?

4. Some philosophers, like Descartes, are dualists who believe that there is both matter and mind, not that one of these categories explains everything. Since mind and matter, on the surface at least, seem to be much different kinds of things, this sort of solution looks like it might help us avoid the difficult problem of explaining matter in terms of mind or vice versa. Can you think of any new problems that might result from arguing that there are two or more ultimate kinds of stuff rather than only one kind?

Chapter 3

1. The theory of evolution is constantly referred to when questions about God are asked. This theory has several forms (stellar, biological, etc.) which can be related to the arguments presented in this chapter in a variety of ways. Consider the following statements. What does "evolution" mean in each of these statements and which ones, if any, do you agree with?
   - **a.** Evolution shows that there was no designer of the universe.
   - **b.** Evolution shows that the designer included the process of evolution in the design.
   - **c.** Evolution shows that the universe was not created.
   - **d.** Evolution says nothing about creation; it only attempts to show how things developed.
   - **e.** Evolution is the cause of the universe.
2. Hume does not want to give intelligence a special place in the universe ahead of other principles, like the "vegetative" principle, which might explain other things, including intelligence. Do you think that intelligence is the cause of order or that order is the cause of intelligence? Is there some other alternative?
3. If the idea of a "necessary being" made perfectly good sense, which of the following statements do you think would be true and why? Which arguments in this chapter refer to a Necessary Being?
   - **a.** The Necessary Being must actually exist.
   - **b.** The Necessary Being either must exist or cannot exist.

c. The Necessary Being might just happen to exist.
d. The Necessary Being might pop into existence sometime.
e. There would be nothing if there were not some Necessary Being somewhere.

4. B.C. Johnson argues that God could work many minor and subtle miracles to keep innocent babies from dying without ruining the universe as a place where humans could morally develop. John Hick does not think such a world would work at all. Assume that God did constantly intervene and that no innocent babies suffered and died. Would this make it possible for people to have "baby dropping and burning contests" since no harm would ever come? Would this kind of world trivialize human choice and life or would it merely provide a safe and secure world in which to develop character? What do you think?
5. Do you think, contrary to what C.S. Lewis says, that it is possible to believe in the existence of a personal God and rationally avoid confronting the issue of one's relationship to God? There are many things which we believe exist and which we feel we can ignore. Is God one of those things or is God something entirely different, something which could not be rationally ignored? Would God's existence change everything, some things, or nothing? Give reasons for your answers.

Chapter 4

1. John Stuart Mill, Immanuel Kant, and Aristotle explain morality differently. What reasons do you think each of them would accept for or against each of the following actions? To what extent would they agree on which actions are good or evil?
   a. I decide to to lie to avoid taking a test.
   b. I decide to risk my life to save a friend.
   c. I decide to lie to save a Jew from a Nazi death camp.
   d. We all decide to eat plenty of nutritious foods.
   e. We decide to get really drunk to celebrate a victory.
2. Consequentialistic theories depend upon being able to predict the consequences of actions. Do you think this is a problem for consequentialism? What might a consequentialist do if the results of an action were totally unpredictable? Could some other moral theory deal with these cases? Are there cases which the other theory could not deal with but

which consequentialism could?

3. Assume that, in a certain culture, it is believed that children must kill their parents before the parents reach the age of fifty because nobody over fifty can be happy in the next life. Consider the Western ideal that children should make every effort to protect and extend the lives of their parents. How would Ruth Benedict explain the different rules? How would W.T. Stace? Do you think the moral values are different in these two cases? Explain.
4. Given Russell's conception of morality, what percentage of people do you think can actually be considered moral? Is this an important consideration in evaluating Russell's claim? Why or why not?
5. George Mavrodes does not think we can be obligated to sacrifice in a universe where morality is not deeply grounded. Does this mean that all obligations must ultimately hold some payoff for the moral person? Do you think, for example, that you could be obligated to die for another person? To go to Hell for all eternity to save someone else? Discuss.

Chapter 5

1. How do Thomas Hobbes and Locke differ in the laws they ascribe to the state of nature? How do each of them understand the transformation that takes place when government comes into existence?
2. John Rawls defines several different kinds of justice. Given Rawls's classification, what kinds of justice do Hobbes, Locke, Karl Marx, and Hospers each consider?
3. Which philosopher in this chapter argues for the most powerful form of government? Which argues for the weakest? Why?
4. John Locke believes that God grants certain rights to human beings. Do you think it is possible to grant the same rights to humans without recourse to God? How?
5. Marx argues that economic reality determines what people believe about philosophy, morality, religion, etc. If this is the case, how is it possible for Marx himself to develop beliefs which are different from the beliefs of his own society? Do you think Marx can answer this question?

Suggestions for Further Reading

General

F.C. Copleston, *History of Philosophy.* Westminster, MD: Newman Press, 1966. This nine-volume set is the most comprehensive contemporary work in the history of philosophy. Individual volumes can be read independently.

W.T. Jones, *History of Western Philosophy*. New York: Macmillan, 1976. A five-volume set written for college students.

Chapter 1

Augustine, *Against the Academicians, Volume 3*. Translated by Sister Mary Patricia Garvey. Milwaukee: Marquette University Press, 1957. Contains early arguments against skepticism that predate Descartes. Excellent.

Brand Blanshard, *The Nature of Thought*. 2 volumes. New York: Allen & Unwin, 1940. A brilliant work by an idealist. Currently out of vogue, but worth reading.

James Jean, *The New Background of Science*. 2nd edition. New York: Macmillan Co., 1934. A mathematical physicist uses quantum mechanics to demonstrate how scientific method cannot lead to truth. Fascinating and controversial.

Oliver Johnson, *Skepticism and Cognitivism*. Berkeley: University of California Press, 1978. A fine, in-depth treatment of practically every skeptical argument ever presented.

Immanuel Kant, *Critique of Pure Reason*. Unabridged edition. Translated by Norman Kemp Smith. New York: Macmillan and Co., 1929. Reissued by St. Martin's Press, New York. The German master's argument that knowledge is obtained using both the reason and the senses. Difficult reading made easier by an excellent translation.

G.E. Moore, "A Defense of Common Sense," *Philosophical Papers*. London: Allen & Unwin, 1959, pp. 32-59. A common-sense critique of skepticism by an important philosopher.

Plato, *Theaetetus*, in *Collected Dialogues of Plato*. Edited by E. Hamilton and H. Cairns. New York: Bollingen Foundation, 1961. Plato's classic text on the nature of knowledge.

Bertrand Russell, *Human Knowledge: Its Scope and Limit*. New York: Simon and Schuster, 1948. Russell writes with his usual clarity for the lay reader.

CHAPTER 2

Aristotle, *Metaphysics*, in *The Complete Works of Aristotle, Volume 2*. Edited by J. Barnes. Princeton: Princeton University Press, 1984. This is the work that defined metaphysics. Worth the effort for an introductory student.

Augustine, *Confessions*. Translated by John K. Ryan. Garden City, NY: Image Books, 1962. The philosophical and spiritual journey of a great thinker. Touches upon many areas of philosophy. Great reading.

George Berkeley, *Three Dialogues Between Hylas and Philonous*. Indianapolis: Hackett, 1979. First published in 1713; a clear, systematic version of idealism. A philosophical classic.

Brenda Dunne and Robert Jahn, *Margins of Reality*. San Diego: Harcourt Brace Jovanovich, 1987. A readable introduction to PEAR, the Princeton Engineer Anomalies Project, which challenges materialism.

Charles Hartshorne, *Creative Synthesis and Philosophic Method*. London: SCM Press, 1970. The final work of this important twentieth-century philosopher and student of Alfred North Whitehead.

Immanuel Kant, *Prolegomena to Any Future Metaphysics*. Translated by P. Carus. Indianapolis: Hackett, 1977. This is Kant's own simplified introduction to his thinking about metaphysics and epistemology.

C.P. Snow, *Two Cultures and a Second Look*. New York: Cambridge University Press, 1969. Snow reopens the debates between science and humanism that Spencer and Huxley began at the end of the last century. He raises important questions about approaches to humans and reality.

A.E. Taylor, *Plato: The Man and His Works*. New York: Methuen, 1960. A standard introduction to Plato's life and philosophy.

Richard Taylor, *Metaphysics*. Third Edition. Englewood Cliffs, NJ: Prentice-Hall, 1983. An understandable introduction to popular metaphysical issues. Highly recommended.

CHAPTER 3

F.C. Copleston, *Aquinas*. Baltimore: Penguin Books, 1955. This contains the best, most understandable introduction to Aquinas's Five Ways.

W. James, *The Will to Believe and Other Essays in Popular Philosophy*. Edited by Frederick H. Burkhardt. Cambridge, MA: Harvard University Press, 1979. Contains highly influential and understandable essays.

Charles Hartshorne and William Reese, *Philosophers Speak of God*. Chicago: University of Chicago Press, 1953. A comprehensive introduction to the philosophy of God. This collection includes several process perspectives.

John Hick, *Evil and the God of Love*. New York: Harper & Row, 1966. A highly influential attempt to solve the problem of evil by a religious believer.

————, *Philosophy of Religion*. Englewood Cliffs, NJ: Prentice-Hall, 1983. An excellent, easy-to-understand introduction.

C.S. Lewis, *Mere Christianity*. New York: Macmillan, 1967. Lewis's famous argument for God's existence based upon moral experience. A classic that is easy to read.

Edward H. Madden, "The Many Faces of Evil," *Philosophy and Phenomenological Research, Volume* 24 (1964), pp. 481-92. An examination of the problem of evil by a nonbeliever.

Wallace Matson, *The Existence of God*. Ithaca, NY: Cornell University Press, 1965. A critical perspective on arguments in favor of God's existence.

Bertrand Russell and F.C. Copleston, "The Existence of God: A Debate," *Humanitas*. A lively debate between a Roman Catholic believer and a famous skeptic. Essential reading.

R. Swinburne, *The Existence of God*. Oxford: Clarendon Press, 1979. Contains Swinburne's original "inductive" proof of God.

F.R. Tennant, *Philosophical Theology, Volume* 2. New York: Cambridge University Press, 1928.

CHAPTER 4

Aristotle, *Nichomachean Ethics*. Translated by T. Irwin. Indianapolis: Hackett, 1986. The source of virtue ethics. Essential reading.

Kurt Baier, *The Moral Point of View*. Ithaca: Cornell University Press, 1958. Baier's theory in detail. A contemporary classic.

N. Gifford, *When in Rome*. Albany: State University of New York Press, 1981. A lucid discussion; good for beginners.

Alasdair MacIntyre, *After Virtue*. South Bend, IN: University of Notre Dame Press, 1981. One of the most important recent works on virtue ethics.

G.E. Moore, *Principia Ethica*. Cambridge: Cambridge University Press, 1903. A seminal work. Essential reading.

Kai Nielsen, *Ethics Without God*. Buffalo, NY: Prometheus Books, 1973. A defense of secular morality.

Louis Pojman, ed., *Ethical Theory: Classical and Contemporary*. Belmont, CA: Wadsworth, 1989. A comprehensive anthology of significant papers.

W.D. Ross, *Kant's Ethical Theory*. Oxford: Oxford University Press, 1954. One of the best introductions to the subject.

Henry Sidgwick, *Outlines of the History of Ethics*. Boston: Beacon, 1960 and *The Methods of Ethics*. New York: Dover, 1874. These are classic works in ethics. Sidgwick raises issues many philosophers miss.

J.J.C. Smart, "Extreme and Restricted Utilitarianism," *The Philosophical Quarterly, Volume 6* (1956), pp. 344-54. An influential defense of utilitarianism.

CHAPTER 5

C. Cohen, *The Four Systems*. New York: Random House, 1982. A useful, systematic survey of democracy, socialism, communism, and fascism.

John Hospers, *Libertarianism: A Political Philosophy for Tomorrow*. Los Angeles: Nash Publishing Company, 1971. A lucid defense of libertarianism by its premiere philosophical defender.

John Locke, *Second Treatise on Government*. Indianapolis: Bobbs-Merrill, Library of Liberal Arts, 1952. One of the most influential liberal political theories of government in terms of influence on the American Revolution.

Karl Marx, *Karl Marx: Selected Writings*. Edited by David McLellan. New York: Oxford University Press, 1977. The best anthology of Marx's writings.

Robert Nozick, *Anarchy, State, and Utopia.* New York: Basic Books, 1974. The most important defense of libertarianism to date; essential reading.

Plato, *Republic.* Translated by G.M.A. Grube. Indianapolis: Hackett, 1974. Perhaps the most important work in political theory in Western thought.

John Rawls, *A Theory of Justice*. Cambridge, MA: Belknap Press, 1971. Already a classic, this work defends a version of liberal–social contract theory.

INDEX